The Virgin Sailor

The Virgin Sailor

Peewee Hunt

Cover artwork conceived and designed by Nick Withers Design

Additional artwork by Danielle and Katie Harbord

Book layout by Tim C. Taylor

ISBN: 978-1490912042

Visit the author at www.peeweehunt.com

CONTENTS

FOREWORD

I was born in Sparkbrook, Birmingham, and grew up there, a Brummie, just as far away from the sea in any direction that is possible in our little island. My mother worked as a housekeeper for a posh elderly lady and my father worked as an inspector in the enamelling plant at the Rover Car factory where I was assured of a job waiting for me when I finished school. So, why did I suddenly get this overwhelming urge to join the Royal Navy and go to sea with the brave and honest intent to serve my Queen and country?

It was all down to a *Pearl & Dean* film advertisement for cigarettes, shown between *Tweety Pie,* and *Flash Gordon,* at the ABC Minors Club that my little gang and I used to attend at the Piccadilly cinema on the Stratford Road on Saturday afternoons. The commercial showed a jet fighter catapulting off the flight deck of an aircraft carrier followed by a camera as it zoomed over the ocean and crossed over a coastline to attack a mocked up enemy military installation hidden deep within a desert landscape.

After successfully strafing the target with rockets and seeing it blown to smithereens, the pilot wheeled his aircraft back out across the waves and made a dramatic ear-splitting, tyre-screaming touchdown back aboard the carrier. As the aircraft came to rest, the camera closed in to focus, first on the pilot, as he slid back his canopy and gave a thumbs-up of success to the deck crew. The camera then zoomed in more closely on the packet of cigarettes that the pilot produced, and then slowly zoomed back out to reveal him making a great show of lighting one and exhaling a stream of blue smoke as he sat back comfortably in his seat. The pilot's face registered a relaxed smile of content at his nicotine reward for a job well done.

I was hooked. Not by the attraction of the cigarettes, I didn't smoke and didn't want to start; but I knew there and then that as soon as I was old enough, I was going to join the Royal Navy. Four years later at the age of fifteen, I did.

This story is inspired by actual events, and characters, drawn from the memory of my maiden voyage as a boy of sixteen aboard HMS *Ark Royal,* the flagship of the Royal Navy in the early sixties.

Welcome aboard...

1

We all pull together…

'PULL YOU BASTARDS, PULL,' roared the chief. 'You bastards are gunna pull sir up-and-down this fuckin' river all fuckin' morning while sir sits in the back smoking baccy. Pull, you bastards, pull.'

At 0730 on a dank October morning, the choppy, muddy-grey waters off the Shotley Peninsula slapped solidly against the wooden hull of the thirty-two foot cutter as the crew of twelve, fifteen-year-old-boys, dutifully bent their backs to heave on the heavy oars and continued to haul the four tons of mahogany, oak, and ash through the murk. If any of them resented the words, or the sight, of Old Thunderguts, Chief Petty Officer (Instructor) Townshend, sitting at the helm in the stern sheets puffing away at his pipe, it would be difficult to tell as each boy's face wore the same tortured grimace.

At this hour, the harbours of Felixstowe and Harwich were busy with shipping. Commuter ferries and workboats in the main but there were much larger craft also on the move. Bells clanged incessantly from vessels hove to and foghorns sounded constantly from those cautiously manoeuvring in the thick, damp mist. If the Chief PO was concerned, he was keeping it well concealed from the junior seamen in his charge. As a CPO (I) at HMS *Ganges*, the boys saw him as God, and in him, they held absolute trust and with good reason. They all knew that they were close to the mainland even if they couldn't see it, but in this weather, should anything go amiss, they might just as well have been in the middle of the North Sea.

It came as a shock then, when the high, dark prow of the British Rail workboat *Pinmill* suddenly emerged from the gloom, looming towards them like some giant behemoth. 'Port your oars,' bellowed Thunderguts, making himself heard even over the ear-splitting blast from *Pinmill*'s horn...

2

A rude awakening

THE BOY SNAPPED AWAKE, eyes-wide, body tense with nerve-ends tingling, as the screech of the boat's siren faded along with the nightmare. His sleep-drenched mind fought to remember where he was, then, as his head began to clear, he dismissed the reminder of the near miss with the workboat *Pinmill*. He was lying in the bunk that had been his aboard the aircraft carrier HMS *Ark Royal*, the Flagship of the Royal Navy, for almost a whole week. He remained lying on his back, closed his eyes, and allowed his body to relax.

Overhead the night light shone dully, its dim blue glow successfully illuminating his own six-by-two feet of space but casting the neighbouring block of bunks into deep and eerie shadow.

He was lying on his back uncomfortably conscious of the narrowness of the bunk. His crossed feet were stiff and cramped and he was becoming aware of a slight discomfort where his testicles hung trapped between his thighs. A warm hand gently probed, and a crooked finger eased them free, then, joined by its fellows, began massaging the tender and slightly sweaty underside of his genitals, gently but firmly, as if trying to restore lost circulation. It was at that moment, his relaxed body snapped taut as it received the warning signals from his brain. The hand beneath the blanket was not his own!

It did not take the boy long to discover who the owner of the intruding hand was. A panic-stricken grope between the bedclothes confirmed that it belonged to the occupant of the adjoining bunk, Tactical Operator "First Class" Clive Appleby.

"Adjoining bunk" meant literally that. An iron bar some two inches in diameter ran horizontally between the two bunks. Apart from being the support on which the bunks were hinged, it also served to provide the physical barrier that the naval architects who had designed the sleeping accommodation considered proper, necessary, and adequate to afford each man his bedtime privacy and to ensure that there was no risk of forbidden intimacy. Not surprisingly, throughout the fleet, it was generally referred to as "the buggery bar".

However, as Junior Tactical Operator Alan Hunt had just discovered, Appleby, in common with every other man aboard HMS *Ark Royal* – including the ship's cat – had an arm reach of well over two inches.

'It's all right, kid, no one can see us,' Appleby whispered from out of the gloom.

Too scared to reply, the boy rolled quickly away from the older man, forcing him to let go suddenly. For a few moments, the young sailor lay on his side, struggling to collect his thoughts. Then the fingers returned. Cold now, they sent even colder shivers down his spine as they tickled their way lightly across the sensitive cleft of his buttocks.

Frantically he thrashed over onto his back but the hand neatly avoiding becoming trapped underneath swept up smoothly over his thigh catching hold of him again in an even tighter grip. Using his own hands now, the boy tried desperately to prise the other's fingers loose, but Appleby maintained his grip and was obviously prepared to apply more pressure if necessary.

'Kid, listen,' he whispered sharply. The young signalman lay still, his heart thumping painfully in his chest. 'For Christ's sake, keep quiet and enjoy it. If you make any more noise and we get caught, we'll both be in the shit – and you can stand by to have your fucking head kicked in; by me. Got it?'

The harsh words seemed to carry more emphasis for being said in whispers, and they had the desired effect. Frightened and subdued, the sixteen-year-old boy sailor lay shivering as the strong fingers stroked and fondled him. Mercifully, nature took over, bringing rescue and release surprisingly quickly.

3

Charlie Charlie

'WAKEY WAKEY NOW, OUT you get. Let's be having you. Hands off dicks and on knicks. Jesus Christ! It hums like a bloody Chinese brothel in here. Come on then, I said out. Oh yoo tee – out.'

The Duty Petty Officer was still at the far side of the bunkspace, but his voice, after recently completing a six-week course at the Royal Navy Gunnery School, HMS *Excellent*, carried strongly, bouncing from bulkhead to bulkhead, reverberating around the vast metal chamber. The voice had a penetrating quality to it as well. It bit deep into sleep-ridden brains like a saw-toothed knife, thrusting and gouging, its serrated edge grating against bone.

At least it felt like that to the boy as he fought his way back into the land of the living. His eyes felt as if they had been sealed with glue and it took several attempts before he succeeded in keeping them open.

The bunk above him began to creak noisily and then sagged suddenly in the middle as its occupant sat up. A pair of slim hairy legs swung down and Hunt flinched as one foot came precariously close to his face. The foot stretched down and waggled about until it found the boy's shoulder which it prodded none too gently.

'Hey, Peewee, are you awake yet you lazy sod?'

'I was until you waved your great smelly foot in my face,' Hunt replied, 'It's enough to knock any bugger out for good.'

A slow, warm smile had spread across the boy's face during the short exchange. When he had joined the ship a week earlier, the older hands who had greeted him on the mess deck had unanimously decided to give him the nickname of Peewee, after the well-known American jazz musician with whom the boy shared his surname. He was still getting used to it and no one had called him Alan since.

The owner of the foot dropped easily from his bunk, grimacing as the unyielding iron deck transmitted a cold shock to the soles of his feet.

'Bloody Hell! You would think that they'd have the decency to put a carpet down or something. 'This deck is fucking freezing.' JTO "Toz" Tozer was slim and muscular with a pleasingly soft East Yorkshire accent. Like Peewee, Toz was an ex-*Ganges* boy but had been in a different division at the training establishment. While Peewee had been in Keppel Division, Toz had trained in Duncan. He had been a Badge Boy and also successfully boxed for the division. They had both passed out of training school at the same time and been drafted to HMS *Mercury*, the Royal Navy Signalling School at Petersfield. There they had spent a short period of time in-transit while waiting to be drafted to their first sea-going billets, which in both their cases turned out to be HMS *Ark Royal*. Despite this, they had only first met properly while on the train from London to Plymouth, en-route to join the ship. They were the same age, and had already become the closest of friends.

'Come on then, lads, you should be up top and about by now - hey, just a minute, you are both juniors aren't you?' The petty officer who had been sailing past stopped in mid-stride and wheeled upon the two boys. Toz nodded cautiously but said nothing while Peewee scrambled from his bunk, nearly landing on the PO's feet in his haste.

'Well, well, well,' the petty officer grated, 'then please tell me why you two are still farting about down here when you should be up on the flight deck doing physical exercises with all the other juniors?'

'It's alright PO, they're both watchkeepers in the Main Signal Office so they're excused keep-fit musters.' The petty officer half turned to see a fully dressed Clive Appleby appear from the other side of the block of bunks.

'Bunting tossers!' The petty officer made it sound like a dirty expression. Glaring at Appleby, he carried on, 'Well, some of my junior seamen are doing watch-keeping as well, but do they get excused; do they bollocks. Right now, there are forty-two of them freezing their knackers off up there. I'll be seeing your chief yeoman about this and no mistake. You just see if I don't.'

The petty officer moved on, mumbling obscenities about the stroppy yobs you get in the navy these days, and about bunting tossers in general. Bunting tossers get the name from waving flags made out of bunting stitched onto sticks, in a mysterious pattern of communication known as semaphore in which the tactical operators of the branch are highly trained. Some people could never get their heads around this and thought it a weird practice. Presumably, the Duty PO was one of those who subscribed to this school of thought.

When he was comfortably out of earshot Toz said, 'Cheers, Clive, that got the bastard off our backs.' Peewee smiled woodenly but said nothing. The memory of what had taken place during the night was too vivid and he sensed a barrier of embarrassment between Appleby and himself.

At that moment, the ship's Tannoy system crackled into life and the raucous, bugled strains of Reveille, referred to in the navy as Charlie, echoed around the bunkspace.

'Bloody typical,' grunted Appleby, 'Charlie goes at half-past-six and the Duty PO comes round five minutes earlier to wake us up just to make sure we all hear it.'

'Yeah, bloody typical,' Toz agreed. 'Anyway, I'm going up to the dining hall for some breakfast. Someone was doing the *Shotley Shuffle* down here last night and I had a job getting off to kip, what with the bloody bunks shaking and all. Not only am I half knackered, I'm also starving.'

'Scran,' Appleby said.

'What?' enquired Tozer.

'Breakfast, dinner, food whatever, it's called "scran". And butter; that's called "grease" or "slide". You'll learn a lot more before long. You're in a real ship now remember. Not some bloody stone frigate made out of concrete and bricks.'

'Cheers, Clive,' Toz grinned at the TO (1) and looked at Peewee. 'How about you, are you coming up?'

Peewee hesitated for a moment before replying. 'Not just yet,' he said. 'I feel a bit crabby. I think I'll go down to the mess and get washed first.'

'Can't say that I blame you,' Toz said, still smiling. 'It was probably you that was pulling your pudding all night anyway. I'll see you when you get there, but you'd better hurry if you want any bread rolls. There was sod all left yesterday if you remember. I'm sure the bloody chefs keep half of them back for themselves.'

After Toz had gone, Peewee finished dressing and began to make his way out of the bunkspace taking care to avoid the still present petty officer who was now bemoaning, "The filthy buggers who sleep down here." There was a look of pure revulsion on his face and he was shaking his head in disbelief as he stared down into the contents of the main rubbish bin. 'Just look at the state of that bastard thing,' he was saying to no one person in particular.

The bunkspace was the sleeping quarters for some five hundred of the ship's crew, and the rubbish, or gash bin, a huge circular affair that measured some six-feet across by about four deep, contained a thick, greasy, foul smelling mixture consisting mostly of food remains, urine, and vomit. The usual in-harbour spillage. For some it was an unpleasant reminder of how pleasant last night's run ashore had been.

'Bloody animals,' the PO was now complaining to naval airman Milligan as Peewee slid quietly past. Milligan, who slept in the block of bunks nearest to the bin, was lying half-raised on one elbow, his left eye screwed firmly shut while the other blinked rapidly in an effort to remain open. Only just awake, he was already sucking on his first cigarette of the day, a blue liner - so called because of the blue stripe printed along it that denoted Royal Navy issue.

Poor old Spike, Peewee thought, chuckling to himself as he slid quietly past. Looks as if he had a good run ashore last night.

In truth, Milligan was not feeling very well. He was suffering from the after effects of binge drinking countless pints of scrumpy and large measures of Irish whiskey in the pubs of Plymouth the previous evening. He was finding it difficult to focus his vision on the petty officer, let alone understand him.

'Why can't the dirty bastards use the heads like every other bugger,' the petty officer was snarling as Peewee made his escape from the bunkspace.

Judging by the smell of it I should think every other bugger uses the gash bin as well, thought Peewee as he sped nimbly up the steel ladder into the canteen flat above.

The Regulating Office, disciplinary headquarters of the ship, was situated at the far starboard side of the canteen flat from where the NAAFI conducted their business. To reach his mess the boy would have to walk right past the office, and, as he could see the figure of a leading regulator inside, he knew that if he was going to report the incident with Clive Appleby that now was the time.

Pausing at the open door, he stood hesitating, still unsure until the man turned a sour, enquiring glance in his direction.

'What?'

'Er... good morning, sir,' he said quickly, then, totally losing confidence, turned and pushed open the adjoining steel watertight door and stepped through, out into the dark, open air beyond.

It was late January and the sharp wind whipping across the murky dockside water instantly cut through his shirt like a knife. Pity those poor sods up on the flight deck, he thought, giving an involuntary shudder. Behind him a hard voice called, 'Oi. Do not call me sir. You are not at *Ganges* now. You call me Leading Regulator. Now, how's about shutting the fuckin' door then?'

Peewee turned to see the angry face of the regulator glaring out at him. 'Sorry, Leading Regulator, I was just about to close it,' he replied.

The regulator mouthed something hostile in return and jerked two fingers savagely at the boy before heaving the door closed himself.

'Balls to you too, mate,' the boy muttered indignantly. The action of the regulator had left him with little light to see by. It was still almost an hour until dawn and there were several tricky obstacles to be negotiated as he made his way along the starboard weather deck.

Eventually reaching the next watertight door without mishap, he was annoyed to find it firmly battened down. All eight of the heavy steel clips securing it had been jammed on tight and he swore inwardly as he struggled to get it open. Finally, he succeeded and stepped thankfully through into the comparative warmth and light of the Stores Accountants Mess, narrowly avoiding leaving a leg outside as a particularly strong gust of wind slammed the heavy door shut with a bang. Cursing softly to himself, he made his way down the ladder towards his own mess.

Two decks down he was greeted by the domestic odours of stale tobacco, canvas, cordage, metal polish and feet. The mess was still in darkness and he had to grope uncertainly between the canvas hammocks and camp beds until he reached his personal locker. Trying to make as little noise as possible, he turned the key in the lock quietly, but the inset metal lever that opened the door when lifted was stuck, and he was forced to rattle it several times until without warning, it jerked upward, trapping his fingers painfully within its narrow recess.

'Oh ffffuck,' he swore, bringing the bruised knuckles to his lips.

'For crying out loud, give the watchkeepers a chance will ya?' The strings of a nearby hammock creaked furiously as the complainant thrashed around beneath his blankets.

'Sorry, mate, I caught me bloody fingers in the door,' Peewee whispered into the gloom.

Those who were fortunate enough to have a sleeping billet in the mess were not subject to early morning visits from Duty Petty Officers and strongly resented any intrusion that took place before the Leading Hand of the Mess decided it was time to get everybody up.

After collecting his toilet gear from the locker the boy made his way silently to the bathroom outside which he took the precaution of removing his shoes and socks. This was necessary as the floor of the bathroom had been flooded with an inch-or-two of scummy water for almost a week. The pungent blend of stagnating water, urine and other noxious odours was becoming most unpleasant.

In the light of the bathroom, he discovered that the injured knuckle was bleeding from a small gash. Pressing the cold tap lever, he held it under the icy running water for a few seconds until it became almost numb. When he couldn't bear the cold water any longer he pressed the hot tap and jumped back smartly, startled as a cloud of rust coloured steam almost scalded his other hand.

'Jesus Christ! That's bloody dodgy,' he complained aloud.

'Good morning lad, having trouble with the taps again are we?' The massive figure of "Robbie" Robson paddled up alongside him at the next sink.

'Yes, I'm afraid so, Hooky,' Peewee replied, using the traditional nickname for a leading seaman. Robson was the senior leading hand of their department with the official title of Leading Hand of the Mess.

The very size of the man had an unnerving effect on the boy. Robson was powerfully built, and stood well over six-feet tall in his bare feet. He had a kindly nature however, and treated those junior to him in a firm but fair manner. In the short time that Peewee had been aboard the ship, he had formed a great deal of respect for the big leading hand.

'Oh shit!' Robson said after pressing his hot tap and getting the same result. 'The bloody stokers have been working overtime again, plenty of steam but no hot water.'

At that moment, Steve Tredrea, another junior who was one of the lucky ones with a billet in the mess, came into the bathroom.

'Mornin', young Tredders,' Robson greeted the boy by his nickname. 'Better watch the hot taps, they're bloody dodgy again as usual.'

By alternately squirting a few inches of cold water and several jets of steam, they managed to get enough warm water into the bowls to enable them to have a decent wash.

'It's nice to find that we have a couple of juniors who don't need to be taught the facts of navy life,' Robson said as he carefully negotiated his Adam's apple with an ancient cutthroat razor. 'Where are Tozer and Piper? They should have been down here by now.'

The question was not merely out of interest. Robson was responsible for the actions of the men under him, including their adherence to strict domestic discipline, in this case, their personal hygiene.

Tredrea said that he thought they had both gone to breakfast.

Robson nodded, 'I see,' he murmured in reply.

With their ablutions completed, the boys left the mess together and made their way up to the main dining hall, leaving Robson to the unpopular task of rousing the rest of the hands.

At any other time, the dining hall was probably the most cheerful place on the ship, particularly at lunch time after the rum and beer issue had been made. Then, the large compartment would be crowded and the air filled with the noise of men eating, talking, laughing and arguing, with the latest buzzes (rumours and gossip) the usual topics of conversation.

At breakfast on this cold dark morning, it had all the cheeriness of a funeral parlour. The men, some on their own, others in groups of various sizes, sat picking listlessly at their food.

As always, a surly group of MUPs (Men Under Punishment) had a table of their own close to the galley door where they sat separated like lepers from the other crewmembers. Soon they would take their places in the galley and be up to their elbows in scalding water that would rapidly turn into a greasy mess as the mountains of dirty eating and cooking utensils piled up, waiting to be scrubbed clean.

One of these, a young stoker, was idly flicking breadcrumbs at a life-sized painting of a moorhen, part of a group of wildfowl that had been painted on the walls of the dining hall by the celebrated naturalist Peter Scott. The crumbs had been dunked in tea so that they stood a better chance of sticking to the surface of the wall.

After collecting their breakfasts, Peewee's, a well burned sausage with canned tomatoes on fried bread, known as train smash, while Tredrea opted for the more exotic braised kidneys on toast, or, shit on a raft, as it was called, the boys joined Toz and the fourth the ship's new complement of junior signalmen, JTO "Pip" Piper.

Piper had finished eating and was lethargically sipping tea from a bowl normally used for soup or cereals.

It was not surprising that the most popular item on the breakfast menu were the warm bread rolls. Freshly baked each morning, they were sent up as soon as they came out of the oven in the bakery below the dining hall. They were in such demand that men would be queuing at the bakery door, long before they had finished baking.

'All the rolls have gone then,' Peewee grumbled at Toz, disappointed that his friend hadn't kept any back for him.'

'They've scoffed the bloody lot I bet,' Tredrea sneered. 'They're a right pair of shite-hawks these two.

'Toz stood up without a word and made a show of unbuttoning his shirt. Leaning forward slightly he extracted six thickly buttered rolls, leaving a bright yellow smear across his chest in the process.

'Three each,' he said, treating Tredrea to a scornful look of disdain. 'Poke them up your arse if you like, Tredders, I won't save you bugger all in future.'

'Oh, cheers Toz,' replied Tredrea happily, ignoring the remark. Stuffing a roll into his mouth, he took a large bite. 'Shit hot,' he mumbled through a mouthful of bread and butter. 'They're still warm as well,' he added.

'That's because he's had them next to his tits for the last twenty minutes,' Piper informed him.

'Well they taste great anyway,' Tredrea replied, already tucking into his second one.

'Eh up,' Toz said suddenly, nudging Peewee. 'Here comes our glorious leader, and he looks as if he's in a bit of a mood! Wonder what's up with him then.'

The burly figure of LTO Robson strode purposefully towards them, a dark frown set upon his normally cheerful face.

'Tozer, Piper,' he barked without preamble. 'Away you go. Get yourselves down to the mess and wait for me there. No but's,' he glared at Piper who looked as if he were about to protest. 'Leave your tea. Thumbs out of bums and move your backsides. Now!'

Robson was obviously in no mood for argument. Pip and Toz got up and left the hall immediately.

'I just can't stand,' Robson said as he lowered himself onto one of the vacated chairs, 'men who don't wash in the morning, especially before having breakfast. I'll give them a bit of a bollocking this morning and they'll remember in future.'

'Did they save that for you?' he went on, pointing at the last bread roll in front of Tredrea.

'Well, yes,' replied the boy worriedly. 'But that's alright isn't it?'

'Of course it is,' Robson said, 'provided you're not bothered by the fact that whichever one of them saved it for you has probably been scratching his arse and fondling his meat and two veg all night. Men do that kind of thing in their sleep you know, and I'm afraid it puts me off the idea of eating anything they might have handled, especially when you know they haven't bothered to wash their filthy hands.'

Steve Tredrea stood up quickly, his face stricken. 'Oh bloody cheers, Hooky,' he said, pushing the roll away from him. 'That's really made my day that has!'

Robson smiled at the boy and slowly shook his head in mock sympathy. 'A bit squeamish are we son? Well there's nothing wrong with that,' he sighed, picking up the discarded roll and stuffing it firmly into his own mouth.

4

A game of Chuffs and Puffs

SQUEEGY LIPS WAS A BASTARD. This was the considered and combined opinion of the whole of the signals department, and an opinion shared by a good many others aboard the aircraft carrier who had been unfortunate enough to cross his path.

His sole pleasure in life – or so it seemed to those who knew him – lay in causing as much distress and misery as possible to those junior to him. The fact that he had recently been elevated from Leading Tactical Operator, to Communications Yeoman, the equivalent in rank to Petty Officer, meant that he had a large and varied supply of victims from which to choose.

Among the men of the lower deck, there was a standing joke that claimed that during the war Squeegy Lips had defected to Germany and joined the Gestapo, only to be kicked out after just one week on the grounds of excessive cruelty.

Like a cat at a mouse hole, he was waiting expectantly at the top of the ladder that led onto the flag deck. His watch, which he always kept exactly three minutes fast in order to give him an advantage, showed the time at one minute past eight in the morning.

Any second now, he was thinking; any second now and I'll have them. He gazed searchingly around the flag deck, and for the first time that morning, he smiled. With the coming of daylight, his eyes had picked out a multitude of jobs that needed doing, and he was never happier than when he had a full list with which to greet the hands when they turned-to for work.

The flag deck atop the carrier's command superstructure known as the island was his personal pride and joy. In his capacity as Yeoman I /C FD, he was responsible for the efficiency of the signalling equipment and, of course, its cleanliness and tidiness.

Squeegy was particularly proud of his equipment. His private inventory was almost endless but the official one was short. It comprised of two pairs of signalling projectors, eight battery-operated Aldis lamps, six pairs of binoculars, four sets of semaphore sticks, and, stored in a huge iron locker, a vast bundle of assorted bunting stitched onto more than five-hundred yards of wire rope for use on dress ship occasions.

A Very pistol and box of flares were also listed and these were kept locked in a specially constructed metal container fixed to the starboard bulkhead. In an emergency, it would be the yeoman's responsibility to unlock the box and personally supervise the firing of the pistol.

There were two flag lockers mounted either side of a hooded signals desk and these were pigeonholed to enable storage of the large assortment of signalling flags. Finally, there were a number of metal cleats welded to the port and starboard bulkhead rails. These were used to secure the signal halyards that stretched down from various positions on the mainmast.

The mast was not the responsibility of the communications department, but as the signal halyards were attached to it, and given that he had the use of the small store in its base, Squeegy saw things differently. Unbeknown to his men, he had just obtained permission from the delighted radar and meteorological departments to assume responsibility for its paintwork.

As his eyes wandered around, he noted with perverse satisfaction, the pockets of rainwater that had collected in the large depressions caused by natural warping of the steel deck. Earlier he had sprayed the deck with salt water from the fire hydrant and it was particularly deep under the raised wooden boards known as sponsons, on which a man operating the signalling projectors would stand.

To improve things even further for himself, he had gone to the considerable trouble of crawling beneath them in order to shove some dirty rags into the concealed drains.

Yes. Squeegy Lips was a bastard!

His fat face suddenly broke into a large grin and the thick rubbery lips from which he earned his nickname, compressed with satisfaction. He could hear the sound of hurrying feet racing up the series of ladders below.

'About bloody time,' he bawled, as a string of men emerged onto the flag deck.

'We're not late, Yeo,' one of the older signalmen began, only to be cut short by an angry gesture from the yeoman.

'Not late! You are by my watch, Collins.' He shoved a thick hairy wrist to within an inch of the signalman's nose. 'Look here,' he went on, tapping the face of his wristwatch. 'It's nearly three minutes past.'

'By your watch that means it's not quite eight o'clock yet. So, in fact, we're all a few seconds early,' a dry voice broke in.

Squeegy whirled on the speaker. 'What did you say Allen?' he bawled.

Before Tactical Operator "Second Class" George Allen could reply, they were interrupted by a sudden outburst from the Tannoy speaker. 'Out pipes. All hands turn-to,' a metallic voice commanded.

'Never mind,' the yeoman snapped at Allen, inwardly also cursing himself for forgetting to turn down the volume on the loudspeaker.

Standing next to Peewee, Toz was having trouble suppressing a snigger until the yeoman turned on him.

'Find something funny do we, lad?' he demanded ominously.

Toz shook his head but was unable to maintain a straight face.

'Right,' spat Squeegy, glaring at the faces around him. 'I'll give you all something to laugh about. Before you do anything else this morning, and there's plenty, believe me, I want this deck mopped until it is dry. And by dry, I mean, as the proverbial bone. And as for you two,' he continued, glowering at Tozer and Green, 'any more out of you and you'll find yourselves working right through stand-easy. Now, cut the cackle, and get bloody moving - the lot of you.'

The small group broke apart and as if by magic, buckets, cloths and mops appeared in their hands. The yeoman strode amongst them like an admiral directing a battle. His shouted orders clearly heard by those working on the flight deck some forty-feet below.

'Bastard petty officers,' grumbled Naval Airman Milligan to his friend Riley, a flight deck stoker and fellow Irishman.

Riley nodded, 'They're all the bloody same - bastards,' he agreed.

Milligan had been detailed to clear out the gash bin in the bunkspace by the Duty PO that morning. He still did not look very well.

On the flag deck the men worked liked slaves for the next twenty minutes or so. With Squeegy Lips ready to pounce on the first one to slacken, they had no alternative.

It seemed that George Allen was wise to the yeoman's tricks. Either that or he was possessed of a remarkable sixth sense that directed him to check each of the drains in turn. It took him very little time to discover the cloths that were preventing the water from running away. Once these had been removed, the mopping up operation progressed smoothly and quickly and before long, the deck was as dry as it possibly could be.

Squeegy Lips had been looking forward to this moment. 'All right you lot, let's have you gathered around so as you can hear what I've got to say. Come on, chop chop, look lively now, I don't want to have to repeat myself.'

The men, a morose bunch now that the combination of freezing water and the chill wind had taken its toll on their hands and fingers, formed a ragged semi-circle and stood watching him, an air of suspicion about them.

'Right then,' the yeoman began when he was sure that he had their complete attention. He had been savouring this moment and wanted to enjoy it to the full. 'As from this morning, our department has assumed responsibility for the cleaning and painting of the mainmast!'

He paused, expecting a loud chorus of protest but was disappointed when it did not come. Instead, the men remained silent and continued to stare at him sullenly.

A puzzled frown appeared on the yeoman's face. 'What's the matter with you lot?' he demanded. 'Surely one of you must have something to say.

'I thought that radar and met were in charge of that,' George Allen spoke out.

'Well you thought bloody wrong, Allen,' the yeoman sneered. 'For your personal information, Chief Communications Yeoman Wilcox had a meeting with the chiefs of those departments earlier this morning and the upshot of it is, is that as from today, I am in charge of the mast, which in turn means that you lot are going to scrub it and paint it - twice a day if I say so. So, it's tough titty,' he ended with almost childish emphasis.

The men shuffled restlessly, faces dark and scowling.

'Now look lads.' The yeoman's voice had taken on a softer, almost apologetic tone. 'I don't like it any more than you do but I have to take orders as well you know, and what the chief yeoman says, goes.'

'I still don't reckon it's our job,' George insisted stubbornly.

'Well hard bloody shit Allen. It is now, and that's final, so stow the bloody drips or you'll find yourself in the rattle.' The old voice was back.

'Hunt and Tozer, you two shoot off and get a couple of buckets of fresh water. I'm going down to the PO's mess for a cup of coffee and when I get back I want to find that mast gleaming.' He stabbed a thick forefinger at George Allen. 'In the absence of a TO1, you're in charge while I'm gone, and I'm holding you personally responsible for seeing that the job is done properly. Nobody leaves the flag deck until I say so. Got it?'

The men broke up again, muttering cheerlessly as they retrieved their buckets and cloths.

As Yeoman Jolly – for that was his name – went down to his mess he was grinning broadly. Jolly wore truculence like a second skin, and it was far too thick to be pricked by something so trivial as a pang of conscience. On the contrary, he was feeling good. Very good indeed.

Up top, the signalmen approached their new task with something less than enthusiasm.

'What an absolute bastard!' Tom Collins complained bitterly.

'Too bloody right,' Allen agreed. 'He could have told us about the mast before we dried the bloody deck out.'

'Yeah, why not,' Toz said, echoing all of their thoughts. 'Now the deck's going to get soaking wet again.'

'So, let it get wet,' a signalman by the name of Olly Green said. 'All he told us to do was to mop it dry for a start. He never said anything about mopping it up again.'

Nobody bothered to reply. Green was the glamour boy of the department with darkly handsome good looks. He was well liked by his messmates but suffered with a reputation for making stupid observations.

'What?' he enquired, puzzled by the looks the others were giving him.

At that moment, the door to the Main Signal Office opened. The MSO was a box-like structure situated at the forward end of the flag deck. It was a tiny place about ten feet square, its main equipment comprising two desks, a typewriter, duplicating machine, three electric fires and two telephones. Tucked away on the end of one of the desks was a battered aluminium tray on which stood an equally battered kettle surrounded by an assortment of cracked and stained mugs, together with tea, coffee, sugar, and a tin of condensed milk.

It was from here that every signal sent or received by the ship was processed. Once typed, duplicated and distributed by messenger to the persons concerned, the original copy was then filed away for posterity.

The MSO never closed. It was manned around the clock by a small team of watchkeepers headed by a leading hand who was designated LHOW – Leading Hand of the Watch, currently, Leading Tactical Operator "Topsy" Turner.

'Oi, you lot,' he yelled from his position of warmth inside the door. 'The chief yeoman has just been on the phone. He wants two juniors to go down to his mess to lend a hand with cooks.'

'Balls!' Toz swore under his breath. Cooks was the navy term for mess deck cleaning. He shot Peewee a look, 'You and me again I'll bet.'

'I'd rather be down there than up here anyway,' Peewee replied. 'At least it's out of the bloody cold.'

'Sorry, Topsy, Allen called back. 'I'm not letting anybody go anywhere.'

Turner reluctantly stepped out of the office into the cold air. 'And just who are you to ignore the chief yeoman?' he demanded belligerently.

'Squeegy put him in charge,' proffered Collins.

'And threatened to put him in the shit if anyone leaves the flag deck,' Olly Green added.

'Suit yourselves then,' Turner shrugged. 'I'm not getting myself caught between the chief and the bloody yeoman. As far as I'm concerned I've passed on the message, so fuck your luck when the CCY gets here. I'm going back inside for a smoke.' He went quickly back into the office, slamming the door behind him.

Peewee gave George a worried look. 'That's going to stir things up a bit,' he said. 'Me and Toz would have been happy to go down and put the chief in the picture about Squeegy.'

'That's okay,' George smiled at him. The rule is, always obey the last order, and that is just what I intend to do. Let's crack on with the mast and give Squeegy his money's worth,' adding with a wink and a grin, 'If you catch my drift.'

The boy thought it over for a moment, then, as the meaning behind Allen's words sank in, he smiled in return before saying, 'You don't think the chief knows about the mast do you? Well, for all our sakes I hope you're right.' The office door swung open. 'I don't want to worry you lot but the chief is on his way up.' The door slammed shut.

'What are you going to say then, George?' Olly Green asked.

'God knows. Just keep working. I'll think of something.'

'We'll stick by you,' Pip Piper said encouragingly, but nobody believed him.

The next few minutes passed with agonising slowness but eventually there came the sound of heavy feet clambering up the ladder.

'Stand by, lads.' George murmured.

'Where's bloody Jolly?' It was almost a scream.

'He's gone below Chief,'' George replied simply.

'Gone below!' It was a scream. 'What the bloody hell for, eh?'

Chief Communications Yeoman Sam Wilcox looked positively evil. He had a naturally red face but at that moment its colour could be more accurately described as vivid purple.

'Alright then,' said Wilcox thickly, as the men remained silent. 'If none of you can explain why the yeoman has left the flag deck, perhaps one of you would care to tell me who was detailed to go down to the chief petty officers mess to help out with...' His voice trailed off as he caught sight of Tozer and Tredrea perched on a cross member of the mainmast about fifteen-feet above the flag deck.

For a brief second he paused to suck in air, then roared, 'What are those two juniors doing up the bloody mainmast? This is supposed to be a warship, not a fucking circus.'

'They're scrubbing it down,' George said carefully. 'Yeoman Jolly detailed us to do it. He put me in charge of the working party.'

'Jolly told you to scrub the mast down!' The chief sounded incredulous. 'Since when did my staff assume the responsibility for the work of other departments?' he demanded.

'Since this morning, Chief,' George replied promptly. He was beginning to enjoy the exchange. 'The yeoman told us that you had authorised it.'

'Jolly said that? Well he's very much mistaken.' Wilcox's voice had dropped and taken on a low, menacing quality. 'Right then. I want to see him in my mess in precisely ten minutes. Piper,' he snapped at the junior. 'Hop to it, lad, find the yeoman and tell him.'

As Piper sped gratefully away, Wilcox fixed George with a baleful eye. 'Alright, Allen. Accepting that you were put in charge of this fiasco, I'm holding you responsible for not obeying my order as given to you by the leading hand of the watch. Get your hat and report to the Regulating Office. You, my lad, are in the rattle.'

'If he goes, Chief, then we're all going as well,' a defiant voice spoke out firmly.

Five hearts stopped in mid-beat and five pairs of eyes turned in horrified disbelief on the speaker. Peewee Hunt, his voice thickening with emotion could only go on. 'Yeoman Jolly told Allen that he would put him in the rattle if he allowed any of us to leave the flag deck before he got back so it's not his fault and it's not fair to punish him.'

Staggered by the boy's outburst Wilcox hesitated. To the surprise of everyone, his voice was calm when he replied. 'Belay the last order, Allen. Thank you, Hunt,' he continued, turning to face the junior. 'Instead, you and the rest of this bloody shower will work an extra half-hour this morning.'

'You stupid little bastard,' Collins sneered after the chief had gone. 'Why couldn't you keep your stupid mouth shut?'

'At least he had the guts to speak up though,' Toz said, defending his friend.

'Yes, and it's a good job he did if you ask me. At least he managed to keep George out of the rattle,' Steve Tredrea put in, adding, 'even if you don't care, the rest of us bloody well do.'

'You cheeky little sod, don't you talk to me like that,' snarled Collins, grabbing a handful of the junior's number-eight shirt. He would have hit the boy but for the intervention of George Allen who pulled him away.

'Easy, Tom,' George said soothingly. 'No need for that, mate.'

Peewee tried to apologise for his action but Collins turned his back on him sulkily.

'Forget about it,' George told the junior. He turned to the others looking at his watch. 'Seeing as I'm in charge we'll all go down for stand-easy now. Squeegy and the chief are going to be tied up for a while yet, so with a bit of luck we can pinch an extra ten minutes.'

The tension was immediately broken and the mood was far more friendly as they trooped below.

Down in the mess they found Robbie Robson engaged in an excited discussion with a number of other mess members including Clive Appleby.

'What's up, Hooky?' George enquired.

'Haven't you lot heard?' Appleby answered. 'Topsy just phoned down. He's just got the signal. The ship's been put under sailing orders!'

'You're kidding us of course aren't you, Clive,' Olly Green said. 'This heap ain't ready to cross the Serpentine yet.'

'Well, you'd better believe it, Olly,' Robson told him. 'We're sailing for Gibraltar on Friday. After that, it's through the Med and down the Suez Canal. It looks like we'll be in Singapore for Easter. I hope you lot weren't planning to go home for a dirty weekend,' he finished with a chuckle.

This was bad news for some, particularly the married men who lived ashore in their quarters. Leaving their families for what might turn out to be many months or possibly years was not good news for them. For the juniors though who had yet to make their first trip to sea, the news was not only good, it was extremely exciting.

Further good news arrived that morning when the chief yeoman reappeared on the flag deck.

'Listen up, lads. As of now, responsibility for the mast is back in the hands of the radar and meteorological departments.' He paused for a moment, enjoying the suspense on their faces as they waited, knowing there was more to come. Suddenly his face broke into a big round grin. 'You've all done well enough this morning, so clear away below and get your dinners.'

'He's not such a bad bloke after all,' Peewee said to the others as they raced down to the dining hall – exactly three minutes early.

5

Last run in Guzz

WITH THE NEWS OF THEIR impending departure made known to the crew, a remarkable change had occurred in the atmosphere onboard.

The great ship had lain alongside her dockyard berth for almost five months. Peaceful and unmoving, she had lain breathing gently, like an anaesthetised iron giant at the mercy of the surgeon's knife.

The surgeons in this case had been an army of plumbers, welders, electricians and a dozen or more other trades who had probed expertly into the metal body, ripping-out, repairing, and restoring wherever they went.

Now, the slumbering leviathan had awakened and was already beginning to flex huge muscles. Deep inside its cavernous iron belly, vital organs once again began to function with renewed vigour.

Now, all was hustle and bustle as every one of the ship's diverse departments became alive with activity and the days went flying by.

New men were arriving all the time. Some after long periods of shore duty were keen to get back to sea again. Others, like the juniors, were eager to get to sea for the first time.

There were those who were not so keen, and on arrival could be heard complaining bitterly about the terrible injustice that had befallen them.

'I've been a barrack-stanchion for so long, that I've forgotten the arse end of a ship from the other,' dripped one bewildered stores accountant who wore three stripes on his left sleeve. Officially termed good-conduct badges, one stripe was awarded for every four years of satisfactory naval service. 'After I did me twelve, I only signed on again because I liked it where I was, up there in the country, miles away from the soddin' oggin.'

39

The Commodore Naval Drafting (CND) had unearthed the man and finally drafted him back to sea after he had enjoyed years of a cushy little number in HMS *Royal Arthur*, the Royal Navy Leadership School at Corsham in Wiltshire.

On the Wednesday afternoon prior to sailing, the aircraft carrier temporarily left the berth to which she had been attached for so long and assisted by a flotilla of tug boats, moved out into midstream. Here she had room to carry out a full three-hundred-and-sixty degree swing in order to check and calibrate the ship's compass. This was a very necessary operation following a major refit. The banging and hammering of the workmen could have altered the magnetic properties of the ship, which would affect the ship's compass readings at sea, possibly with disastrous results. It was a routine and somewhat boring manoeuvre requiring little or no assistance from the majority of the crew. Nevertheless, Squeegy Lips considered it important and dangerous enough to justify ordering the whole of the tactical communications department to close up on the flag deck.

Although Robbie Robson and some of the other senior men had squeezed into the MSO for a cigarette and a hot drink, and despite the fact that Squeegy had gone to assist the chief yeoman on the compass platform, the flag deck was still overcrowded. Men wandered about aimlessly like cows in a field, while some sat on the sponsons, squashed like sardines. Others lined the port side rail trying to summon up some interest in the slight activity on the flight deck below. As the aircraft would only arrive onboard when the ship was clear of land, there was precious little of that.

Peewee and Toz were at the starboard rail taking in the general scene across the water when George appeared alongside them.

'Are you two planning to go ashore tonight?' he enquired.

'Dunno yet,' Toz replied.

'Of course we are,' corrected Peewee. 'It's the last chance for us before we sail, remember?'

Toz grinned. 'I suppose we are then, seeing as you're twisting my arm.'

'I didn't know you could be so hard to convince, Toz,' George chuckled. 'Well, seeing as how you've made up your minds, do you want to come ashore with some of us? It's going to be a good run tonight, the last one in dear old Guzz for a while. Almost the whole ship's company will be on the town.'

Plymouth and Devonport get their endearing nickname almost certainly thanks to a Captain Frederick Bedford who wrote a pocket book for sailors in the late nineteenth century. In it, he uses an Asian word, Guz, to represent a measurement of one yard. It did not take long for the romance and poetry of the ordinary West Country sailor's language for this to become used as a term for returning home to the dockyard, or more simply, yard, hence, returning home to Guzz.

'He's dead right, lads. You'll be letting the side down if you don't.' Olly Green joined them. 'Besides,' he went on, grinning at the boys, 'A load of sparkers are coming as well so we might end up with a half-decent punch up.'

'Brilliant!' Toz laughed, balling his fists and shadow-boxing the air. 'Nothing like a bit of sparker bashing to make a good night out,' he joked.

'Definitely not,' Peewee agreed with a smile, pleased by the invitation. It was an indication that they were beginning to be accepted by the older hands.

Of course, there would be no sparker bashing. The radio operators out -numbered them by at least three to one, and while a good deal of professional rivalry existed between the radio and tactical departments, it was extremely rare for it to come to blows.

With the operation successfully completed and the ship back alongside, George and the two juniors joined the crowd of men filing over the gangway when shore leave commenced at 1800 hours.

Leaving the dockyard via the Albert gate, their first stop was the Keppel's Head, a spit and sawdust pub just across the road from the dockyard gate. Here, the landlord kept a good supply of wine and spirits and took reasonable care of his beer, but at ninepence a pint the Scrumpy was understandably his best-seller.

The air was thick with tobacco smoke and the place crowded with sailors, many at the bar jostling one another in an attempt to catch the barman's eye. He was working at a furious speed, pulling pints as if his physical well-being depended on it, and it was not long before he served the three friends their drinks.

They moved away from the bar, Peewee and Toz following George Indian-style as he picked a way through the crowd. Early evening was the busiest time for the pub as it had long been a tradition for sailors to call there for the first pint of the night before heading off into the city.

There were no vacant seats, so the three had to content themselves with leaning against the dirty stone wall facing the door.

'Nice drop of scrumpy this,' commented Toz after gulping down a couple of large mouthfuls.

Peewee grinned. 'Shame about the colour though. It looks like the urine sample I gave at the recruiting office in Birmingham.'

'I can see that I've landed myself with a right pair of wise guys,' George said. 'One's a connoisseur of fermented apple juice at the tender age of sixteen, and the other knocks it back like orange juice.' He pointed at Toz's glass, already nearly empty. 'You need to go careful with that stuff - it's bloody lethal.'

The bar counter was now so solidly packed that at George's suggestion they left the pub and hailed a fast black, a taxi in navy parlance, to take them into Plymouth.

The driver dropped them outside the Westward Television building and they walked back along Union Street to the London Inn, a favourite and notorious haunt of the servicemen based in and around the city. In addition to serving cider, although at the more costly price of elevenpence a pint, it also boasted a live band. It was also well known as an establishment from where many ladies of easy virtue conducted their business, thereby ensuring its reputation as a popular place.

If the Keppel's Head had seemed crowded, it was nothing to that which greeted them now. The enormous open-plan bar was heaving with a multi-uniformed crowd of servicemen, singing, shouting and arguing. Some made obscene gestures at the brassy women who either smiled or swore in reply.

'Bloody hell,' breathed Toz. 'Just look at it!'

'I told you it was going to be a good one tonight,' George said. 'Come on, let's mingle, some of our lads are bound to be in here somewhere.'

He led the way weaving a zigzag course between the overcrowded tables, peering through a haze of tobacco smoke as he went. Following last in line, Peewee found his path suddenly blocked by a middle-aged woman of generous proportions.

'Hello, sailor boy – looking for me are you?' She smiled, displaying a dazzling row of even white teeth.

'Er, no. Not exactly.' The boy flushed with embarrassment.

'Eee'r Mary, leave the little prat alone,' a coarse voice called from a nearby table. 'Eee won't `ave no money. You're supposed to be getting the bleeding drinks in, and finding us some good looking blokes to pay for them.'

'On me way, Sal,' the big woman yelled over her shoulder. Grabbing the young sailor by the back of the neck with one hand, she roughly pressed his face against her bosom, slapping him hard between the shoulder blades with the other. 'I'll be seeing you later, me darlin',' she growled, then shoved him aside and strode off to the bar.

Shaken, but otherwise unhurt, Peewee caught up with the others who had discovered Collins, Green and a number of their messmates sitting around two tables which had been commandeered and hauled together.

To ease the crush at the bar, the landlord had deployed a number of staff to act as waiters. One of these had just delivered a tray of drinks to the table and George ordered another three pints of cider before he disappeared.

'Becoming a sea-daddy then, are we?' leered a thickset sparker with a Welsh accent, winking suggestively at the men around the table who responded with coarse laughter and grins. 'Never knew you were like that, Georgie,' he pantomimed with an exaggerated lisp.

'Balls to you, mate,' George retorted good-humouredly. 'These two don't need any sea-daddying. They could drink a sparker lightweight like you under the table anytime.'

'That's what I like to hear, boyos,' the Welshman laughed, 'Baby sailors who can hold their booze. Grab some chairs, lads, and join the party.'

As the evening progressed, the conversation was mostly concerned with their ship's future programme and colourful tales of previous adventures abroad.

Peewee and Toz said little. Unlike the others, they had no sea-stories to tell, but they were content to listen happily and join in with the laughter and general banter.

At nine o'clock, "Mike Mamba and The Cobras" struck up. Mike, an ex-dockyard policeman, played the trumpet with more than enough energy to make up for his lack of musical skill. His band, The Cobras, were made up of Ron "Rhythm" Rawlings, a former army drummer and veteran of the Great War who was fast approaching senility. A local builder called "Gem" Stone on electric bass, and Freddy "Fingers" Philpott on guitar. The landlord had given Philpott the nickname as he doubled as a barman when not playing in the band. The man had no idea that it had been derived from his dubious till keeping rather than his skill as a guitarist. The quartet had been in residence at the pub since they had formed almost a year earlier. It was not that they were particularly popular, but that the landlord found it extremely difficult to persuade any other bands to return to his premises to play there again after a first visit. The London Inn was not the ideal place for the expression of genuine artistic talent.

By this time, Peewee, who had been nursing his drink and was only on his third pint, was becoming slightly concerned for Toz who had manfully been keeping up with the others. He had consumed two or three glasses of whisky along with the cider.

Olly Green must have been thinking along the same lines. 'You'd better hope that the weather holds out tomorrow. Whisky and scrumpy are not the best of pals when taken together,' he warned from across the table where he was sitting with an attractive but hard-faced girl, perched on his lap.

'Stow that for a load of bollocks, Olly,' Taff Jones butted in. 'George reckons the kid can handle it.' He threw an arm around Toz's neck, 'That's right isn't it, boyo, you can handle it can't you?'

Toz managed the Welshman a squiffy smile by way of answer.

A leading signalman sounded concerned as he asked what time the juniors had to be back onboard, pointing out that 2230 hours was normally the limit for boys of their age.

'It's okay,' George Allen told him. 'The chief has given them watchkeepers leave so they've got until midnight.'

'Bloody Cinderella leave!' Tom Collins snorted. 'I just don't know what this bloody mob is coming to. When I was their age, I had to be back onboard by ten o'clock every night.'

'Aarrr, but that were a long time ago, Tom,' a sparker by the name of "Bungy" Williams, teased.

'Aarrr, you be right there, Bungy me hearty,' cried Taff Jones, picking up the theme. 'That were back in the days when the men had to be separated from the boys! In your case, boyo, I bet they had to use a crowbar!'

Everybody laughed aloud at that except Collins who remained silent, glowering in the direction of the two boys.

'Hello again, my little darling, fancy a dance then?'

Peewee looked up to find the big blonde woman towering over him, her neat white teeth exposed in what she supposed to be her brightest smile.

'Go on, boyo,' chortled Taff Jones. 'Consider yourself honoured. Bloody Mary doesn't dance with just anybody.'

'That's because just anybody won't dance with Bloody Mary, the fat cow,' Collins sniggered, keen to re-establish himself among the group.

Peewee shoved his chair back quickly as the woman's large hand closed around his pint glass. Collins ducked, but he was too late. The glass and its contents struck him squarely in the chest. He leapt to his feet cursing, cider soaking his jacket and shirt, running in swift rivulets down to his crotch and legs.

'Fucking cow!' he yelled, shaking his fist as Mary dragged the reluctant boy away to the dance floor.

The band was struggling painfully through their own arrangement of the Bobby Vee song, *Poetry In Motion*, while Bloody Mary displayed a style of dancing which had more in common with heavyweight wrestling than Victor Sylvester. Peewee soon abandoned any idea of using his own feet as the woman clamped his head between her breasts and swung him from side to side with his legs dangling like those of a rag doll.

The boy was made to suffer through two more dances in this manner when to his great relief the band decided to take a break, and the woman escorted him back to his friends. After shooting Collins a look that could have sunk a battleship, she said, 'I'll be back for you later, my luvver,' before heading back to re-join her unsavoury friends at their own table.

'Jesus H. Christ! I wouldn't fancy being in your shoes, Tom,' Bungy Williams spluttered through a mouthful of ale. 'Bloody Mary's been known to sort out a few Royal Marine commandos, all by herself.'

'I don't think he's got anything to worry about,' said Peewee. Picking up the fresh pint that George had bought for him, he took a big swallow.

'How d'you mean?' Williams asked.

'I mean that I'm the poor bugger who should be worried,' the boy explained. 'It's me that she meant she'd be coming back for!'

They all looked at him, grins spreading across their faces, even that of Collins.

'Well! Fuck your luck, my son,' said one incredulous voice.

Peewee was soon proved correct as he and a staggering Toz tried to slip out of the pub quietly, unseen by Mary. George Allen was staying on with the others but had insisted that his two young friends make their way back to the ship in order to be onboard in good time.

The band were playing their final number which was also their party piece - a passable rendition of *Ceremonial Sunset* - as the pair wove an unsteady path towards the door.

'Wait for me, boys, I'm coming with you,' Bloody Mary called across the room.

Groaning inwardly, Peewee hustled Toz out into the street, praying that they would find some form of transport close at hand.

They were out of luck. Outside a fine drizzle slanted down, it's pattern clearly visible under the brightness of the street lighting. A bus had just pulled away from the nearby stop and there was not a single taxi in sight.

Peewee had a sudden idea. There must be an alleyway somewhere along the street, he reasoned. If they could find one, they could hide in it.

'Wass goin' on,' Toz slurred as Peewee took his arm and towed him along the pavement as fast as he could. Luckily, an alleyway soon appeared and Peewee wasted no time in bundling Toz inside and herding him to the far end which was in deep shadow but blocked by a locked wooden gate.

'Bloody hell!' mumbled Toz. 'Are you after my parts?'

'You must be joking,' Peewee told him. 'Have a piss or something but for Christ's sake, keep your mouth shut for a few minutes.'

'Good idea, I'm breaking my neck anyway.' Toz fumbled clumsily with his zip, hampered by the effect of the alcohol inside him.

Peewee stood still, listening. He could hear the sharp click of high-heeled shoes coming from the direction of the pub. Please keep it quiet Toz, he prayed to himself. The clicking slowed its beat, stopped, then started slowly again. Peewee got a good look at the bulky figure as it went by along the pavement, passing the open end of the alley.

'Oh shit! It's her alright,' he whispered under his breath. His heart missed at least two beats as the sound of Toz urinating loudly against the wall made him jump. Oh shit!' he repeated, breathing raggedly, 'that must have buggered it.'

Indeed it had. The lumpy figure reappeared, starkly silhouetted against the lights in the street.

'I was wonderin' where you'd got to, my luv. Having a slash are you?' Her large body all-but blocked out the already dim light in the narrow passageway as she moved towards them.

Peewee stood and waited, mouth dry, his heart thumping.

'Ooohh,' she shrilled, 'You've still got your mate with you - it must be my lucky night!' In the blink of an eye, Peewee found himself pinned against the wall and as the woman dealt expertly with his belt and trouser fastenings, the combination of stale gin, cheap perfume and her rank body sweat almost caused him to vomit.

'Hey, wass you two doin'? Don't I get a bit as well?' Toz, having fully relieved himself was keen to get in on the action, but in his befuddled state it was obvious that he had not recognised the woman in the dark.

You wouldn't be so keen if you knew who it was, Peewee thought to himself grimly.

'Of course you do, sweetie,' murmured Mary, beckoning with the fingers of her left hand. She already had Peewee exposed and was gently fondling him with the other. As she took hold of Toz, she gave a little gasp of pleasure at finding him ready. 'It's still a bit wet at the end, my luv,' she whispered. Toz groaned softly as she ran the ball of her thumb over the tip of his gland.

Without warning, she dropped to her knees in front of the two boys, and Peewee looked down at her. Oh my God, what is she up to now? He worried briefly, but then his back arched and instinctively he placed both hands on the woman's head as she engulfed him with her mouth.

While most of his brain was preoccupied with incredible new feelings, a small part of it kept insisting that something was not quite right. It was only when Mary turned her attention back to Toz that he discovered what it was. As he zipped up his trousers, his eyes caught a glimpse of an odd-shaped, pale looking object that seemed to glisten on the wet ground in the dark alley. He reached down, brushing against the woman's knee as he picked the object up. It was a beautifully made, gleaming white pair of false teeth!

The taxi ride back to the dockyard was conducted in silence. Toz slept all the way and the driver was seemingly indisposed toward conversation. Peewee paid the fare and gave the driver his last sevenpence as a tip before pointing Toz in the direction of the gangway.

It was a steep climb for the tide was in and it had lifted the ship. The gangway was at an angle of almost forty-five degrees, and the Royal Marine Corporal of the Gangway and the Duty Petty Officer eyed their progress with interest.

'Names?' The DPO demanded when they finally reached the top and stepped aboard.

'JTO Hunt and JTO Tozer, communications mess,' Peewee answered smartly.

As the petty officer turned to the index box that held their shore leave cards, Toz said loudly, 'JTO Tozer and JTO Hunt, communicaty chest.'

The DPO swung back and eyed the boy with suspicion. 'Are you drunk, lad?' he rapped. The marine corporal looking on was grinning broadly.

'No, PO, he's just a bit tired that's all,' Peewee explained anxiously.

'He looks as pissed as a rat to me,' the petty officer said coldly. He handed Peewee the two cards. 'Get him below and turned in before I turn nasty.'

Gratefully taking their cards, Peewee murmured a quick, 'Aye aye, PO,' and hurriedly propelled Toz through the watertight door into the canteen flat.

Once inside the bunkspace Toz collapsed completely and Peewee was reduced to half dragging and half carrying his friend the considerable distance to their bunks. There he laid him on the deck for a couple of minutes while he fought to regain his breath.

Toz's bunk was the top one. How am I going to get him up there? he wondered helplessly, before hitting on the idea of putting Toz in his own bunk, which was the middle one.

As part of the duty watch, Clive Appleby had not been ashore. The signalman was turned in and had been fast asleep until Peewee heaved the fully dressed and already loudly snoring Toz into the empty bunk alongside him.

'What the fuck is going on?' he demanded angrily.

'We're just swopping bunks for the night,' the boy replied.

'Well think of the bloody watchkeepers,' Appleby grumbled. 'I've got to get up again for four o'clock.' He rolled over, pulling the blankets over his head.

Peewee licked the end of a finger and drew a line on an imaginary board. 'Score one to me,' he said under his breath.

After undressing, he swung up into Toz's bunk and arranged the cold blankets around his body, then lay back and closed his eyes, but not for long.

Until then, he had been so concerned with the task of looking after Toz that he had not realised quite how drunk he was himself. He opened his eyes and waited for the ship to stop revolving.

Suddenly he found himself having to swallow rapidly as his mouth filled with salty spittle, then without warning his stomach began to churn.

Panic stricken, he rolled out of the bunk forgetting about the extra height until his feet hit the steel deck with a nasty thump. Cannoning from one block of bunks into another, he lurched crazily towards the bulkhead door already knowing that he was not going to make it to the heads in time.

Milligan and his chum Riley had just returned from shore and were standing by the gash bin. Barging them aside, Peewee hung himself over the side of it and heaved.

'Dirty little bastard,' said Milligan to Riley.

'Yeah, crabby little sod,' grunted Riley, narrowly missing the boy's head as he urinated into the bin.

6

Bon voyage

AT 1000 HOURS ON Friday morning Her Majesty's ship *Ark Royal* was in all respects ready for sea. Groups of seamen who had been working feverishly throughout the early morning now stood in idle readiness at several casting off stations from the focsle at the bow, all the way aft to the quarterdeck at the stern of the ship almost a thousand-feet to the rear of the huge vessel. They were awaiting final orders to slip the last of the heavy steel wire ropes or "springs" that would allow the *Mighty Ark* her freedom.

The ship's ladders had been swung in and were securely lashed and stowed. The three heavy gangways positioned forward, midships, and aft, had all been detached and lowered onto the jetty. These had been hauled clear by gangs of dockyard workers and now lay alongside the tangled assortment of redundant power cables, air, water, and diesel hoses that had bled life into the ship during her long rest in port.

It was a cold, wet, and cheerless morning but for the ceremony taking place. Many of the wives, girlfriends, and families of the crew, had come to wave their good-byes and to blow kisses and safe wishes to their loved ones while a Royal Marine Band assembled on the jetty delivered a stirring medley of soul-stirring patriotic music - *A Life on the Ocean Wave*, *Rule Britannia*, and, of course, the official march of the Royal Navy, *Hearts of Oak*.

The *Ark Royal* had a Royal Marine band of its own but they were formed in ranks along with the ship's small detachment of commandos, no doubt grateful for being excused the task themselves given the weather conditions. From the dockside, the marines were hidden from view by a cordon of blue-suited sailors, more than a thousand in all who lined the side of the flight deck end to end.

High up atop "the island" on the compass platform or ship's bridge, the captain was ready to proceed. 'Stand by for'ard, stand by aft.' The second officer of the watch, a young midshipman, instantly relayed the order over the command intercom.

Lieutenant Commander Cousins, the ship's navigating officer, was bending over the chart table making last-minute corrections. He straightened suddenly, smiling sheepishly as the captain calmly murmured, *'Pro bono publico no bloody panico*, Navigator.' It had been a popular saying by the officers and men of the previous *Ark Royal*, fondly known by its crew as the *Lucky Ark*. During the first two years of The Second World War, she had served with distinction in several theatres of naval operations and won a number of battle honours and awards. The most memorable of these, perhaps, was the crippling of the German battleship *Bismarck* that had famously sunk the Royal Navy's largest battle cruiser HMS *Hood* on the 24th May 1941. Two days after the loss of the *Hood*, *Swordfish* bombers of *Ark Royal*'s 820 Naval Air Squadron located and successfully attacked the German Chancellor's pride and joy, leaving her damaged and unable to steer. The *Bismarck* was finished off and sunk by British Naval Forces the following day. Despite her success at sinking the *Hood*, since departing Gotenhafen on May 19th, two weeks after Adolf Hitler had proudly inspected her, *Bismarck*'s first and only wartime deployment had lasted just eight days. It was not true that the German fleet commander, Admiral Lutjens, was a fervent Nazi who died on the bridge of the *Bismarck* clutching the birthday telegram that he had received from Hitler earlier that day. Lutjens certainly died on the bridge of the *Bismarck*, but he was no Nazi as he was unkindly portrayed in the film, *Sink the Bismarck*.

Luck eventually ran out for the *Lucky Ark* when she was torpedoed off Gibraltar on13th November1941. After a desperate thirteen-hour night-time struggle to save the ship, she was abandoned shortly before she finally capsized and sank. The attack by the German submarine *U81*, cost the aircraft carrier the loss of all her aircraft, one rating, Able Seaman E. Mitchell, and the ship's cat.

Cousins realised that the captain must have noticed the crossed fingers of his free hand as he worked at the chart table.

'Sorry sir,' he replied dutifully. The captain raised an arm dismissively, brushing the apology aside. A blushing smile then spread across the navigator's face. The captain also had his fingers crossed.

Chief Communications Yeoman Wilcox hovering in the background had observed and enjoyed the subtle exchange. He was old enough to remember the expression that had become known around the fleet, back when he was just a boy signalman himself. Turning to the tactical operator at the small desk aft of the port side of the bridge he snapped, 'Tell the flag deck to standby.'

Olly Green pressed the transmit button on his handset. 'Stand by the ensigns,' his voice squawked over the intercom circuit.

On the flag deck, Clive Appleby stood on the wooden sponson at the port ten-inch signalling projector, ready to give the brief prearranged flash to the men waiting at the sea and harbour ensign positions.

The main command intercom burst into life and crackled, 'Let go for'ard...' Each man waited for the second order that would galvanise him into action. It soon came.

'Let go aft.'

'Change ensigns,' Green's voice ordered. TO (1) Appleby flashed a crisp, two-second burst of light, and the large White Ensign and Union Jack were swiftly lowered from the collapsible flagstaff's positioned at either end of the flight deck. Simultaneously, the smaller sea ensign was broken out at the mainmast only to be instantly seized by a gust of wind that wrapped the flag around its halyard. HMS *Ark Royal* was now officially at sea.

'Clear that, ensign,' Wilcox roared over the intercom but an alert signalman was already attending to it.

On command, the men on the flight deck came smartly to attention as the marine band broke into the national anthem. Astern of the attendant tugboats, *Alsatian* and *Boxer*, the water churned into a thick, creamy froth as they heaved ahead together, gently easing their fifty-five thousand ton burden clear of the sea wall.

From somewhere in the dockyard a siren screamed a salute that was echoed by every ship in the harbour, including the tiny *Torpoint Ferry*. The carrier gave a short answering blast that sent a cloud of soot high into the air. Most of it was caught and swept away by the wind, but not before the men on the flag and after decks of the island received a generous dusting.

The fine drizzle that had persisted throughout the proceedings had increased to a steady downpour of freezing cold rain. Because of the worsening conditions the men formed up on the flight deck were prematurely given the order to dismiss. Most of them scuttled away quickly, keen to get below and out of the biting wind and rain. Some, chiefly those with loved ones still on the jetty, remained there waving their last farewells in the direction of the rapidly vanishing sea wall. The strains of the Royal Marine Band could still just be heard on the gusting wind. They were playing *Auld Lang Syne*.

With their towlines recovered, all that remained for the tugboats was to escort their charge safely through the narrow doglegged channel into the deeper water of Plymouth Sound where the great ship would increase speed and head out towards the breakwater and the open sea.

As junior of the watch, Steve Tredrea had the distinction of being the first of the four junior signalmen to receive the first signal at sea. It came by flashing light from the old signal fort perched atop the massive breakwater that protected the Sound and was now lying some distance astern. Despite the poor visibility, Tredrea was able to pick out the Morse symbols without difficulty. The message read simply, *Bon voyage Mighty Ark.* It was not considered necessary to send a reply.

An hour after clearing the breakwater, the ship increased speed to a business-like twenty-six knots as it went to Flying Stations in readiness to receive her aircraft.

Peewee Hunt who had taken over from Tredrea for the afternoon watch was alone on the flag deck. It was bitterly cold and the boy was grateful for the protection of his foul-weather clothing.

As he dutifully scoured the horizon in all directions, he was thinking enviously of his watch-keeping colleagues whose duties kept them warm and snug within the shelter of the bridge or the Main Signal Office. He was therefore, pleasantly surprised, and pleased, when the door of the MSO opened a few inches to reveal an outstretched hand proffering a mug of steaming hot tea.

As soon as he had taken it, the hand shot back inside and the door clanged shut like a steel trap.

'Bridge to flag deck,' the chief yeoman's voice called over the intercom.

'Flag deck,' the boy responded promptly.

'Well done, flag deck,' the chief's voice came back, pleased to find the young tactical operator on the ball. 'We will shortly be taking aircraft on board, so have your flying signals at the ready and keep a sharp lookout. I expect your visual sighting report in advance of the seamen lookouts down here on the bridge. Got it? Bridge out.'

Hunt grinned despite the cold. At least it had stopped raining and the hot tea helped. He knew that the chief yeoman saw it as a matter of pride that his department was always a couple of jumps ahead of the opposition provided by the navigating officer, and the junior did not intend to let him down. He was already experiencing a surge of excitement with the arrival of the squadrons of warplanes, rapidly becoming imminent.

He was not the only one to experience such feelings. As he snapped to the task of bending-on the bulky flying signals for hoisting, the afterdecks abaft the mainmast and funnel were beginning to fill with a good number of spectators, or goofers, as they were derisively called.

Below the island, the flight deck was a hive of activity. To the young signalman it appeared a chaotic sight with groups of men dressed in overalls of various colours, heads adorned with protective helmets and bulky ear protectors, all seemingly milling around with no apparent sense of purpose.

Several strange looking vehicles painted in yellow and black stripes appeared to be driven around with the gay abandon of dodgem cars at a fairground, and it seemed to the boy that it could only be a matter of time before an accident took place.

In fact, he could not have been more wrong with his assumptions. What he was observing was the incredible teamwork of the Fleet Air Arm specialist deck crews as they made ready to receive and welcome their pilots and aircraft aboard.

With the flying signals ready to hoist, Peewee adjusted his binoculars and concentrated on the skies to port and starboard astern of the ship.

'Bridge to flag deck.'

Peewee lowered the binoculars as he turned to answer the chief and was surprised to find LTO Ash at the signals desk, already making the response.

'Flag deck!'

'Radar indicates a wave of aircraft at forty miles on the port quarter. By their speed of approach I think we can assume it's Eight One Five Squadron. I expect your visual confirmation at any moment. Bridge out.'

Adrenaline coursed through the boy as he resumed his stance, raking the port quarter through the binoculars. 'Come on, come on,' he murmured to himself, then spun round in disbelief when he heard Ash's voice shouting over the intercom. 'Flag deck to bridge – aircraft closing on the port quarter – range approximately twelve miles.

'Very well done, flag deck.' Wilcox's reply came in a voice rich with satisfaction.

Peewee stared in awe at the LTO. 'How on earth did you spot them so soon Hooky?' he asked. 'I couldn't even see them through these,' he added, indicating with the binoculars.

'Neither could I, lad. I just used one of the tricks of the trade that you'll learn soon enough. The chief had just told us where they were on the radar screen, so I just made an educated guess. I bet if you take a look now, they'll just about be in sight.'

Raising the binoculars, the boy studied the sky above the horizon on the port quarter and there they were - a group of helicopters some ten miles distant.

'Flag deck to bridge.'

'Bridge!'

'Confirm helicopters on the port quarter.'

'Thank you, flag deck. Well done again.'

'It was JTO Hunt who made the first sighting chief.'

'Thank you, Ash. Bravo Zulu Hunt. Bridge out.'

'Wow! Cheers for that, Hooky,' Peewee said feeling doubly pleased with the fact that the chief had used the phonetic code for "well done" to congratulate him personally.

'S'only fair innit,' sniffed Ash. 'Now, get those fucking flying signals up the mast while I go back inside for a warm.'

Within minutes, the Wessex helicopters of 815 Squadron were approaching the ship in a line formation from astern. One broke away and took up a hovering station at five-hundred yards on the port beam, ready to act as rescue chopper in the event of any mishap. Sounding like airborne tractors the remainder flew straight in to land, blue and yellow shapes settling like giant bees on the flag deck to be seized by the handlers and whisked away via the pair of giant lifts down to the vast hangars below.

Next came the fighter squadrons, *Sea Vixens* and *Scimitars*, startling everyone up on the island as they swooped from the sky like monstrous birds of prey to buzz the ship before forming into a circular landing pattern.

It was a very exciting experience for Peewee as one after another they came in to land from astern. An illusion of slow motion was created during their approach, but this was quickly shattered by the noise itself as the extended landing hooks caught one of the five arrester wires, bringing the aircraft to an abrupt, engine-howling, tyre-screaming halt.

One *Scimitar* pilot misjudged his touchdown and overshot the wires, causing Peewee to experience shock, horror, amazement and relief in the space of a few terrifying seconds as the aircraft scorched the full length of the deck before climbing back into the sky and hurtling away from the ship with incredible velocity.

Last to arrive were the *Fairey Gannets*. Slow and ungainly they might be when compared to the sleek jet-fighters, but for Peewee they held an almost comical beauty as they danced an aerial ballet around the ship, engines and propellers droning like angry hornets before alighting gracefully, if not gratefully, onto the flight deck.

Finally, the crash-guard helicopter touched down and Peewee was about to lower the flying signals when Ash came out of the MSO looking annoyed.

'Where's the relief watch?' he demanded, pointing at the shiny gold Rolex on his wrist – a sure sign that he had visited the Far East Station in the past where such items were relatively cheap. 'It's ten-past-four and there's no bloody sign of them.'

The boy froze and inwardly swore. He should have asked the bridge for permission to leave the flag deck in order to rouse the next watch at least forty minutes ago, but he had been so absorbed with watching the landings that he had completely lost track of the time.

'I'm sorry, Hooky, I'm afraid I forgot,' he offered, staring apologetically at the leading hand.

'You forgot!' Ash glared back at him. 'Well you'd better get down there and wake the bastards up. We've got the middle-watch tonight remember. That's from midnight until four in the morning in case you'd forgotten that as well.'

As Peewee rushed below, he could feel his face burning. Oh well, he thought to himself, I've only dropped one bollock so far. He was wrong, for in fact he had dropped two, but at that moment he was unaware of it.

Calling first at the bunkspace to wake Clive Appleby and Pip Piper, he found it strange to find the place in complete darkness at that time of the day. Now that they were at sea, the vastly increased numbers of watchkeepers had lost no time in settling into a new sleeping routine that demanded most electric lighting in sleeping areas switched off.

Piper slept on the opposite side to Peewee, underneath Clive Appleby, but both bunks were unoccupied when Peewee arrived there. Surprised, but assuming that they were already on their way up top, he hurried on to the mess to wake the others.

Here too the lights were out, except for one where he was surprised to find Appleby smoking a cigarette while sitting at one of the mess tables writing a letter. Despite his secret sexual tendencies, Appleby was a happily married man with two children. His chief pastime, whether in harbour or at sea, was writing letters home to his family. At sea, he marked each envelope with a serial number and posted them in huge batches whenever one of the *Fairey Gannets* was tasked to fly off mail. By the time they reached his wife, she would know by the serial numbers in which order he intended for her to receive them. She reciprocated by using the same system when replying, which she did often, though not in quite the same quantity as her husband.

As the boy's shadow darkened his writing pad, he glanced up. 'You're a bit late shaking the hands,' he uttered through a stream of cigarette smoke.

Peewee was somewhat annoyed, and rightly so as the TO (1) was a member of the relief watch. It wouldn't have hurt you to have given the others a kick, he thought, but said, 'It's just been a bit busy up top, that's all.'

Appleby merely shrugged, stubbed out his cigarette into an overflowing tin ashtray, and began stowing his writing gear away.

After successfully rousing LTO Robson and the rest of the watch, he looked into the now serviceable bathroom where he discovered Pip Piper scrubbing his teeth. 'Won't be a minute,' he spat through a mouthful of toothpaste after catching sight of Peewee behind him in the mirror. Peewee raised a hand in acknowledgement then sped back up to the flag deck and found himself confronted by a savage looking Yeoman Jolly.

'How long does it take to shake the next watch, Hunt?' he bawled. 'I've been up here for the past half-hour doing a sodding junior's job, looking out for you.'

In fact, the young signalman had been away no longer than fifteen minutes, but he was given no chance to defend himself as the yeoman carried on, 'And what about flying stations, eh? Can you see any bloody aeroplanes flying about then?'

Peewee shook his head uncomprehendingly. What's he going on about flying stations for? He wondered, bewildered, then, following the yeoman's eye he looked up at the mast where the bright red and white flying signals were still swinging briskly at the port yardarm.

His heart sank. He had been about to lower them when the leading hand had interrupted him and despatched him below. To make things worse, Chief Communications Yeoman Wilcox chose that moment to put in an appearance on the flag deck. Stepping through the hatchway at the top of the ladder he stood, hands on hips, gazing calmly up at the yardarm.

The boy's heart sank even further. First, it had been Ash, then Jolly, and now, all in the space of less than twenty minutes, the impending wrath of the Chief Communications Yeoman.

'Good afternoon, Chief,' Jolly greeted him solicitously.

Wilcox merely grunted and said, 'Who is in charge up here, yeoman?'

Squeegy Lips scowled accusingly at the junior. 'Well, this bloody idiot is supposed to be, but as he was off the flag deck, I've had to do his job for the last half hour.'

'I see,' Wilcox said quietly. Then thundered, 'Well tell me what those flying signals are still doing up the fucking mainmast then? Flying stations secured fifteen minutes ago!'

Squeegy Lips, well and truly wrong-footed, stuttered and stammered in a hopeless attempt to get the right words out. 'It was...' he blustered, pointing at the boy. 'I mean... I was just...'

'You're always *mean*, but never fucking *just*,' the chief yeoman thundered. 'Now, get those bloody flags down before I find it necessary to get a leading hand up here to take over.'

By now the relief watch were beginning to arrive, and Robson, embarrassed at being witness to such a public dressing down of a superior in front of them passed quickly into the MSO. Appleby on the other hand, made an excuse of rigorously checking all the halyards for tautness. It was not because he felt uncomfortable with the situation (bollockings such as this were usually carried out with more discretion and out of earshot of the lesser ratings) it was because he did not want to miss a thing.

Pip Piper hung back at the hatchway, genuinely reluctant to approach any further, but Peewee joined him saying, 'Come on mate, it's your watch now. Flying stations are secured, speed was twenty-six knots but I think it's back down to twenty-one by now. I'd check with the bridge if I were you. Got it? Great, I'm away then.' Squeezing past his dazed looking relief, he ducked through the hatchway and scrambled below, breathing a huge sigh of relief, thankful to be clear of the fireworks above.

As the ship steered for Gibraltar, the remainder of the passage remained uneventful until the morning prior to their arrival, when sparks began to fly once again on the flag deck.

It all began with the afternoon watch being summoned to turn-to at 0830 hours that morning by Yeoman Jolly. Normally they were excused from mustering on the flag deck as they were responsible for cooks, a job which left them a little more time to relax and have an early dinner before taking over the watch at midday.

'What's going on, Yeo?' grumbled LTO Toby "Tubbs" McEwan.

'You ought to know what's going on, Hooky,' Jolly retorted in a voice that suggested that the leading hand would have to be a complete idiot if he didn't.

'Well I'm sorry, but I don't,' McEwan replied, sounding puzzled. 'We're supposed to be doing cooks down in the mess.'

Squeegy Lips smiled unpleasantly. 'We're also supposed to be arriving in Gibraltar tomorrow, so your mess will just have to wait. The Flag Communications Officer will be paying us a visit, so I want this place looking ship-shape and Bristol fashion when he arrives.'

'All the same, cooks has still got to be done,' the leading hand insisted. 'The mess looks like a shithouse.'

'Well it will have to stay looking like a shithouse for a bit longer then, won't it?' Jolly was getting angry now. 'I've spoken to Robson about it and he's in the MSO right now. If you've got any more drips about it go and see him.'

McEwan gave a resigned shrug, and moved towards the office, but George Allen said, 'Do we take it that we are excused turning-to tomorrow morning instead then?'

'Leave it, George,' Collins cautioned quietly, tugging at the TO's sleeve, but he was too late.

'You what! Allen!' Jolly exploded.

'I said,' George went on, 'Do we take it that we're excused from turning to tomorrow?' He said the words slowly and with exaggerated emphasis, as if speaking to a child.

Collins stepped away, rolling his eyes at the others who had gathered there watching. They all knew what the outcome of this must ultimately be.

Jolly paused dramatically for a brief second, then spat venomously, 'The only thing that you do take, Allen, is your hat. Get it and report to the Regulating Office right this minute. You, my lad, are in the shit.

'But if I do that, then surely you won't have enough hands to clean up your bloody flag deck for you!'

'Still trying to be a smart arse are we, Allen,' the yeoman purred silkily. Then, raising his voice so that the others could hear clearly, continued, 'Seeing as how you've suddenly taken an interest in the appearance of the flag deck, there's a special job that you can do on your way down. Take the slop bucket out of the store and empty it. Then, take it with you to the Regulating Office. After you have reported there, you will wash it out and polish it until it is gleaming. I want it back here for me to inspect, no later than twenty minutes after the Duty RPO has finished charging you. Now, get on with it.'

Allen shrugged, 'Fair enough, Yeoman,' he said easily. Whistling to himself he collected the foul smelling bucket from the small store beneath the mast and departed with it below.

Although Allen had not given Squeegy Lips the satisfaction of showing it, insult had been added to injury. The responsibility for emptying and cleaning the bucket rested strictly with the juniors. Over the course of a few days the bucket would become filled with left-over tea, coffee, cocoa, sour milk, cigarette ends and the like. During the night watches, it was even occasionally used as a urinal by the flag deck lookout.

When it was full, or nearly so, the juniors would draw lots for the dubious privilege of emptying it. Although it was not in the same class as the bunkspace gash bin, it was nevertheless a pretty revolting proposition.

In accordance with this unwritten code of conduct, no one higher than a junior rating should have been ordered to deal with it.

But then - Squeegy Lips was a bastard.

7

Gibraltar

THE SHIP ARRIVED IN Gibraltar at 0930 the following day, berthing with little ceremony alongside the King George V dock. The only musical contribution was that made by the quartermaster of a Daring Class Destroyer who whistled a salute on his bosun's pipe as the senior ship slid majestically past.

It was to be a short, two-day visit, just long enough to take on supplies of fresh food, water and oil, for the carrier's appetite was enormous. It was also long enough for most of the ship's company to enjoy a run ashore, with the exception, of course, of those men who were under punishment.

George Allen now fell into this category. Following his dispute with Yeoman Jolly, the signalman had been placed on Officer of the Watch's report. From there he was subsequently passed on to "Commander's Table" where he was awarded five days "number-nine" punishment for his insubordination. Although five days' stoppage of pay and leave, plus the mustering for extra work at inconvenient times of the day and night would have bitterly aggrieved most people, George shrugged it off in his typical cool, relaxed, and casual manner.

'Don't worry about it,' he had told Peewee and Toz when the boys expressed their disappointment at him not being able to go ashore with them. 'I've been here before and no doubt we'll be stopping here again on the way home.'

Cheered by George's optimism, the two friends went ashore immediately after lunch for an exploratory tour of The Rock, as Gibraltar was affectionately called. As some of the older hands had promised them, it did not take long. By mid-afternoon they had visited the Moorish Castle, the Galleries, St. Michael's Cave, and the famous Ape's Den where Toz came close to losing his hat to an over friendly baboon. With time to spare, they decided to take a walk along Main Street.

Crammed from one end to the other with bars, cafes, and duty free shops, each a miniature emporium and run mainly by Asian or Moroccan merchants, the atmosphere along Main Street was very much in keeping with the boys' perception of an eastern bazaar. Fascinated, they spent the remainder of the afternoon touring the street and spending money. When they returned to the ship for supper at 1800 hours, they were laden with souvenirs. Gaily coloured head scarves, silk cushion covers richly embroidered in gold and silver thread, and an assortment of other cheaply obtained goods. In an effort to beat the rain, for the weather was not much better than it had been in Plymouth, Peewee had bought an automatic spring-loaded, self-opening umbrella. Toz had splashed out the princely sum of one pound two shillings and sixpence on a wristwatch, a hefty chrome plated affair that sported a calibrated bezel and which claimed to be waterproof for depths of up to one thousand feet! Inside the glass, the maker's name could be clearly distinguished. It read, Ben Hur.

While proudly displaying their purchases to an admiring Pip Piper, they found themselves treated with something approaching scorn by some of the older men.

'Typical bloody juniors,' Tom Collins observed loftily while Olly Green simply treated them to a mocking, superior sort of smile.

'If you keep on buying "rabbits" at this rate, boyo's, you'll have to put in a request to the air department for storage space in one of the hangars,' Taff Jones joked, using the navy slang word for gifts or souvenirs.

After supper, in company with Jones, Green, Collins and a few others, they sallied forth again, stopping for a while at the NAAFI Club for a couple of quick drinks as a starter for the main course, the evening to come.

Just around the corner at the top of the short hill from the dockyard gate, a few yards from the ancient castle, the servicemen's club boasted among its other amenities the cheapest bar in Gibraltar. The quick drink soon turned into several and before long, Toz was not only feeling a little drunk, but he was also running out of money and decided to return to the ship.

Despite the short distance to the dockyard gate, Taff Jones insisted that Peewee should go with his friend, at least as far as the gate and see him safely into the dockyard.

By the time Peewee returned to the club, the others had disappeared. Disappointed that they had moved on without him he was on the point of calling it a day and going back onboard himself when his attention was caught by a smartly dressed man in civilian clothes who was sitting at the bar apparently signalling to him.

Puzzled, the young sailor turned and looked around behind him but could see no other person who the man might be trying to attract. When he faced the bar again the man was smiling and shaking his head at the boy's obvious perplexity. He beckoned again and Peewee walked towards him. What on earth does he want with me? he wondered.

'Hi there,' said the man with a slight trace of accent as the boy joined him. 'I guess you're wondering where your pals have gone, right.' The accent was light but unmistakably American.

'Well, as a matter of fact, yes,' Peewee replied hopefully. 'Why, do you know where they've gone then?'

The stranger chuckled. 'No, but I was talking to one of them, a stocky kind of feller with black curly hair and a weird voice. Said his name was...' he paused, snapping his fingers as if to aid his memory.

'Taff Jones?' Peewee prompted him.

The fingers snapped again. 'Taffy, yes, that was it. I remember thinking what an unusual name for an Englishman.'

'Taffy is a Welshman,' corrected the boy.

'What! Oh, yes of course. Well, anyhow, he told me that you would be coming back and left me with enough loose change to buy you a drink when you got here.'

Peewee smiled and nodded. 'Yes, that sounds like Taff alright. I'll thank him when I catch up with them later.'

'I wish I had friends like yours,' the man chuckled as he fished around in a pocket and produced a crumpled one-pound note. 'Name your poison,' he drawled in an exaggerated western style.

It was Peewee's turn to laugh. 'Why thank yuh pardner, I'll take four fingers of red-eye,' he responded, managing a passable W.C. Fields impersonation.

The man raised a hand to the barman who had been watching the charade with mild interest. 'One double scotch, and a gin and tonic on the rocks,' he ordered quickly.

'Cheers, or is it, "Down the Hatch" that you sailors say,' he smiled raising his glass as soon as the drinks arrived.

Returning the salute, Peewee swallowed about half of his drink and suddenly found himself fighting back an unexpected wave of nausea as the strong, unfamiliar spirit burned its way down to his stomach. Forcing himself to appear casual, he slowly lowered the glass onto the counter but was unable to hold back the coughing fit that seized him.

'Good stuff, huh?' said the American, still smiling.

Recovering sufficiently enough to reply, Peewee nodded, coughed once more and said, 'It certainly is, I don't think I've ever tried a brand as strong as this before.' He picked up the drink and swirled the liquid around inside the glass, pretending to examine it with what he hoped would give the impression of experience, noticing at the same time that the American's glass was still full.

As if in answer to the boy's unspoken question, the man raised his glass and took a tiny sip. 'My gosh, I wish I could knock it back as easily as you can,' he said, casually putting the glass down. 'I guess you sailors get a lot of practice one way and another.'

Peewee smiled and nodded, pleasantly flattered by the compliment.

'Yes, you might say that,' he agreed, 'especially in some of the places that I've been to.'

The man chuckled, then slid suddenly from his stool and rose to his feet all in one smoothly oiled motion. 'Goodness me,' he exclaimed, 'I must be forgetting my manners. My name is Robert,' he said extending his right hand.

The boy accepted the hand that felt rather soft and unpleasantly clammy. 'I'm called Peewee,' he replied, shaking it and letting go almost instantly.

'Peewee?' Robert laughed. 'Why, that's even more unusual than Taffy.'

'It's a nickname really,' the boy explained uncomfortably. 'My real name is Alan,' he said, feeling a little foolish.

'Ah, that's much better,' Robert said. 'I like Alan. Would you mind if I called you that? I'd feel much happier if I could.'

'No, I don't mind,' Peewee replied, wondering what all this was leading up to.

'Well Alan it shall be then,' Robert said decisively. 'Now, why don't you finish your drink and let me get you another.' He laughed again and patted his pocket, 'This time with my own money.'

'Well, alright, but this time I'd prefer a small beer if that's okay with you,' Peewee said cautiously. He managed to swallow the rest of the whisky in one gulp, this time more prepared, but still not enjoying it.

Robert's glass was still more than half-full, so he only ordered for the young sailor, this time a small bottle of expensive German beer. As the boy sipped the icy drink, he thought that it too was rather strong, though certainly preferable to the whisky.

They chatted for a while and soon Peewee began to feel more at ease in the man's company. Robert had a charming way about him and directed the conversation skilfully, oohing and aahing in all the right places, pretending to be enthralled as the boy told him some of the sea stories that he and Toz had overheard in the London Inn a few nights earlier.

'What on earth did you do with your friend, the drunken one you took outside?' he asked eventually, then, eyes twinkling, followed this with, 'I bet you had his trousers down!' He waggled a finger in mock accusation, 'I've heard all about you sailors you know.'

Peewee laughed. 'We're not like that really. That was my best mate Toz. I just went with him as far as the dockyard gate. He'll be back on board by now. Anyway, if he'd been really pis…, er, sorry, I mean drunk, I'd have taken him back all the way.

'You mean pissed,' Robert said easily. 'Well I think it's really decent of you. Not many people that I know would go out of their way to take care of their friends like that. By now, he was beginning to sound to the young sailor, as sincere as the Archbishop of Canterbury.

'Oh, it was nothing really,' Peewee said. 'Toz would do exactly the same for me. We matelots like to take care of each other, that's all.'

'Yes, I just bet you do,' Robert chuckled suggestively.

Peewee grinned, accepting the joke in man-to-man fashion. He downed the remains of his beer and offered to buy another round.

'I've got a better idea,' Robert answered with a quick shake of his head. 'How about we go and find somewhere a little livelier. This place has become so quiet it's starting to make me feel sleepy.'

Peewee looked around and had to agree. The club was now deserted but for themselves and two sailors who he did not recognise. One, a burly looking stoker with a bushy ginger beard caught his glance and gave the boy a big grin that was accompanied by a broad, conspiratorial wink.

Puzzled by the stoker's behaviour, he turned to face Robert again. 'Yes, I see what you mean. Okay then, let's find somewhere else, but remember, the next round is on me.'

Robert raised both hands in a gesture of surrender. 'Sure thing, pardner,' he grinned. 'Anything you say. Now, let's go and find the action in this here town.'

The pair left the club and walked briskly in the direction of Main Street, stopping now and then to peer through the windows or open doorways of several uninteresting looking bars. Eventually they came to one which had a large, hand-painted poster pasted to the outside wall. It read...

The Trocadero Bar
TONIGHT

Proudly Presents
The Lovely
Senora Carmen Hernandez
Exotic Flamenco Dancer

At the bottom of the poster, the words "Men of Ark Royal Most Welcome" had been roughly scrawled in thick black ink.

'Shall we?' Robert looked at the boy who shrugged and replied simply, 'Suits me.'

In every seaport in the world, there is always one bar, pub or club, that for a time, is the place where visiting seamen frequent more than any other. Where in Plymouth it had been the London Inn, in Gibraltar the Trocadero was currently enjoying such status. The furniture was simple and designed more to withstand punishment than to appear tasteful. The tables were sturdily built of rough-cut wood, while the folding chairs were obviously cheap and could easily be repaired or replaced. The small circular stage was about twelve inches high, laid with bare planking and sited in the centre of the room surrounded by a jostling horde of high-spirited sailors. There were a number of men from other warships in harbour, but most of the cap ribbons bore the name, HMS *Ark Royal*.

Drinks could only be bought from the white coated waiters who moved among the tables at bewildering speed, delivering and taking orders non-stop. Peewee caught hold of one by the sleeve as he bustled past, but again it was Robert who ordered, and insisted on paying when the waiter returned, bringing a gin and tonic for himself, and a rum and coke for the boy.

'Stop worrying about it, Alan,' he said when the young sailor protested, 'I happen to have a great deal of money and I enjoy spending it on people I like. Hey look,' he carried on, touching Peewee's arm with one hand and pointing with the other, 'I think the cabaret is just about to start.'

Peewee followed Robert's pointing finger to where two heavily moustachioed men, flamboyantly attired in Gypsy costume had emerged through a door at the back of the room. A terrific roar went up from the men crowding around the stage as they appeared with their instruments. One carried a guitar and the other was proudly waving a gleaming, gold-coloured trumpet above his head. One of the waiters went before them clearing a pathway through the closely packed throng. The musicians were forced to endure a good deal of raucous heckling as they followed their escort towards the stage.

'Hello, sweetie, who's your tailor?' a big Royal Marine shouted, and someone – Peewee thought it looked like Milligan but couldn't be sure in the dim lighting – stuck out a foot which succeeded in tripping up the guitarist who went down on one knee, desperately clinging onto his instrument.

Finally battling their way onto the stage, they opened with a fast flamenco piece that had the effect of cooling the unruly audience a little. The music reached a crescendo, then came to a sudden stop as the trumpeter removed the instrument from his lips with a flourish and announced dramatically. 'Laydees and gentlemans, iss with much pleasure we 'ave tonight of giving thees exeebeetion...' He was interrupted by loud cheers and roars of laughter, for the word "exhibition" held a special meaning to the men of the Royal Navy.

'Plees, plees, gentlemens!' The noise abated slightly and he continued, 'Thees exeebeetion of flamenco dance. To performa for you now, we 'ave, from the 'eart of Espagna...'

'Bloody La Linea more like,' a loud voice yelled, bringing more hoots of laughter and derision from the crowd. 'Plees, plees, the musician continued to plead, glaring in the direction of the voice, then got out quickly, 'From the 'eart of Espagna, the lovely Senora Carmen Hernandez!'

The guitarist began strumming in dramatic style but the sound was smothered by the noise erupting from the crowd as another waiter carved through their ranks to admit the senora, a plump but firmly built woman in her forties. She was suffering even more abuse, including that of a physical nature, as she ran the gauntlet of drunken servicemen.

Groping hands reached out from all directions, finding their way underneath and inside her dress. One sailor, a leading chef who went by the proud nickname of "Fucker" because his messmate's felt that it went so naturally with his surname, Duck, grappled the lady from behind and squeezed her breasts with both hands.

'Get in there, Fucker,' one of his friends yelled.

The woman stamped hard and accurately on the chef's left foot with the spiked heel of her right dancing shoe. He released her instantly giving an agonised yell as she turned smoothly and brought her right knee up squarely into his groin. The chef sank to his knees with a soft groan. The crowd roared their delighted approval.

The escorting waiter had turned back to help but his assistance had suddenly become superfluous. Seeing what had befallen the unfortunate chef, the crowd now parted before Senora Hernandez like the Red Sea before Moses. Soon, she was being helped onto the platform by several pairs of willing hands.

As the musicians struck up, the senora went into her dance, moving superbly and capturing the attention of her audience for a full ten minutes. Sadly, after that she began to flag as her age and weight began to tell. It was when she stamped up to the edge of the stage, almost breathless with her arms held high, castanets clicking and legs astride, that it all happened.

Somebody placed an empty beer bottle between her feet and shouted, 'Let's see you get that between your lips grandma!' Snorting like an enraged bull, the senora reached down, grabbed the bottle by the neck, and hurled herself bodily from the stage. Wielding the bottle with a technique that would have gladdened the heart of a Royal Marine commando instructor, she demolished the first three rows in moments.

From there the terrified musicians sat with their heads tucked between their knees in the middle of the stage, clutching their instruments tightly as missiles flew all around them. Bottles, glasses, ashtrays, and chairs crashed and shattered as men from the smaller ships rallied joyfully to fight those from the *Ark Royal*.

The senora was in the thick of it. Her costume had been ripped open to the waist, exposing heavy breasts that were supported by an outsized, black-laced brassiere. Still gripping the bottle, she was finding a target with every blow.

Robert threw an arm around Peewee's shoulders and yelled into his ear, 'Come on, Alan, let's get the hell out of here,' but the boy held back, watching open-mouthed as Fucker Duck caught hold of the dancer's bra-strap and began to drag her backwards.

Taken by surprise, the woman looked as though she might lose her balance but she recovered amazingly quickly and lunged powerfully forward.

Still rooted to the spot, Peewee stared in fascination as Duck and the senora strained to win this bizarre tug of war. Suddenly, no longer able to withstand the tremendous pressure exerted upon it, the strap snapped and the bra shot into the air and wrapped itself around the neck of a sailor who was on his knees a good fifteen-feet away.

Screaming unintelligibly in Spanish the woman spun round to face her assailant, droplets of sweat glistening on her face and breasts. Duck panicked and tried to run, hobbling on his injured foot, but he could not escape. The senora had recovered her wind and was upon him in an instant, screaming and clawing like a wounded tigress as she dragged him effortlessly to the ground.

Peewee had seen enough. Together with a very frightened-looking Robert, they made their way, unscathed, out into the street.

Outside, one of the waiters, bleeding from a nasty-looking cut on the temple, was blowing on a police whistle and shouting for help from the Royal Navy Shore Patrol.

Peewee and Robert wasted no time and crossed the road quickly, running along the pavement until they came to a suitable shop doorway in which to hide. They stood there quietly for a few minutes, sheltering from the sheer bedlam that had now spilled into the road outside the bar.

'Well!' Robert said eventually. 'That was a bit of fun wasn't it.'

Peewee looked at the American who seemed to have recovered some of his former self-assurance. 'It certainly beats the NAAFI for excitement,' he replied.

Robert glanced at his watch. 'Oh my!' he exclaimed. 'It's almost eleven o'clock. Have you got time for another drink, Alan? If you have, I've got a very nice idea.'

'Well I have to be back onboard by midnight so I should be getting back really,' Peewee answered cautiously.

'I'll tell you what,' said Robert. 'I'm staying at the Rook Hotel which is really close to the dockyard. Why don't we take a taxi there? You'll easily have time for one quick drink to say good-bye with, and I'll order another cab in time to take you straight back to your ship.' He smiled reassuringly, 'How does that suit you?'

'Well... I suppose that would be alright,' Peewee agreed uncertainly. 'But it will have to be a quick drink I'm afraid. I'll end up in big trouble if I'm adrift by even one second.'

'Let's get a move on then,' smiled Robert, stepping out smartly onto the pavement.

The night porter at the hotel handed the American the key to his room with a polite, 'Good evening, Mr Birnbaum,' then returned to his little glass cubicle, hardly giving the young sailor so much as a passing glance.

Robert led the way across the thickly carpeted foyer, bypassing a door marked Lounge Bar and headed straight for the lift. 'I thought we could give the bar a miss as I happen to have a good choice of drinks in my room,' he explained plausibly as the lift rose silently upward.

The sumptuously furnished room was brightly lit when they entered, but Robert turned the main lighting down with a dimmer switch and flicked on a low, red-coloured wall light, creating a subdued rose-tint effect.

Gesturing towards a sumptuous silk-upholstered armchair, Robert said, 'Make yourself at home, Alan, while I fix us that drink.'

Peewee sank into the deep, comfortable chair and watched as Robert lowered a mirror-fronted wall panel to reveal a well-stocked drinks cabinet.

'I'm afraid I don't have any beer here but I know that you'll enjoy this.' He came across with a large, cut-glass tumbler that was three parts filled with a green, oily looking liquid.

'Thanks,' said the boy, taking the glass and sniffing at its contents. 'What is it?'

'It's called Green Chartreuse, a rather nice liqueur, and very expensive you know,' Robert told him.

Peewee took a cautious sip and finding it rather pleasant, took a large swallow. 'Mmm, it certainly tastes good,' he agreed.

Robert looked pleased. 'Good,' he said. 'I was sure you would like it. Now, you drink that up while I get a glass for myself and bring the bottle over.' He went back to the cabinet, returning with the bottle just as the boy downed the rest of his drink. After pouring himself a small measure, he leaned over the boy and splashed a generous quantity of the liqueur into the empty glass. 'Well, pardner,' he drawled, 'I guess this is it.' Raising his glass in a salute, he said seriously, 'Cheers, Alan, here's to both of us.'

Peewee tried to stand and return the salute but found that the best he could manage was an unsteady wave of his glass and a slurred, 'Cheers!' His eyes felt heavy and he was finding it extremely hard to focus. He tried to get up from the chair again, fighting the urge to succumb to the friendly beckoning fingers of sleep, but it was no use.

Attentively, Robert pressed the boy's shoulder. 'It's okay, Alan,' he whispered quietly. 'You just relax for a few moments while I go and find you a cab.' There was no reply from the young sailor. He was already asleep.

Perhaps it was instinct or a subconscious defence that he had developed since the incident with Clive Appleby that triggered it, but the boy suddenly awoke, clear headed despite the alcohol. His eyes immediately took in the gross scene with shocking clarity.

Robert, now naked except for a pair of bright orange socks, was standing over him masturbating violently.

Anger and revulsion welled up inside him as he pushed himself out of the armchair. 'You filthy, perverted bastard, I ought to kick your fucking head in,' he raged. 'This is what you've been planning right from the start, you slimy piece of shit!' He stood swaying over the homosexual who had curled himself into a protective ball on the floor of the hotel room and was now quietly sobbing to himself.

'I'm sorry, Alan,' he whimpered.

Feeling even more sickened, Peewee said nothing else but threw a contemptuous glance at the American as he stalked out of the room, not bothering to close the door as he left.

He stepped over the gangway exactly as the dockyard clock began striking midnight. His first stop after collecting his card from the Corporal of the Gangway was the mess deck bathroom where he spent nearly an hour under a hot shower.

As he washed, his thoughts kept returning to the scene in the hotel room. Although he had walked away unscathed, he had the sense to realise that things could have been a great deal worse. You've certainly learned a valuable lesson today, he told himself grimly.

He was suddenly struck by a curious thought that for some obscure reason he found hilariously funny. Where the fuck did he get those horrible bright-orange socks from? he wondered, chuckling as he scrubbed away at himself under the steaming shower.

8

Along came a spider

'HERE, YOU LOT, COME and have a butchers at this!' Holding a sheet of pink message form aloft, Tom Collins came to a stop at the edge of the imaginary line that effectively divided the mess between the sparkers and the signalmen.

Peewee Hunt and Olly Green were the duty cooks, and under the watchful eye of Knotty Ash had just finished mopping the whole of their area of the mess deck. Collins was politely obeying the customary law that forbade anyone but the duty cooks from walking across a wet deck.

'What's the buzz then?' Olly Green enquired as he strode across the glistening wet linoleum leaving a trail of footprints in his wake.

Knotty and Peewee looked first at the deck and then at one another, shrugging shoulders and shaking their heads in mock dismay. 'Oh well,' Knotty said resignedly, 'I suppose you can go back over it with the mop again. Come on, let's go and see what Tom's got to show us.' Following Olly's trail across the deck they joined the other two. Olly was reading the signal, his eyes alight with speculation and excitement as they took in the boldly printed words on the message form.

'Bloody Hell,' he whooped, thrusting the form at Knotty Ash. 'This is definitely going to stir some shit!'

Peewee watched as the leading hand studied the contents of the signal. His reaction appeared to be one of stunned disbelief. Collins looked on with satisfaction, pleased with the result of his buzz spreading.

'So the bastard's coming back after all then,' said Ash, passing the paper on to Peewee. 'I honestly thought that we'd all seen the last of him.'

The older men, Collins now following by invitation that overruled the law of cooks, moved back into their part of the mess leaving Peewee to read the signal alone. It was from the Commodore Naval Drafting and addressed to both HMS *Ark Royal* and the Royal Naval Provost Marshal, Gibraltar. The addressing preamble also showed that an informatory copy had been sent to the Royal Naval Detention Quarters at Portsmouth.

The signal read: TO (2) WEBB C.A. D/055615 Ex-RNDQ PORTSMOUTH ARRIVING GIB. BY SERVICE FLIGHT AT 1745 HOURS LOCAL TIME TO REJOIN ARK ROYAL. REQUEST PROVOST STAFF ARRANGE FOR RATING TO BE MET ON ARRIVAL AND ESCORTED TO SHIP.

Apart from informing him that they were to receive an unexpected addition to their department, the signal meant nothing to the boy, unlike the others who were still busily discussing it when he re-joined them.

'I'll bet you a month's pay that he's back in jankers again before we reach Singapore,' Olly Green was saying as Peewee handed the sheet of signal form back to Collins.

'No way,' Collins disagreed, as he carefully folded the form and re placed it in his shirt pocket. 'It'll be services no longer required the next time. I'll bet you anything you like on that.'

'Where is he going to live though?' Knotty Ash wondered aloud. 'We don't want him back down here in this mess again, and that's for sure. There's no bloody space, and anyway, I doubt whether Robbie would put up with it.

'It's got sweet fuck all to do with Robson though,' Olly Green said pointedly. 'If the Mess Deck Officer billets him down here – and no doubt he will – Robbie and the rest of us will just have to put up with it, won't we.'

Collins and Ash both nodded grimly and murmured in agreement.

'Who is this bloke, Webb?' Peewee asked, thoroughly intrigued.

The three looked at him for a moment as if he were mad, then Olly Green snorted, 'Who is Spider Webb? I'll tell you who he is. He's the most thieving bastard that I've ever met in this man's mob. Christ, he must have knocked off hundreds of quids' worth of stuff the last time he was onboard. I'm telling you mate, don't ever leave your wallet, your watch, or even your fucking socks lying around when he's about, 'cos you'll lose the bastards.'

'He's a crabby piece of shit as well,' Collins joined in. 'He doesn't like to wash or shower, wears the same knicks and socks for months unless he can nick yours or mine in the meantime, even if they're fucking manky. I absolutely fucking hate the bastard!'

This last was said with such vehemence that Peewee actually shuddered. 'Can't you do anything about him then?' he asked. 'I always thought that blokes like that got sorted out by you older hands.'

They all laughed at that, but coldly, without mirth. 'You must be joking,' Green said cynically.

'But why? Surely you don't allow him to get away with it. I certainly wouldn't if he's as bad as all that.'

'Just wait until you see him then,' Collins said. 'You might not feel quite so sure then. Spider is a big bastard and hard as nails with it too. Oh, and by the way, he fucking hates juniors - so you and the rest of your sprog mates had better watch out,' he added nastily.

'Wind your bloody neck back in, there's no need to talk to the boy like that,' Ash snapped at Collins. Turning to the young signalman he said, 'Spider's problem is with authority and messmates of the same rate as him, or higher. As long as you and the other juniors don't rub him up the wrong way you'll be alright. The one *good* thing I can say about him is that I have never known him to be a bully with young un's. Mind you, he will still nick stuff from you if you give him half a chance, so it's simple; just make sure that you don't. Now, let's get this deck touched-up and dried off.'

It was unusually quiet in the Main Signal Office for the first part of the afternoon watch. The few signals that arrived were soon dealt with and Peewee found his job operating the Banda graph, a spirit-alcohol duplicating machine, a pleasant change from standing outside on the flag deck in the fine drizzle that had persisted throughout most of the day.

There was plenty of time to talk and the topic of conversation revolved around the buzz of the day. The impending arrival of Tactical Operator "Second Class" Webb.

'What about that time in Plymouth when he rolled that dodgy leading steward,' Olly Green reminded them. 'The poor sod had been buying drinks for him all night and Spider just kept leading him on, letting him think that he was going to be all right for a bit of the old pork sword. When they went into the bushes in the garden behind Aggie Weston's, the queer bugger really believed that Spider was going to shag his arse for him!'

'What happened then?' asked Peewee, passing Olly his fourth cup of coffee in less than an hour.

'What happened…?' Olly gulped at his coffee before continuing. 'What happened?' he repeated, 'Spider filled him in, that's what happened. And when I say filled him in, I mean that he did it good and proper. Ruptured the bloke as well. After that, he pinched his bloody Saint Christopher. Real gold it was too, a present from his parents to keep him safe on his travels. It didn't keep him safe from Spider though. As the silly sod had already taken his trousers and knicks off, he nicked them as well. That's what fucked Spider up in the end. The Master-at-Arms discovered the steward's ID card and wallet stuffed at the back of his locker when they searched it. Spider had found them in the poor sod's trouser pockets after he'd done him in. They never found the Saint Christopher though. I expect Spider had probably sold it in a pub or swapped it for a drink before he came back onboard.'

'What a bastard! I'm surprised that he didn't get kicked out of the mob for that,' Peewee said incredulously.

'Yeah, so were we,' Knotty Ash put in. 'Spider's a flannelling bastard though. He only got off light by saying that he'd lost his temper after the steward made an unnatural suggestion to him. He blamed it all on that, and having had too much to drink. Ninety-days detention was all he got and now they've sent him back here again. Christ knows why!' he finished disgustedly.

Olly Green took up the story and carried on, 'The steward got kicked out though,' he said. 'He spent nearly six weeks in hospital and then they chucked him out, SNLR - services no longer required, just because he admitted that he was queer. The poor sod,' Olly went on, shaking his head sympathetically, 'He really loved this mob as well. Even if he was queer, he seemed to be a pretty decent bloke all the same.'

Peewee nodded but said nothing. He was thinking about his encounter with the predatory American homosexual the previous night. There's no way I could describe that cunning bastard as decent, he told himself grimly.

The conversation was suddenly interrupted by the arrival of a messenger from the Naval Stores Office bearing a wad of signals for despatch. The prospect of further gossip was finally curtailed when the Leading Hand of the Watch in the wireless office two decks below sent up a thick batch of incoming signals to be dealt with by the team in the MSO.

'Bloody sparkers,' Green complained. 'They must have been saving this lot up for the last couple of hours!' He had more complaining to do when the relief turned up at 1600 hours for the first dogwatch minus George Allen.

'Where's George?' he demanded of Tubbs McEwan who had entered the office followed by Tozer. 'Every other bugger has got a relief except for me.'

'He won't be long,' the leading hand replied. 'He's still under punishment remember, and there's a 1600 muster at the regulating office.'

'That's bloody charming that is,' Green grumbled. 'We're doing a twenty-four-hour, watch-and-watch-about you know. I've only got two hours before we're back on for the last dog.'

'Sorry, mate, it can't be helped,' McEwan shrugged. 'If you want to blame anyone, blame Jolly. He's the one who put George in the shit.'

'You can go on down if you like,' Peewee offered, talking to Olly Green. 'I don't mind staying up here until he arrives.'

Olly gave him pleasant look of surprise. 'Cheers, mate, that's brilliant. I'll give you a sip of my tot tomorrow. See you all later then.' With that, he shot out of the office and disappeared below before McEwan might realise that he now had a junior standing-in for an able rated signalman.

Knotty Ash turned to the boy and said, 'Tell you what you can do while you're waiting for Allen. You can take those dirty cups into the store and give them a dhoby.' He grinned at the other leading hand. 'No doubt Tubbs will get one of his lads to do the same for us before we come back on again.'

'Don't take the piss,' McEwan growled indignantly. 'My watch don't only just wash the cups - they even have them filled with fresh coffee for our reliefs.'

'We'll believe it when we see it,' Knotty laughed as he stepped out through the steel door, ignoring the mock jibes of protest that followed him.

Toz followed Peewee to the store in the base of the mast and made pretence of tidying around while his friend rinsed the cups in the far from fresh looking water in the fresh-water bucket.

'Sorry for being such a lightweight yesterday,' Toz said eventually.

Peewee chuckled. 'You bloody pisshead. Maybe one of these days you'll learn how to stand the pace. You missed a good run last night you know. I had a pretty interesting time by myself.'

'Yes, so I hear. Were you in on the big punch-up in a bar called the Troc?' Toz asked casually.

Peewee hesitated before replying, 'Well, sort of, but we got out before the shore patrol arrived.'

'We?' Toz enquired, giving Peewee a peculiar smile. 'Do you mean you and that bum-bandit who picked you up in the NAAFI?'

Peewee felt his face starting to burn. 'How did you know about that?' he asked. 'I haven't said anything to anyone but I was going to tell you later.'

'Just wait until you get down to the mess then,' chortled Toz. 'Apparently one of the stokers who kips in the bunkspace saw him with you. He told one of the sparkers, who, being a typical sparker told everyone else.' He laughed again. 'I didn't know you were like that, mate. Was he nice then?' he carried on, nudging his friend teasingly.

Peewee scowled. 'As a matter of fact, he was a bloody nice bloke - and you can take that stupid grin of your face straight away. He didn't try anything on if that's what you're thinking,' he lied. 'He just bought me a couple of drinks, that's all, and if you hadn't gone and got yourself pissed-up so early, you'd have been alright for a few free wets as well.'

Still grinning, Toz held up his hands protesting. 'It's OK. I believe you. Thousands wouldn't, but I do. Honest. Anyway, I couldn't give a fish's tit. If you want to go off trapping brown-hatters, that's your business, mate.'

Just then, George Allen appeared in the doorway. 'Ooh, hello sailors,' he lisped effeminately. He grinned at Toz and said, 'What's a nice boy like you doing in a place like this with a boy like him?' Pursing his lips he blew Peewee a silent kiss.

'Oh Christ! Not you as well, George,' the boy groaned. 'I've had enough of this, I'm going to bugger off below.' He flicked the excess water off his fingers into George's face and stormed out of the store in mock temper, ignoring their laughter and fighting to keep his own face straight.

Thankfully, Peewee was spared any further ribbing regarding his encounter with Robert. The imminent and unwelcome arrival of Webb had seen to that. Nobody wanted to talk about anything else and the atmosphere in the mess was calm but tense as the evening wore on.

After completing the last dogwatch at 2000 hours, Knotty Ash and the members of his watch would normally have headed straight for their bunks as they were due back in the MSO from midnight to 0400 in the morning. As Webb was due to show up at any moment, they decided to hang around in the mess for a while.

They did not have to wait long. Spider Webb's arrival was heralded by the sound of the heavy kit bag that preceded him, landing with a thud at the bottom of the ladder.

Apart from the duty watchkeepers, everyone else was ashore enjoying the last night in Gibraltar. Olly Green and Taff Jones had paired up in a card game against Knotty Ash and a Leading Radio Operator called "Jumper" Cross. The four of them were sitting shrouded in a haze of cigarette smoke, engrossed in the game when they heard the noise. Sitting facing the ladder, Knotty glanced up from his cards to see a pair of long legs descending through the hatch. 'Don't look now, lads,' he murmured softly. 'Here he comes.'

While the card players studiously ignored the new arrival, Peewee, who was lying sprawled on one of the empty bunks, looked up from the book he was reading to get a look at the man who had caused such a stir amongst his messmates. From hearing so much about him the boy had formed a vivid impression of how the signalman would look. He was not disappointed.

Webb was indeed a big man. Not as tall perhaps as Robbie Robson, but he was at least six-feet tall, with a build that was in perfect symmetry with his height. He was said to be bone-idle and a terrific beer guzzler but any spare flesh he may have carried in the past had been whittled away by the Spartan regime of the Detention Quarters.

The one thing that surprised Peewee was Webb's face. The boy's impressionable young mind had conjured up a coarse, brutish image, which would have gone well with the prison haircut. Instead, beneath his shaven skull, the man had a rather pleasant, almost boyish face.

Nobody spoke or offered any form of greeting as, unperturbed by the lack of welcome, Webb went straight to his locker which had remained empty and unopened for the past three-and-a-half months. Five minutes later, after stuffing the contents of his kit bag into the locker, he slammed the door and tossed the empty bag carelessly into the pile of tightly rolled hammocks that nestled snugly in their stowage space looking like plump canvas sausages.

In the middle of dealing a fresh hand, Ash paused and raised an eyebrow, looking for a moment as if he were about to say something regarding the misuse of stowage space, but Webb, hands on hips, stared challengingly down at him. Ash, deciding not to push the matter, avoided the man's gaze, and continued dealing, saying nothing.

It had been an uncomfortable moment. When the big signalman eventually went back up the ladder and left the mess, everyone breathed more easily.

Olly Green stuck a cigarette firmly between his teeth and rolled three more onto the table. 'That was a try-on if ever I saw one,' he said with a grimace, chewing on the cigarette.

Ash picked up one of the loose cigarettes and leaned forward to accept a light from Olly. 'Well I'm not going to be the first to bite,' he replied, drawing deeply on the cigarette before leaning back in his chair and exhaling a cloud of blue smoke through pursed lips.

'Don't blame you at all, boyo,' Taff Jones said. 'After all, Robbie's the senior hooky in your mess. He can sort Spider out if he wants to and he's bloody welcome to the job if you ask me.' He looked around at the others as though appealing for their agreement.

LRO Cross chuckled, and said, 'Well I'm just glad that we haven't got to put up with him on our side of the mess. You lot are bloody welcome to him.'

'Ah! Well, we've struck lucky there,' Knotty told them. 'He's been allocated a pit in the bunkspace among the hairy fairies from the Fleet Air Arm. One of them has just been made up to PO and Robbie has managed to con them into letting Spider have his old bunk.'

'I'm bloody glad that I don't have to sleep down there then,' Cross said to a chorus of agreement from everyone except Peewee who had returned to his book. The boy was experiencing a strange tightening inside his stomach as he sought to regain some interest within the pages of his book, *Tom Brown's Schooldays*.

Shortly after the incident with Webb, Knotty Ash and the others wound up their game in order to get some sleep. As Peewee made to leave for the bunkspace, Ash called him back to tell him that he could have a stand-off from the middle watch that night.

Surprised by yet another streak of generosity shown by the leading hand, Peewee was quite pleased but guessed that there would probably be a catch in it somewhere.

He was right. Just as he reached the foot of the ladder, Ash called out to him again. 'Oh, by the way,' he said as if it had only just occurred to him. 'The chief wants you to close up on the flag deck with Tozer for sea stations in the morning. We're sailing at 0800 so you'd better be up there standing by, around sixish. Tubbs McEwan knows, so he'll make sure that your mate Tozer has a hot drink waiting for you. Is that okay?'

'Yes, of course, Hooky,' he replied, knowing that he had no choice in the matter anyway.

The main lighting was still on when Peewee entered the bunkspace. The first thing he noticed was Webb lying on the bottom bunk below the one in which Milligan slept. As he tried to creep past, Webb called to him softly, 'Oi you, come here.'

The boy froze. 'Do you mean me?' he asked nervously.

'Yeah, you. I wasn't talking to myself. Come here a minute.'

Timidly he walked back the half-dozen steps to where Webb was lying on his side, propped up on one elbow. His muscular body looked unnaturally white in the glare of the fluorescent lighting, causing the vividly-coloured picture of a hooded cobra that was tattooed coiled around his left bicep to appear as if it was indeed about to strike. For a long moment, he continued to stare at the junior as if sizing him up.

Peewee stood waiting anxiously for Webb to continue. Finally, the stare dropped, and Webb's face softened a little. 'What's your name?' he demanded.

'JTO Hunt,' the boy replied nervously.

'Don't be a prat,' Webb said tersely. 'I mean your first name. What is it?'

'Everyone calls me Peewee,' the boy said.

Unexpectedly Webb grinned as if he had just realised the effect he was having on the young signalman. 'That's more like it,' he said easily. ''You can call me Spider then, alright.'

'Yes, of course.' Surprised, Peewee took the hand that reached out to him. It was a firm hand, warm and dry as he shook it.

'Don't believe everything those bastards have told you about me. I'm not as bad as they try to make out.'

'Nobody has told me anything about you,' he lied awkwardly.

Webb grunted something unintelligible in reply then rolled over in his bunk, bringing the conversation to an abrupt end.

'Goodnight then,' Peewee said quietly, moving cautiously away. He hesitated for a moment, just in case, but Webb remained silent.

That night the young sailor dreamed vividly. Once again, he was in the hotel room with Robert, except that Robert kept changing into Spider. At times, he became Spider himself, attacking the American viciously. Then the scene would change as he found himself running down a never-ending dark alleyway desperately trying to escape with the bright orange socks he had found on the floor of the alley. Behind him in the glare of the street lighting he could make out the huge figure of Spider advancing upon him. At least, it was Spider's figure, but it had Bloody Mary's face!

9

A Sad Day

ON DEPARTING GIBRALTAR, THE captain sent a signal to the station Flag Officer, "*Ark Royal leaves Gibraltar as a giant refreshed*". As a result, the fourteen-day operational visit to Malta proved to be something of a disappointment for many of the ship's company. In need of no further replenishment, the carrier did not enter the harbour at Valletta as had been expected but dropped anchor half a mile off the coast near Marsaxlokk, a small, dreary town that was a long and bumpy bus ride away from the capital.

Shore leave was restricted and expired at midnight for all except officers and senior ratings who enjoyed privileged leave until 0200, and the juniors in the communication division who were limited to 2100 hours only.

Peewee and Toz went ashore only once during the whole period. They could not afford the time to travel by bus or taxi to Valletta City and guarantee returning in time to catch the ship's boat, so they had spent a bored two hours sipping warm Hop Leaf beer in one of the few unappetising looking bars that were dotted along the waterfront.

At 0800 each morning, including the weekend, *Ark Royal* weighed anchor and proceeded to sea for a day of intense exercises involving a number of other warships, mostly frigates and destroyers, but also an unknown number of submarines that would be participating in the role of enemy.

It was during this time that the junior signalmen got their first opportunity to work on the bridge. They would be under the supervision of CCY Wilcox or Communications Yeoman Tom Blowers, a newly appointed petty officer who had joined the ship on its arrival at Malta.

Back in his classroom days at the training ship HMS *Ganges*, JTO Hunt had excelled in voice-radio operating procedure and had passed-out with flying colours in the subject. Now, he found himself communicating with real ships for the first time and his initial confidence was shattered within minutes.

The very speed at which the orders were given unnerved him completely, and the growing fear that he might relay a wrong course or manoeuvre which might result in a disaster, only served to make him become more confused and hesitant.

He lasted for just quarter of an hour. As he was asking the destroyer that steamed in crash-guard station on the *Ark Royal*'s port quarter to, 'Say again your last,' Sam Wilcox was telling the flag deck to send a replacement voice operator to the bridge.

'Take over, Webb, and look sharp about it,' snapped the chief as the big tactical operator appeared at the desk looking smugly amused. There was no time to give him a briefing on the tactical situation for the captain was already ordering the next course and speed change.

In one fluid movement, Webb took possession of the microphone and removed the earphones from the boy's head. He began speaking calmly and precisely, 'Execute to follow, wheel two four zero, speed two one...'

Trembling so violently that he actually found difficulty in walking, the young communicator left the bridge and made his way along the passageway towards the flag deck ladder. His first stop was at the bridge heads, a small toilet cubicle tucked away behind the ladder that led up to the flag deck. Here, after several painful attempts he managed to urinate and so relieve the painful pressure that had developed within his bladder.

When he eventually climbed the ladder and stepped out onto the flag deck, Yeoman Jolly was waiting to pounce on him.

'Kicked off the compass platform, eh! He sneered. 'Christ knows how you ever managed to pass out of *Ganges* if you can't be trusted to carry out a simple bit of radio procedure.'

Thoroughly chastened and feeling sick with shame, it did not help to see that most of the others on the flag deck were either grinning or openly sniggering at his discomfort.

One face was not smiling though, and there was an edge to George Allen's voice as he said, 'Get off his back, Yeoman, the first time on the bridge is always pretty rough for anyone. There's no need to make him feel worse than he does already.'

Jolly whirled around angrily. 'You mind your own bloody business, Allen, and don't tell me what to do or you'll find yourself outside the Regulating Office again.'

'Yeah! Bloody typical that,' George said derisively. He turned his back on the yeoman and walked across to the port bulkhead rail from where he could watch the furious activity below on the flight deck.

Squeegy Lips waited until the signalman had crossed the flag deck, and then bawled, 'Come back here, Allen.' There was no response so the yeoman yelled, 'Do you hear me, lad? I said, come back here!' Still Allen showed no intention of obeying.

Jolly took a deep breath. 'I'm going to give you one more chance, Allen. One more, and that's your lot. Now, turn yourself around and come back here – that is a direct order.'

TO (2) Allen carried on leaning over the rail, studiously ignoring the shouted commands.

Squeegy Lips fully erupted. 'Right then! You all saw that,' he appealed to the others. 'Direct disobedience of orders! You lot are all witnesses. Did you hear that Allen? I'm having you up for direct disobedience. You'll get cells for this, my lad.'

George Allen turned around ever so slowly and faced the yeoman. 'Big fucking deal,' he said, clearly and quite calmly, looking the yeoman directly in the eye.

At Commanders Table the following morning, Yeoman Jolly presented his case without the benefit of witnesses. It appeared that none of those who had been present at the time of the incident could remember the yeoman giving any orders to Allen at all. The commander, a highly experienced officer who had dealt with many such cases before where witnesses were lacking, naturally accepted the word of the communications yeoman. Without hesitation he sentenced George Allen to fourteen days loss of pay and seven days in cells to be followed by seven days number-nine punishment.

Squeegy Lips was more than satisfied. Serves the stroppy little bastard right, he told himself as he watched Allen being escorted away by a pair of dour leading regulators.

His satisfaction was to be short-lived as the signalman's imprisonment was to create a number of problems unforeseen by the yeoman and which would result in a further lowering of his popularity with Chief Communications Yeoman Wilcox.

On a modern warship, the material aspect of being locked in a cell is generally considered to be not that much of a hardship. In fact, depending upon the type of job you had it could almost be considered as a rest. The real punishment carried more subtle implications as it was not the defaulter who was made to suffer physically. It was his messmates.

The procedure was this. Four men from the prisoner's own department had to be detailed to act as guards. To make things worse, this duty required the reluctant detail to be temporarily assigned to the dreaded regulating staff. This meant the inconvenience of having to wear the uncomfortable – and detested – Royal Naval Provost uniform, complete with freshly Blancoed white belt and gaiters at all times, and around-the-clock cell duties for each of them.

Naturally enough, these unfortunates could not vent their feelings to their superiors so they would often protest loudly and bitterly in the presence of the prisoner. In this way, the hapless man was obliged to endure a psychological punishment that was far worse than his loss of liberty.

Sam Wilcox was furious. He had more than his fair share of problems without the added one of how his now seriously undermanned department would cope during the current busy operational period. His anger was further compounded when his order detailing the four juniors to report to the Regulating Office for Provost Duties was countermanded by Lieutenant Commander Buckfawn, the Signal Communications Officer.

'I'm very sorry, Chief,' the SCO had said, 'but I must insist that these boys receive the full benefit of the valuable experience that these exercises will give them.'

Reluctantly, Wilcox was left with no other choice but to release three of his most experienced staff, Collins, Green, and Webb for sentry duties.

Thankfully, his friend and colleague, Chief Radio Supervisor Harrison had loaned a sparker from the radio office to make up the fourth sentry required, but at a price. It had cost the chief yeoman two days personal rum rations.

The reduction in staff saw to it that Peewee Hunt was given a chance to redeem himself far sooner than he had expected. That afternoon he found himself back at the signalman's desk on the bridge, vowing not to make a fool of himself this time.

Luckily, the first hour had been uneventful and passed quietly. Flying stations had been secured for the duration of lunch, and for the time being there was very little to be done. Voice communication between the ships was limited to the transmission of a few routine messages and this slow and easy start helped the boy to relax and greatly restored his battered confidence.

By the time things started happening on the flight deck again he was completely at ease and more than ready for the hectic period to come. At the time, he had no idea of just how hectic it was going to be.

From his position on the port side of the bridge at the rear of the compass platform, he had a clear and unrestricted view of the flight deck and he was able to enjoy the launching of the *Scimitar* squadron without suffering the discomfort of the terrific din which they made. The compass platform was totally enclosed, and through the inch-thick, armour-glazed windows only the faintest rumble of engine noise could be heard.

Now, two Sea Vixens, engines warming, waited for the order that would send the ground crews racing in to release them from the steel retaining shackles and wheel chocks, leaving the pilots free to taxi their machines along to the giant steam-driven catapults.

The order came, and a group of four chock-men sprang towards the aircraft. Bending low as they ran, the group split into two as they approached their designated aircraft from either side. One man from each pair seized and freed the wheel chocks on his side, then immediately ran clear of the aircraft as soon as his task was completed.

The teams worked swiftly and expertly, competing with each other until only one chock-man remained, still working feverishly below the forward end of his aircraft. He appeared to be having some difficulty and there were a few more seconds delay before he finally had the shackles freed.

Bloody wanker, Peewee thought, watching.

To get clear of the aircraft the man should have gone to the side, keeping beneath the wing, but for some reason he decided to take the shorter route around the nose. Still bent almost double he ran straight out in front of the aircraft and that was when it happened!

Like a piece of straw, the man was plucked clear off the deck and sucked head and shoulders first into the port engine intake.

The pilot reacted instantly, shutting down both engines, but it was of no help to the aircraft handler. The pilot had known that it was a futile gesture, but there was no other action that he could have taken.

On the bridge, the young signalman stood frozen, unable to do anything but stare in horror as the rest of the man's body disappeared through the protective grid inside the intake opening. Like a potato pressed into a chipping machine it went, drawn by the power of the *Rolls-Royce Avon* engine that sucked in air at the rate of twenty tons per second.

By the time the Senior Medical Officer and a team of assistants had raced up from the sick bay, the only persons found to be in need of attention were the pilot and his navigator, and some aircraft handlers who had been on the spot as soon as the engines had stopped.

On peering inside the intake one of the medical attendants had collapsed, vomiting violently, and was clearly in a state of severe shock.

The pilot, although looking outwardly calm did not fool the SMO, and he, along with his navigator, the medical attendant, and several others, were quickly escorted below to the ship's hospital.

It took a team of Fleet Air Arm mechanics and technicians less than half an hour to dismantle enough of the engine housing to enable what remained of the body to be reached, but it took the medical staff a further three and a half hours to remove those parts of it that could still be found. The man's head, and one of his hands, were the only whole parts that could be salvaged and identified. The rest was indescribable.

The man had been a mechanical engineer who had recently completed a course to qualify as an aircraft handler. It had also been his twenty-first birthday. Later, it emerged that his messmates had contributed to his first tot of rum, all adding just a little each of their own to his glass that lunchtime.

The following day HMS *Ark Royal* duly proceeded to sea at 0800 and headed for a point twelve miles off the island of Malta. Here the aircraft carrier hove to in order to carry out the burial-at-sea of the engineer. The majority of the crew were formed in divisions on the flight deck while the service was relayed over the Tannoy system from the quarter deck, crammed with officers and men from the air departments.

JTO's Hunt and Tredrea were detailed to attend the burial party under the watchful eye of Communications Yeoman Blowers. They would be responsible for the handling of the White Ensign that draped the coffin, a hammock, inside which the body was sewn by the ship's sail maker.

They stood smartly to attention at either side of the well-scrubbed duckboard that served as the funeral bier as the chaplain conducted the service. Finally, after a solemn rendering of the hymn, *Those in Peril on the Sea*, the chaplain concluded the service. As the bearers, men from the air engineering department, raised and tilted the board, Yeoman Blowers muttered quietly, 'Steady, boys, don't let slip of the ensign.' The signalmen each caught hold of a corner of the flag and held it tightly as the canvas-wrapped body slid away over the ship's side.

Although the sail maker, traditionally drunk at the time, had done his best to arrange the remains as naturally as possible, no one could fail to notice that it bore more resemblance to a sack of potatoes than it did a man's body.

10

Clapped in Irons

GEORGE ALLEN HAD LIVED well for the past six days. Because of the circumstances that had led to his imprisonment, he was treated as something of a hero by his sentries. Besides, as Olly Green had so aptly put it, 'Loafing about down here is much better than all that farting about up top!'

Many friendly visitors had kept him occupied and cheerful, and his official diet of ship's biscuits and water had been substantially supplemented with donations of cheese or ham-filled rolls, and generously over-stuffed chip butties. He had even enjoyed a number of three-course meals that his friends had managed to smuggle out of the dining hall past the blindly-turned eye of the petty officer on duty there.

He was now serving his final day of confinement. To celebrate this, instead of going ashore at Marsaxlokk, a number of his messmates had planned a grand coming out party to be held in the cellblock that evening.

The *Ark Royal's* cells were conveniently situated in a remote spot amidships, deep in the bowels of the ship and almost immediately above the main engine room. It was Saturday, and with the ship back at her anchorage for the night, there would be no further visits from the regulating staff as happened periodically throughout the daytime. The only persons close enough to hear what was going on were the Chinese crewmembers; cobblers, tailors, and laundry men, accommodated in the compartment above. They were characteristically inscrutable and could be trusted to keep quiet.

Men over the age of eighteen were allowed to buy two cans of beer a day from the NAAFI shop in the canteen flat, and although Admiralty rules and regulations stated that these must be consumed on the day of purchase, many of the men had been saving them up through the week in readiness for the party.

At six in the evening, Olly Green, Tom Collins, and the sparker, Bungy Williams, loaded their canvas holdalls with all of the hoarded cans and slipped down to the cellblock, taking great care to go unseen by anyone who would be likely to make a report of their suspicious behaviour.

Spider took Peewee and Toz up to the main galley where, for the prearranged price of four cans of beer, a leading chef supplied them with three large cardboard boxes lined with greaseproof paper and filled with hot food. Two of the boxes were packed with slices of buttered bread and a stack of thick pieces of fried steak smothered in a mountain of greasy onions. The third was filled with chunks of ham and an un-guessable number of fried eggs welded together so tightly that they resembled a giant unscrambled omelette. All in all the boxes contained everything that was needed for making up perfect sandwiches or *banjos* as they were generally called.

Unfortunately for the trio, the Petty Officers Mess was sited across the passageway aft of the galley, and as luck would have it, just as they were creeping stealthily past, the door opened and out stepped their arch enemy, Squeegy Lips.

'Here, what are you lot up to, and what's in those boxes?' he demanded belligerently.

'Food,' Spider replied simply.

'Food! And what may I ask, are you going to do with it?'

Webb regarded the yeoman disdainfully. 'As a matter of fact we were thinking of eating it,' he answered sarcastically. 'Got any objections to that?'

'Don't be so bloody cheeky, Webb,' snapped Squeegy Lips as he eyed the two juniors menacingly. 'There's something going on that I ought to be told about, isn't there?' He hooked a thumb at Webb as he glared at them. 'You two ought to know better than to get mixed up with a twat like him. Come on then, let's have it. Tell me what's going on and I'll see to it that you don't end up in the shit.'

The boys shared a quick glance of mutual support then stared defiantly back at the yeoman. 'Bollocks,' said Toz. 'Yeah, bollocks,' seconded Peewee.

Before Jolly could recover, Spider had put his box of food down and moved a couple of steps forward until he was standing face to face directly in front of the yeoman. 'First of all,' he said coldly, fixing him with a hard stare, 'I am not a twat - and these two juniors just witnessed you calling me one. Secondly. What goes on in our mess has got fuck-all to do with you. Now, do us a favour you jumped up piece of shit. Piss off and get stuffed!' He turned, bending down to retrieve the box. 'Come on you two. Let's get back down to the mess before this lot gets cold.'

Wearing huge grins, the pair followed the big signalman along the passageway leaving the flustered yeoman standing speechless behind them.

'Don't worry, lads, he won't do anything,' Webb told them once they were out of earshot. 'He's already dropped too many bollocks with the chief, especially with the fiasco over George. He wouldn't dare to have anyone else up before the commander for quite a while.'

'You don't think he'll put two and two together and guess what all this scran is for do you?' Toz asked worriedly.

Webb gave a short laugh. 'No chance. He's as thick as two short planks that bastard. And besides that, he's shit scared of me.'

Toz looked happier but Peewee didn't altogether share Spider's confidence. I wouldn't put anything past that bastard, he told himself as they hurried down to join the party in the cellblock.

When they arrived, the party was in full swing. The doors to the whole of the cellblock as well as George's personal cell were wide open and George was outside with the others. They were all squatting on the steel deck amongst a litter of beer cans.

'Hello hello, here comes the scran. Well done, lads, what have we got then?' George jumped to his feet and took a look inside the box that Spider was about to deposit on the deck. 'Hey, just take a look at this chaps,' he whooped. 'We've got the whole bloody issue - onions, chips and bloody great lumps of steak.'

Even Tom Collins was impressed. 'Spider, I don't know how you do it but sometimes you're a bloody genius.'

'He's probably shagging the chief chef, boyo,' Taff Jones joked.

'Balls, the chief chef is shagging him more likely,' Bungy Williams joined in as he looked up from checking one of the other boxes. 'We've got a stack of ham and eggs in this bugger, so let's get the bastard lot of it passed around and get some banjos made up. Dunno about the rest of you but I'm bloody starving down here.'

There was little conversation for the next few minutes as everyone munched happily away on their individually preferred combinations of banjos, generously washed down with pleasing gulps of Maltese Hop Leaf beer.

As Peewee was hungrily devouring his second sandwich, he watched with quiet amusement as Spider took himself off into George Allen's empty cell. I suppose he feels more at home in there, he thought to himself.

Spider certainly looked at home. He lay on his back upon the solid block of wood that served as a bunk, eating slowly and taking the occasional puff on a cigarette while staring absently up at the deckhead. Wherever his thoughts were at that moment, they were probably far removed from the *Ark Royal*.

With the impromptu meal finished, the serious drinking began. Spider came back out of the cell and joined in the fun with the others, who, for the time being at least, seemed quite happy to have him back in the fold.

As the pile of empty cans grew steadily larger, Tom Collins entered into competition against Olly Green to see who could build the highest pyramid with them. Half a tot of rum was at stake for the one whose pyramid collapsed first. Collins was getting progressively angrier with Toz who was doing his best to undermine their efforts by blowing hard at the two piles of cans.

'You just bloody dare...' he began to warn the boy, but he was the first to hoot and cheer in triumph as Olly's rickety construction collapsed with a tinny clatter to the deck.

Suddenly, the sound of heavy booted feet could be heard coming down the ladder above the Chinese mess.

'Don't worry, mate, it's probably just a stoker on his way below,' George called as Taff Jones ran to the foot of the ladder and looked up. When he looked back at them, his face had lost its colour. 'Sorry to spoil the fun, boyo's, but it looks like we've got a bloody crusher for company,' he said in a matter-of-fact tone of voice.

'Christ! We're all in the shit now then,' Collins muttered, and moments later, a leading regulator appeared in the doorway.

No one else spoke but Webb made a strange noise that could have been a chuckle as he took another drink from his can.

'Well well. There's quite a party going on down here by the looks of things. Which one of you is supposed to be in the cell then? And who's the duty sentry? Or are you going to tell me that he's gone ashore and you're all standing in for him!' The regulator remained in the doorway, blocking the only escape route. He looked very official and rather dangerous, for not only was he wearing full uniform, he was also gripping a long and hefty, well-scarred wooden truncheon.

Webb came smoothly to his feet and moved slowly towards him. 'Well I'll be buggered,' he said disbelievingly. 'It's Leading Regulator Catte. Don't you remember me then Pussy? Spider Webb, the scourge of cellblock number five. Well don't just stand there looking like a spare prick at a wedding - come and have a drink, man. We've got plenty to spare.'

The rest of the signalmen looked at one another in astonished silence, the same thoughts reflected on all of their faces. Spider must have gone mad! Surely he can't get away with this – can he?

The regulator moved forward a little staring hard at Webb. He looked almost as astonished as the rest of them. Suddenly his face broke into a delighted grin. 'Bloody hell, it is you as well,' he said. I didn't know that you were onboard, Spider.' Some of the others almost fainted with relief when he said, 'Pass us a bloody can then, I've been gasping for a wet for the past two hours.'

The regulator sat down amongst the circle of still cautious, but relieved-looking men and gratefully accepted the can that was hurriedly opened and handed to him. "Pussy" as he was known, had been one of the staff at the detention centre during Webb's confinement there. It was widely known that he was not averse to the occasional friendly drink and a game of cards with the inmates whenever it could be done discreetly and unobserved by some of his more conscientious colleagues. It transpired that he had also joined the ship on arrival at Malta. It also transpired that just a short while ago he had received an anonymous telephone call in the regulating office, tipping him off about a suspected "piss-up" in the cellblock.

'Well, naturally I had to investigate,' he said, 'and look what I found.' He held up a beer can and laughed. 'Hooch, lots of lovely hooch, and on the house as well, just the way I like it. Cheers!'

'I wonder which bastard it was who shit on us though,' Taff Jones wondered aloud.

'Hang on a minute,' said Spider. Like most of the compartments inside the ship, the cellblock boasted a telephone. He strode across to it and dialled the number for the communications mess. It rang twice before Knotty Ash answered.

'Listen Knotty, it's Spider. Tell me, has anybody been down to our mess looking for me, Hunt and Tozer?' He listened for a few moments before replying tersely, 'Yeah? Right, cheers mate.' He hung up and turned around to face the others. 'I'll give you all one guess,' he said, at the same time nodding in reply to the question aimed at him from the faces of the two juniors. 'Yes, you've got it. That fat bastard, Squeegy Lips.'

11

It's just not cricket

WHEN THE SHIP FINALLY LEFT the exercise area off Malta and commenced passage to the Middle East, there was a general lightening of the mood on board. The stress that had developed during the pressure of the exercise period had quickly evaporated and the flight deck tragedy was all-but forgotten as *Ark Royal* steamed through the Mediterranean at a comfortable twenty-one knots on an easterly course that would bring them to Port Said, the northern gateway to the Suez Canal.

With the change of mood came a change in the weather as they progressed further eastward, the winds becoming lighter and balmier, and the air drier and warmer. Even the sea changed in colour from deep blue to a fresh translucent green, and for long periods it was as calm and flat as a village pond. Another change was in the uniforms of the officers and men. Until further notice the dress-of-the-day would be tropical whites.

With the aircraft safely tucked away in the hangars for repairs and maintenance the flight deck became a venue for interdepartmental sporting events such as badminton, volleyball and five-a-side deck hockey.

There was never any shortage of competitors as the heads of the various departments always made sure that there were enough "volunteers" to take part. After all, they knew it pleased the captain to see a good representation from everyone and again, after all, everyone wanted to earn smarty points.

It was in the afternoon of the last day of passage through the Eastern Mediterranean and during a game of deck hockey that Peewee and Toz completely outlawed themselves against Squeegy Lips. The yeoman had not forgotten the episode in the passageway outside his mess and his devious mind had been searching for a means of revenge ever since. Now he had it!

The boys were playing in defence, with Squeegy Lips conveniently positioned in the goalmouth. This afforded the artful yeoman plenty of chances to "accidentally" hack away at their legs and feet whenever a skirmish occurred near the net. When the half-time whistle blew and they changed ends, Toz hobbled along complaining bitterly that the referee ought to pay more attention to the fouls going on inside their own team, rather than those against their opponents from the Supply and Secretarial Department. 'That bastard yeoman must have had me about fifty fucking times so far,' he growled. 'He's going to be wearing my hockey stick between his teeth during the next half if he's not careful.'

'I'll drink to that, mate,' Peewee agreed, rubbing a painfully swollen knee. 'Let's hope that the ref stays as blind as he was in the first half.'

After a ten-minute break the game renewed with increased vigour and enthusiasm from both teams. The supply and secretariat were leading four goals to one and during the opening minutes of the second half they made it clear that they intended to improve on that. They had a pair of former Royal Navy hockey team members in their side, and these two were constantly on the attack, running circles around the slow-moving forwards of the tactical communications team. It was only the youthful energy of the two boys in defence which harassed them enough to prevent an absolute massacre.

Peewee closed in to tackle one of the fast-moving forwards, but at the last moment the man jinked neatly sideways and passed, sending the puck skidding away to be smartly intercepted by his partner who was almost on the goal line. Toz came in fast and hard, tackling the man with such ferocity that he was unable to take a clean shot at the goal. Squeegy came forward and crouched low, just inside the semi-circle, weaving his body from side to side as he searched for an opening, his stick held ready to strike.

He looks just like a fat little goblin thought Peewee as he raced in to assist his friend.

Hockey sticks thrashed furiously as each man fought for a clear strike at the puck, with Peewee and Toz desperately trying to get it back up-field.

Suddenly the puck rolled clear of the tangled group and Squeegy Lips seized his chance. Crack…! Toz yelped and fell to the deck clutching his ankle.

The puck had not moved and both Peewee and one of his opponents spotted it at the same moment, each raising his stick high to get a good swipe at it.

Peewee swung his stick like a scythe but was beaten to it. The puck had gone, but as he followed through there was a terrific crack accompanied by a loud roar of pain. The impact of the boy's stick hitting Squeegy Lips full in the mouth almost jarred it free from his hand.

Just then there was another loud roar. This time it came from their opponents' jubilant crowd of supporters as the puck flew into the back of the undefended net.

12

The Suez Canal

LATER, ON THE SAME day at around 1800 hours, the aircraft carrier arrived at the anchorage off Port Said and settled in her designated position among the other vessels assembling to form the southbound convoy through the canal. The canal pilot, an impeccably uniformed plump and jovial Egyptian who would advise and guide the captain and navigating officer throughout the journey, arrived on onboard. The pilot brought with him the news that the northbound convoy coming up from the Gulf of Suez had encountered a delay and would not be cleared before 2200. It was unlikely that the waiting ships would be on the move before midnight.

It was like waiting for the lights to change at the end of a particularly long stretch of road works, for the canal was not wide enough to permit travel in both directions at the same time.

It was several hours before the carrier was under way again, taking station in the rear of the slow-moving convoy where the wash created by her propellers and vast bulk would be of no danger to other ships.

Peewee Hunt had the morning watch, but a strange, almost mystical ambience seemed to emanate from the Egyptian shore. The boy found himself gripped with mysterious fascination and he spent most of the middle watch goofing on the flag deck along with an equally fascinated Steve Tredrea, part of the duty watch, for company. For the first hour, there was not a lot to see except for the myriad twinkling navigation lights that surrounded them, for they were still moving amongst the local harbour shipping. Mostly, this consisted of small tankers and rusty, shabby looking coastal freighters, but occasionally they caught a glimpse of some large ocean-going dhows with their dark hulks illuminated by the line of bright orange lamps that glowed along the eastern shoreline of the estuary.

Suddenly the town closed in around them. The air was filled with a pungent smell of sewage and from both sides of the canal the thin wailing of Arabic music could be clearly heard. On the starboard side, the boys could just make out clumps of square-looking houses that huddled together, occasionally divided by narrow, dimly lit alleys. At one point, the ship passed so close to the bank that had they been standing on a lower deck they could quite easily have leapt ashore.

They were so engrossed that neither boy heard nor saw the figure that appeared quietly on the flag deck behind them. The figure hesitated briefly then glided silently across to the store below the mainmast where it disappeared through the open door. Moments later, mission accomplished, it reappeared and stealthily retracing its steps, went undiscovered back down the ladder

Sometime later, when Peewee went down to the bridge heads to answer a call of nature, to his surprise he found that the door was locked. 'That's a bit strange,' he muttered, rattling the handle uselessly. 'I thought that this place was supposed to be kept open while we're at sea.'

Puzzled, he went back up top and asked Steve if he knew why the heads were locked.

Tredrea was just as surprised. 'I haven't got a clue, mate,' he said, adding, 'As far as I know it's been open all night.'

'Well it's definitely locked now and I'm breaking my neck,' Peewee grumbled. 'I wonder which stupid bastard has got hold of the bloody key!'

'Why don't you nip into the MSO and check with Topsy, he's bound to know where it is,' Steve suggested.

LTO Turner certainly did know where it was and the "stupid bastard" turned out to be Yeoman Jolly. He had recently assumed the responsibility for the locking and unlocking of the cubicle at the correct times. Turner smiled sympathetically and said, 'If I were you lad, I'd go down to the main heads. Yeoman Jolly must have locked the door when we anchored last night and he's obviously forgotten about opening it again.'

'That's bloody typical that is,' the boy complained. 'If one of us forgot something like that he'd be on our backs like a ton of bricks.'

Clive Appleby ripped the signal that he had been typing out of the machine and swung round in his chair. 'Well, to be fair, you can't really hold it against him too much. Apparently he's not feeling all that well at the moment. You clobbered him good and proper with that hockey stick yesterday and I've heard that he's lost at least two teeth!'

'Poor sod,' Topsy chuckled with mock sympathy as he stuck a cigarette between his lips and proffered the pack of blue-liners to Appleby.

'I know!' Appleby said, as if he'd just had a brilliant idea. 'Why don't you go down to the PO's mess and give him a shake? Tell him that you're dying for a piss so you want the key to the bridge heads. I bet he'd be quite happy to give it to you. Cheers, Hooky,' he finished, gratefully fishing a cigarette out of the pack.

Topsy laughed aloud. 'Yes, definitely, but I doubt whether it would be the key though.'

'Sod it then,' Peewee said. 'I'm going down to get an hour of kip so I'll have one on the way. Just remember that it's a long way down to go if you get caught short,' he called over his shoulder as he stalked out of the office.

'See you in about an hour, mate,' Steve Tredrea shouted after him as he clattered noisily down the ladder.

Knotty Ash was in a foul mood. Following his normal routine he had called first at the bridge heads before going on up to take over the morning watch at 0400 in the MSO. Finding the door locked, he had kicked it and sworn loudly. As Peewee Hunt had reminded Turner and Appleby earlier, it was a long way down to the next nearest convenience.

'Why are the bloody heads locked?' were his first words to LTO Turner when he entered the office.

'Jolly forgot to open it last night,' Turner told him simply.

'Jolly forgot! That's just typical that is,' he grumbled moodily. 'If we forgot...'

'Something like that, he'd be on our backs like a ton bricks, 'Clive Appleby finished for him, adding, 'don't look so surprised, that's exactly what your junior said to us about three o'clock this morning when he was trying to get in.'

Knotty directed a puzzled look at Hunt who was busy spooning coffee into some rather grimy cups. 'What on earth were you doing up here at that time? Bloody keen aren't you. And what's the idea of using those crabby cups? I'd like mine washed first, if you don't mind!'

'Aah, that's another thing, Knotty,' Topsy intervened before Hunt could answer. 'There's no clean water in the dhobying bucket because we couldn't get into the heads to use the tap. Not only that, but the slop bucket has disappeared completely.'

Ash was never at his best at four in the morning and this was all becoming a bit too much for him.' The slop bucket has disappeared completely!' he echoed stupidly. 'Where's the bloody thing gone then?'

Topsy Turner stood up and stretched, smothering a yawn. 'Search me,' he replied, shrugging tiredly. 'What I do know is that I definitely need to get some zeds in so I'm off to my pit. No doubt it'll turn up in the morning.'

A sleepy Olly Green had replaced Clive Appleby in the typist's chair. He was slumped over the desk with his head cradled in his arms. As Turner and Appleby were about to leave he lifted his head slightly and croaked huskily, 'Someone must have nicked it.'

'Nicked it!' Ash snorted. 'Who'd want to nick a fucking bucketful of slops? He'd have to be raving mad.'

Topsy paused at the door. 'Well perhaps we've got a phantom watchkeeper who's nicked it. I mean, it wouldn't just get up and walk away by itself would it.'

'Knowing the state that bucket was in yesterday, it might have done,' Peewee said, trying to introduce a little cheer as he arranged Olly's limp hands around one of the cups. Olly's eyes flew open and he sat up quickly, spilling the coffee, almost scalding his hand.

'Christ! That's bloody hot. Didn't you put any milk in it?'

'Well I can see that you lot are coming back to life again so I'll bugger off to my bunk,' Topsy chuckled. 'Oh, and by the way,' he continued, pausing again, 'I hope Collins, your highly alert watchkeeper, has woken up on the bridge by now. Apparently he was sleepwalking when he took over from Spider! Perhaps he's the phantom watchkeeper, eh?'

'Oh, piss off,' Knotty said testily. He waited until the leading hand had disappeared then said more seriously to Peewee. 'You'd better take some coffee down to Tom - hopefully, it'll help to resurrect him. If he doesn't seem too bright, stay there and keep him company for a bit. The last thing I want is for one of my watch to get done for falling asleep on duty.' Turning his attention to Olly Green who had resumed his slumped position, he snapped, 'Olly, flag deck, now! Stay there until Hunt gets back, and for Christ's sake, shut the bloody door behind you. It's freezing in here.'

Tom Collins was quite awake when the junior signalman joined him on the bridge, but he was nevertheless still grateful for the hot drink. It was chilly in the desert night and most of the others on the bridge wore blue sea-jerseys over their shirts or white fronts. Even the canal pilot had donned a double-breasted jacket and was wearing a tri-coloured, red, white, and black silk cravat with two green stars showing on the white area of the material at his throat.

Peewee waited until the signalman had finished the drink then took the empty cup back up to the signal office.

The morning watch was unusually quiet and as there was no need to keep a constant lookout on the flag deck, the boy spent the next couple of hours browsing through some ancient issues of Reader's Digest. Knotty Ash chain-smoked and similarly occupied himself with some well-thumbed copies of Penthouse and Playboy magazines, while Olly Green contented himself with dozing in his chair. The few routine signals sent up from the radio office were plopped into the "For Action" tray, to be dealt with when he felt more like it.

Eventually, Ash ran out of cigarettes and having completed a thorough study of all the colourful pages, decided that it was time to catch up with a bit of work. After tidying up his desk and stuffing the magazines out of sight in a box-file marked Admiralty Fleet Orders, he directed Peewee to make some more coffee and then to keep an eye out on the flag deck as it would very soon be dawn.

Disturbed by the sudden burst of activity, Olly Green began to come round. 'Wassa time?' he mumbled croakily, looking blearily around him.

'My God! Just look at the state of that,' Knotty muttered, glaring at the signalman in mock disgust. 'Time for you to do some bloody work,' he replied caustically.

Leaving them to it Peewee took himself out to the flag deck. It was still cold but not as bitter as it had been during the middle of the night. After the stuffiness of the office the fresh morning air came as a welcome change.

The transition between dawn and full daylight was miraculously quick. One minute it was almost pitch dark, and the next, he was able to see along the canal for miles, both ahead and astern. The dark reddish colour of the water had him puzzled for a while, but he correctly reasoned that the convoy of vessels were churning up the sand in it as they progressed southward.

The view to port was a desolate one for there was nothing but a trackless waste of desert as far as the eye could see. Peewee swept the horizon with his binoculars in the romantic notion that he might see some brightly garbed Arabs mounted on camels, but he was disappointed for there was nothing to see but sand.

The view to starboard was more cheering. Groves of trees dotted the bank, and behind them from his high vantage point he could study the layout of the irrigation system, a vast maze of dull metal piping which carried precious water to the cultivated desert fields.

A number of ancient and badly rusted lorries overtook the ship along a dusty road that ran parallel to the canal. Some of them were loaded with raggedly dressed men, women and children, probably being taken off to their jobs in the fields. Many of them waved wildly at the huge ship and Peewee waved happily back.

Yeoman Jolly came up shortly after seven o'clock and catching sight of the boy, glowered at him for a long moment before stumping off into the Main Signal Office. Peewee continued his sightseeing with a broad smile on his face. The yeoman's thick lips had swollen to cartoon proportions and it appeared that his nose had also suffered some damage. I did a bloody good job there, the boy congratulated himself.

A few moments later, the smile left his face when Jolly yelled for him to come into the office.

'Coming, Yeo.' He called back politely.

The mood inside the MSO was distinctly unpleasant. The yeoman had obviously already succeeded in upsetting Knotty Ash and there were two bright red spots of anger on the cheeks of the leading hand's normally pale face.

'Alright, Hunt,' Jolly spat. 'What's all this bloody nonsense about the bridge heads? LTO Ash tells me that it's locked. Is that correct?'

'Yes, Yeoman,' the junior replied in a respectful tone.

Ash leapt out of his chair and leaned on his hands across the desk to face the yeoman. 'Look here, yeo, I have just told you that I tried to get in there myself. The door is well and truly locked. Why do you need to ask JTO Hunt? Don't you believe me?'

Squeegy Lips glared at the leading hand. 'Of course I believe you, Ash. I never said I didn't. And change the tone of your voice when you speak to me lad, leading hand or not.

''I am not your bloody lad, yeoman, so please don't address me as one,' Ash retorted hotly, 'especially in front of the junior rates.' He gestured angrily in the direction of Green and Hunt.

'Hello hello, what's going on in here? Am I imagining things or did I just hear a communications yeoman and a leading hand arguing with one another?' The rotund form of the chief yeoman filled the doorway.

'No Chief,' Ash spoke up quickly. 'We were just having a minor disagreement, that's all.'

Wilcox stared suspiciously at Jolly. 'A disagreement eh! What's it all about then, Yeoman?'

The way Jolly's injured face looked it was difficult to tell whether or not he was still scowling. 'The bridge heads Chief,' he said. 'Apparently the door has been locked all night, but I know that I unlocked it as soon as we weighed anchor last night.'

The chief yeoman smiled at Jolly, but the smile was without humour. 'Is that so? Well, it is definitely locked now because I've just tried to get in there myself. Anyway, there's no point in standing around here discussing it. You have the key, so let's get it opened up. That ought to relieve the pressure a bit, eh?' He looked round at the others, grinning, but no one else seemed to think that the pun was funny.

'That's just it though Chief,' Jolly said, now definitely scowling at Peewee. 'The key has been hanging on a hook in the signal store under the mast all the time. If one of them had bothered to look for it they could have opened it and saved causing all this trouble.' Pushing roughly past the junior and edging more carefully around the chief, he went out of the office and strode across the flag deck to the store.

While waiting for Jolly to return, the chief stood muttering to himself. He was clearly annoyed. Peewee shot Knotty a furtive glance and found it acknowledged by an almost imperceptible shake of the LTO's head. They both knew that the key was not on its hook as it had been the first place to be checked.

When Squeegy Lips came back empty handed Peewee felt almost sorry for him. There was something pitiful about the expression on his bruised face. 'I'm afraid it's gone, Chief,' he said sheepishly.

'Gone! What d'you mean, gone? Are you sure you put it there in the first place?'

'Definitely, Chief. As God is my witness, I put it there last night.'

'You can call on as many witnesses as you like,' the chief snarled. 'It won't alter the fact that I'm breaking my neck for a piss, will it?'

'No, Chief,' Jolly agreed meekly.

The chief yeoman let out a long disparaging sigh of resignation. 'Alright, Yeoman Jolly,' he said a little less heatedly. 'You must have a spare key so come on, get it out and get the bloody place opened up.'

'It's down in my mess, Chief; I'll send Hunt down for it.'

Wilcox shook his head firmly. 'No. Young Hunt is on watch. Go and get it yourself and be quick about it. In the meantime, I'll have to make do with peeing in the slop bucket. I can't wait any longer!'

'I'm afraid the slop bucket has disappeared as well, Chief,' Knotty Ash broke in.

Sam Wilcox threw his hands into the air. 'God Almighty,' he cried, shaking his head in disbelief. 'What on earth is going on inside this department?'

When Yeoman Jolly returned with the spare key, the chief was waiting in the passageway outside the toilet door. 'About bloody time too,' he grumbled. 'Now get this fucking door opened. I can't hold on much longer.'

Jolly hurriedly inserted the key into the lock, but at first it refused to turn. 'Come on, come on,' Wilcox breathed impatiently standing right behind him. The yeoman fumbled with the key, desperately working it around inside the lock until it suddenly turned with an audible click. Quickly he turned the handle and pushed but the door would only open a couple of inches. It appeared blocked by some resistance from inside.

Putting a beefy shoulder against it, he pushed hard but the door remained shut, stubbornly refusing to give. A second, more desperate shove did the trick though, and the door flew wide open, catching the yeoman off balance and causing him to all but fall through the opening.

'Look out!' Wilcox yelled, backing off quickly, but his warning shout came too late to be of help to the yeoman. There was a loud crash as the heavy slop bucket landed upside down, hitting him half on the head and half on the shoulder. The putrid contents of the bucket smothered his face and neck and ran in thick oozing rivulets down his clothes.

Squeegy Lips screamed as he staggered around inside the compartment. 'Help me, Chief. Please, help me,' he whined, clawing blindly at the muck that plastered his face.

'You'll have to wait, Yeoman,' the chief said as he tried to squeeze by and avoid becoming contaminated himself. 'I've got to have a piss first.'

The nature of the offence committed against the yeoman was considered sufficiently serious by Lieutenant Commander Buckfawn that he ordered an immediate internal enquiry to be convened within the department. The SCO appointed himself as chairman, along with the assistant communication officers, Lieutenant Spencer-Hudson, and Sub-Lieutenant Havers, as investigating officers. Communications Yeoman Blowers was appointed as recorder for the enquiry.

Throughout the morning, they questioned each man in turn starting with the leading hands before working down through the senior signalmen and finishing with the juniors. The questions that had been asked were in general, varied, but one in particular was repeatedly asked of everyone. 'Are you aware of anyone who might hold a grudge against Communications Yeoman Jolly?' The answer in every case had been pretty much the same. 'Yes sir, who would you like me to start with?'

At the conclusion of the inquiry, the board had succeeded in establishing two vital points:

1 .The slop bucket and the key to the bridge heads had been misappropriated by a person or persons unknown at some time between the hours of midnight and 0200.

2. Whoever had carried out such misappropriation was undoubtedly the person, or persons, responsible for the setting up of the booby trap.

Furthermore, going on the assumption suggested by hindsight that whoever had been the spare key holder would almost certainly be the one to open the door, the board was convinced beyond reasonable doubt that the trap had successfully fired against the person for whom it had been intended.

Thus satisfied, the inquiry was brought to a close with Lieutenant Commander Buckfawn ordering their findings to be displayed on the departmental notice board. The SCO added a personal memorandum that stated in concise terms that he would not tolerate "such acts of mindless petty mischief" against his senior ratings. The addendum also carried a dire warning as to the severity of the punishment that the culprit or culprits could expect to receive if discovered.

LTO Turner's quip suggesting a phantom watchkeeper might be responsible, took root, and from there onwards this imaginary addition to the tactical department was blamed for just about anything that went wrong on a day-to-day basis. In the hearts and minds of those who had shared the missing slop bucket and bridge heads key experience though, the fact remained that it *had* actually happened.

Throughout the morning, and early afternoon, the flight deck was transformed into a temporary souk by a number of Arab traders who had joined the ship along with the pilot at Port Said. Dotted at some distance apart from each other among the hastily arranged stalls of the market traders, were two or three Gully Gully men, Egyptian magicians who, like the merchants, plied their trade aboard many of the vessels that transited the canal.

The market stalls were well enough patronised, but the magicians were extremely popular and what the off-duty sailors who had come up to the flight deck for the occasion really wanted to see, Peewee and Toz among them. After the grilling the boys had endured by the SCO's investigation team, they were in need of some light relief. Furthermore, there had been some brief excitement shortly before noon when the ship had been buzzed by a pair of Soviet Mig 21 fighters, *Fishbeds,* as they were code-named by

NATO. While the captain had dutifully signalled a report to Whitehall he had not appeared to be overly concerned by the incident. Peewee and Toz thought differently, and as Toz had put it, 'If those bastards had decided to attack us while we are in the canal, we'd have had no bloody chance!'

They managed to squeeze through the tightly packed crowd that surrounded one of the conjurers in order to get a ringside view, and they were not disappointed at the marvels of close-up magic involving cards, coins, and pieces of rope, performed before their very eyes. The crowd were held in awe, spellbound during the magic, but clapped and cheered heartily in between each trick which the magician concluded with his time-honoured cry of, gully gully gully.

The absolute showstopper was when the Gully Gully man performed a remarkable trick with three small brass cups placed upside down on the flight deck. Placing a small egg beneath one cup, he would slowly revolve and rearrange them before beckoning to one of the sailors to point out the cup with the egg inside. No one managed to do this, no matter how slowly the magician moved the cups until, after several failed attempts, the magician would reward the latest contestant with a nod and a gap-toothed smile before crying, gully gully gully, and carefully raising the cup to reveal, not an egg, but a live chick, much larger than the cup itself. Now, shuffling and lifting the little cups at bewildering speed while still clucking his mystical incantation over and over again, chick after chick after chick, until more than a dozen appeared, each one strutting and fluttering as if on command, into a tall wire cage that had also just as magically appeared on the deck in front of the spectators.

Then, just as the watching sailors thought that it was all over, the robed illusionist once again showed the three empty cups to his audience before placing them back onto the deck, and after shouting a louder, almost triumphant, 'gully gully gully,' slowly eased each one back as though it was hinged to the metaled surface before ever-so-gently and slowly, lifting it. It was unbelievable. As if growing from inside the cups, one-by-one, three white doves miraculously appeared. After flying several circuits around the magician, these birds also went dutifully into the cage to join the cheeping, chirping, fluffy little yellow chicks.

There was a further, solid round of hand clapping as the magician held out his fez for the men to show a more valuable appreciation. This they did with extreme generosity, more notes than coins disappearing into the apparently bottomless tasselled hat.

Shortly after three o'clock that afternoon, after disembarking the pilot, traders, and the Gully Gully men, the aircraft carrier squeezed past Port Tewfik at the southern end of the canal, and surged ahead into the warm embrace of the Gulf of Suez. It was a historic moment as HMS *Ark Royal* had just become the largest vessel to have navigated the narrow man-made channel. The occasion was duly marked by the very short signal that the captain sent to the Admiralty in London. It consisted of just one word. *Pop*!

After increasing speed to a brisk twenty-one knots, the navigator settled the ship on a south-by-south easterly course for the two-hundred-mile run through the gulf between the Sinai Peninsula and the North African Egyptian coast.

By the morning of the following day, the ship and her crew were in the blistering heat of the Red Sea where they kept a rendezvous with the Royal Fleet Auxiliary vessels, *Olna*, and *Reliant* to carry out a replenishment-at-sea.

After reducing speed to safely conduct the manoeuvre, the carrier gorged her fill with oil from the tanker *Olna* to starboard, while simultaneously hauling across a number of vital air stores from the *Reliant* to port. After the RAS was completed, the carrier signalled a fond "*Farewell and thank-you*" by flashing light to the auxiliary vessels as she increased speed and resumed her course for the passage to Aden. There she would be making a brief stop, en-route to the busy East African port of Mombasa.

13

High jinks in Aden

OLLY GREEN WAS BORED. It was still early in the evening but he'd already seen and had enough of the Mermaid Club and its lack of entertainment. He glared irritably at his three companions as he pleaded, 'Come on lads, one of us should be able to come up with something – anything other than this. Are we going to sit here and rot here for the night or bugger off somewhere else?'

Toz replied with a noncommittal shrug, but Peewee looked at George Allen and said, 'How about you? You're the one with all the bright ideas. Got one for us now?'

'Yeah, come on, George,' Olly urged. 'I know that Aden is supposed to be a dump, but there's got to be somewhere a bit better than this place. I don't know about you lot but I'm getting pissed off with hanging about at the bar for hours at a time, just to get a bloody drink. Even then it's warm and all they've got is Red Barrel. In cans!' he finished caustically. To emphasise his point he picked up one of the empty tins that littered the table and smacked it against the palm of his right hand. Wedging it top and bottom between the heel of his hand and his fingertips, he jack-knifed the hand closed. The soft metal can buckled under the pressure and shot forward, skittering across the Formica surface of the table before coming to rest in front of Toz. Olly leaned back in his chair, giving a satisfied grunt at the ease with which he had accomplished the simple feat.

The ship was anchored off the rocky promontory of Elephant's Back, Aden, about two miles out, and the four had left on the 1500 liberty boat, arriving ashore at the Prince of Wales Pier shortly before four. By six o'clock, they had thoroughly explored most of the commercial heart of the

125

main town, The Crescent, and had even taken a good walk around the old Arab quarter where unkempt pedestrian animals, goats, in particular, roamed at will through the hot, dusty streets.

While The Crescent and the maize of narrow shop-lined streets that ran off it, abounded with shops brimming over with tax-free bargains by way of cameras, binoculars, watches, and goods and gadgets of all descriptions (too many to mention) the sailors had noted gloomily that it promised little in the way of nightlife. Eventually, like most of their shipmates, they had ended up at the Mermaid Club where the beer, although canned and warm, was cheap and British. However, as Olly had just complained, the service was poor. At the bar, there was a continuous queue of impatient men waiting to be served by one of the two maddeningly slow moving Arabs behind the counter.

To be fair to the NAAFI manager, the bar normally only catered for the servicemen who were permanently based at Aden, and few of them used it on a midweek evening. It was not often that a ship of such size visited the port and the staff had obviously been quite unprepared for the two-thousand-odd men who had descended upon them en-masse. As the *Ark Royal* would only be there for one day, every man who was not required for duties onboard had taken the opportunity to get ashore and stretch their legs.

George ran a hand through his fine, dark hair, pausing for a moment to allow his fingers to scratch gently at the back of his head. The others watched him and waited expectantly. Suddenly his face creased into a broad grin. 'I've got it,' he said. 'Obviously this place and the town as well, are going to be seething with our lot for the rest of the night. What do you reckon to the idea of a sneaky jaunt across to Little Aden? It should be pretty quiet over there and we might be able to have a good run without having to queue up for beer.'

Peewee stared at him in surprise. 'According to the daily orders, George, Little Aden is out of bounds! We'll all end up in the shit if we go over there.'

'Listen to old mother Hunt spouting on,' Olly sneered. 'If you don't want to come with us that's fine by me. Just keep your gob shut about it, that's all.'

Peewee looked at Toz who grinned back and said, 'I'm going, mate. It's about time I got in the shit for something anyway.'

Peewee faced the other two again. 'Alright then, I'm game. Let's just hope that we don't get caught though. I don't want to be under stoppage of leave when we get to Mombasa next week.'

'Don't be so worried,' George said reassuringly. 'It's going to be all right. The shore patrol won't be going over there. They'll have enough on their hands with this lot in here. As long as we keep out of trouble no one, except us, will ever know that we've been there.'

Olly was already heading for the door. 'Come on then you bunch of wankers,' he called back. 'Last one out pays for the taxi.'

The desert road that connected the main town to Little Aden ran westwards over a sandy isthmus around a bay where the deep-water harbour was overlooked by jagged cliffs of barren volcanic rock. The drive took twenty-five minutes in an elderly Chevrolet saloon driven by an equally elderly, white-turbaned, grey-bearded Arab with crooked yellowed teeth who told them that his name was Omar. The big car had originally been all black in colour when new but the roof and upper part of the bodywork had been crudely hand-painted over in white several times over the years giving the vehicle a two-tone look. If the smell and shoddy condition of the car's interior was anything to go by, it was used not only for transporting people, but diverse forms of livestock also.

Omar asked for twenty East African shillings in payment, but as with everything offered for sale in such regions, taxi fares are negotiable. After a few minutes of hard bargaining, the sailors agreed to pay eight shillings then, and a further ten later if the driver returned to pick them up at midnight. The old Arab assured them that he would be there on time, and, after cautioning them that the local girls were unclean, and that on the return journey, if they wished, he would take them to the house of a friend for a very clean "jig-a-jig," very cheap, he turned the vehicle around and headed back along the dusty road.

Aden, and Little Aden, nestle in the remains of two long dead volcanoes. The two towns appeared remarkably like a mirror image of each other. For hundreds of years they had commanded the sea approaches to the port. It was a perfect stopping-off point for vessels plying the busy trade routes to India, the Far East and along the eastern seaboard of Africa. It had been bitterly fought over, by both the Portuguese who had held it briefly, and the Ottoman Turks who captured the region in the early sixteenth century and continued to hold it for more than a century. Now it was a British Crown Colony with both the Army and the Royal Air Force garrisoned there.

Little Aden, or Jebel Ihsan as it is called in Arabic, was a large village, an extension of the main town. In 1953 the quiet peninsula had been a convenient site for British Petroleum to build an oil refinery, providing many jobs and cheaply built accommodation for the locals. The place where the taxi driver had dropped them was on the fringe of the town that looked to be inhabited on three levels.

A jumble of squalid, oddly coloured houses lay back in the shade of the desolate grey face of the crater wall some distance above the narrow un-surfaced street where the sailors now stood.

In the near distance, a wider road branched off sharply to run downhill and along the shore to the refinery. Several tankers were moored in the harbour and further out, they could see the *Ark Royal*, a potent symbol of British sea power, riding majestically at her own anchor.

The street itself continued for some distance before disappearing from sight around a bend. A narrow road branched off about two hundred yards ahead and wove an uphill path through the lunar-like landscape towards the huddle of dwellings above.

Few buildings lined the street where Omar had deposited them. It seemed strangely deserted, but there was one place that beckoned, vaguely resembling a bar. It was a dirty off-white, squat-looking building built of sand and cement that was displaying clear signs of decay. Above the door hung a sun-blistered wooden board on which the words "CAFÉ AKBAR" were crudely painted. Above it, a small neon *Coca Cola* sign flickered spasmodically in an effort to convince the doubtful that the words on the board were true.

'Here we go then lads,' chirped George. 'Welcome to Akbar's snack-bar.' He pushed open the sagging door and led the way in.

'Looks a bit grotty if you ask me,' Olly Green muttered as they filed through the opening, but they were all pleasantly surprised once inside.

The room was cool and surprisingly large. Apart from a vague smell of stale sweat, it was also quite clean and pleasingly decorated. American-style drinking booths lined the walls, lit by subdued lighting from clusters of ornate brass lamps that hung from the ceiling. Some of the booths were occupied by light-skinned Orientals who turned out to be crewmen from the Japanese tanker in the harbour. They had a few girls for company and they all seemed to be drinking and laughing happily. One or two of the tanker men waved and smiled friendly greetings at the Royal Navy men and they felt quite at ease as they settled into a vacant booth.

'I can't understand why this part of Aden is out of bounds,' Peewee said to the others. 'If this is the only place to drink, hardly anybody would bother coming here so I can't see there being the possibility of any trouble starting, like that punch-up back in Gib.'

George was explaining that the whole region was a hotbed of political unrest and that locally there was particular resentment towards the British service personnel stationed there. When a man appeared at their table to take their order, George felt it wise to stop talking on the subject and prudently fell silent.

The man was no other than Akbar himself, an amiable, plump and pleasant-faced Arab who seemed pleased at their arrival and greeted them warmly. At a gesture from him, four young girls detached themselves from some of the Japanese seamen and came over to join them. There was no animosity from the Japanese group, most of who laughed and waved in their direction, one or two even giving the internationally recognised thumbs up signal for good luck.

'No girls,' Olly burst out strongly, raising a hand, palm outwards. He looked up at Akbar. 'You understand Johnny, we no want any girl, okay?'

Akbar just shook his head and smiled inanely at the sailor.

'Hey! What the matter with you? You queery man or something?' One of the girls came over and stared down at Olly. Her hands rested on her hips and there was a provocative smile on her pretty face.

George laughed and said, 'No love, he's just tight, that's all.'

The girl shot George a puzzled look. 'Tight! What you mean tight? He not drunk!'

She looked at Olly again who was grinning at her understandable interpretation of the word. From previous experience he had guessed that the girls were from the Philippines and were more used to the American expression for someone who was drunk. His guess turned out to be correct when one of the girls told them that they were all Filipinos on a working holiday.

'He means that I don't like spending my money on girls in bars,' he told her.

Toz sitting next to him, gave him a nudge and said, 'Go on, mate, we're not that hard up. We can at least afford to buy them one drink each.'

Olly looked for a moment as if he might still protest but the girl was already ahead of him.

'You don't buy drinks for girls!' She sounded shocked at the very idea. 'Girls buy drinks for sailor mans.' She spun around quickly holding up four fingers. 'Hey, Akbar. Four beer for English sailor mans.'

The operation had been smoothly carried out. Before they knew it, Peewee and Toz found themselves together in the booth with a girl sitting closely next to each of them. Another had enticed George to join her with Olly in a separate booth at the far end of the room.

The drink that Akbar placed before them was a local brew, slightly tepid and looked rather muddy in appearance, but it was palatable enough.

Unfortunately though, it came in rather small glasses that the sailors soon emptied, only to have them refilled just as quickly by the watchful Akbar. This time he also placed a small glass of dark coloured liquid before each of the girls.

Tactfully, he avoided mentioning the cost of this round at Olly's table, standing instead over the two boys, smiling cheerfully. 'Four beer and four rum,' he said. 'Who pay this time?'

Toz's girl smiled encouragingly across the table at Peewee who shoved a hand into his pocket, but Toz said, 'Hold on, mate, I'll get this one, you can buy the next.' He looked up at the Arab and feigning what he supposed to be typical British arrogance and snobbery, enquired, 'How much do you require, my good man?'

Akbar's ingratiating smile broadened even more at this. 'Forty shilling, sir,' he replied.

'Forty fucking shillings!' Toz was aghast. 'That's a bit much isn't it?'

Akbar stopped smiling and his face looked serious as he told them, 'No, is very cheap, each drink only cost five shilling. Other time cost much more, but you very good friend to girl so Akbar sell cheap to you.' The smile returned as quickly as it had left. 'That right, honey,' Toz's girl said while gently squeezing his leg. 'Other time drink cost ten shilling each time.'

The girl's hand moved skilfully along Toz's inner thigh and into his crotch where it came to a stop, nestling lightly against its target. Toz capitulated. 'Well, I suppose that's fair, but I still think it's a bit too much.' He gave Akbar the money and as the Arab moved away, screwed up his face and looked across at Peewee. 'You're bloody welcome to buy the next round at that price,' he said disgustedly.

Peewee grinned back at his friend. His girl was close against him, her leg pressed warmly against his own. 'Never mind, mate, at least we might be in for a bit of fun later on, especially when these two have got a few more tots of rum inside them.'

The Filipinos were experienced conversationalists and their light comical chatter in pidgin English kept the sailors amused. It also appeared that they were equally experienced as drinkers, for as the evening wore on they managed to consume glass after glass of rum without showing the slightest sign of intoxication.

By eleven o'clock, the four sailors had paid for many rounds between them and Peewee was becoming a little concerned. He was down to his last East African twenty-shilling note and was dreading the embarrassing moment that he knew must come quite soon. He was about to suggest to Toz that they should get out of the place, when George appeared at their table and made the suggestion for him.

'I don't know about you two filthy-rich juniors, but us two poor sods are nearly broke. We're going to have a look around outside, so, do you want to come with us, or do you want to hang on here a bit longer?' He winked with a discreet nod in the direction of the two girls.

'We're definitely ready, mate,' Peewee said with a genuine air of relief. The girls had pretty much fleeced them. He looked at Toz and was even more relieved when he too agreed without hesitation.

Instinctively realising that their services were no longer required, the girls slid out of the booth and went over to join the others who had already vacated George and Olly's table. One of them, a girl called Alice who had been George's companion, flashed them a smile. 'Thank you for nice drink. You come again soon, yes?' Peewee replied with what he hoped was a masculine, man-of-the-world smile and said, 'Sure we will, but next time we'll want a bit more than just drinks!' It was a wasted effort for the girl had already turned her back on them and moved away.

There was a half-full glass of rum on the table and as they were about to leave, Toz picked it up and drained it in one gulp. 'Bloody hell, it's fucking *Coca Cola*!' he spat, almost throwing the glass onto the floor.

'Of course it is, mate,' George chuckled softly. 'Didn't you see the sign outside as we came in?' Worried that Toz might do something foolish, he caught him gently by the arm and murmured, 'Come on, let's get out of this bloody place.'

Entirely by accident, just a short distance along the street they discovered another bar. They would probably have walked right past had it not been for the undernourished looking cow tethered to a rusty iron ringbolt that was driven into the grimy wall of the place. Had any of them been able to read Arabic script, the words painted on the strip of rough planking which was nailed over the door would have told them. Otherwise, there was no outward indication to show that it was indeed a bar.

It was while Olly was clowning about, groping around the cow's shrivelled udder and coming out with such lines as, 'Arr, you'm got a luvverly set of titties Daisy me gurl,' that the heavy, brass-studded door opened and several motley looking Asian seamen came out. Most of them ignored the group gathered around the cow and wandered off laughing and chattering drunkenly in the direction of the Cafe Akbar. One of them though, a tall skinny man with a large beaked nose and a badly pockmarked face, hung back, scowling malevolently at Olly while muttering darkly in his native tongue.

Not caring for the look of him, Peewee gave George a meaningful look and said, 'I reckon that this place must be some kind of a bar. Olly's welcome to a pint of milk if that's what he's after, but I fancy seeing what's on offer inside. Besides, I think we should leave this poor thing alone. It's pretty obvious that matey over there isn't too happy with us.

George caught on quickly and nodded. 'Sounds like a good idea to me.' He glanced enquiringly at Toz who grinned back and said, 'Why not,' adding, 'Let's not get involved with any more girls though!'

George tapped Olly on the shoulder. 'Come on, Farmer Giles, you'll end up with a dose of foot and mouth if you keep messing about with that bloody thing.' The tall Asian finally seemed satisfied that the sailors meant no harm to the cow, and headed off to catch up with his companions.

Olly gave the bony animal a final scratch behind the ears and followed his friends into the bar. The placid creature watched him go, idly flicking its tail at the cluster of large red flies that continually circled her rump. Olly turned and gave it a final wink and a smile before passing through the door. Unaccustomed to such fuss and affection, the beast blinked and gazed almost lovingly after him.

The place was in total contrast to the one they had just left. There were no seductively dimmed lights or secluded drinking booths, and perhaps more importantly considering their shrivelled pockets, there were no girls in sight.

The entire clientele appeared to be local men; all turbaned and dressed alike in what looked to Peewee like pyjama jackets and baggy pants. They sat around wicker tables drinking strong coffee out of tiny cups no larger than thimbles, talking quietly amongst themselves. Some of them were sucking on long narrow stemmed pipes, and the air was heavy with the sweet, pungent scent of hashish.

There was a bar servery of sorts, the counter of which was a badly warped and scarred piece of plywood about six-feet long, fronted by a garishly painted strip of corrugated iron nailed to wooden uprights. The most surprising thing of all though, and completely unexpected, was the familiar figure in Royal Navy uniform that puffed away on a cigarette while perched on a wooden stool at the end of the counter.

Spider Webb got up from the stool and stood grinning broadly as they approached. 'Well well, look what the cat's brought in. It seems I'm not the only one who's out of bounds tonight! So what brings you lot over to this booming metropolis then?'

'The same as you I should think mate,' George chuckled. 'We all got fed up with the throbbing night life at the Mermaid club.' He pointed at the smeary looking glass tumbler on the counter in front of Webb. 'What's that stuff you're drinking, some kind of beer?'

Spider picked up the glass and held it up for their inspection. 'The locals call it arak,' he told them, swirling the oily looking liquid around inside the glass. 'Apparently it's made from fermented palm juice and figs and stuff. You ought to give it a go, it's pretty good, and at a shilling a tot, I'm certainly not complaining.'

'A shilling a glass!' exclaimed Toz. 'That's more like it.' He pulled out his last ten-shilling note and slapped it down on the counter. 'Go on then Spider, you order them up and I'll pay for the round.

'Spider picked up the note and waved it at a bearded Arab who was sitting alone, reading a newspaper at a nearby table. 'Fakhir, come and dig out your special bottle out again. These infidel friends of mine are thirsty.'

The man gave them a sour look, clearly unfriendly, but got to his feet and slouched round to the rear of the counter. Taking four grimy tumblers from a rickety wooden shelf, he slowly filled each one to the brim from an unlabelled bottle and stood waiting while Spider sank the drink in a single swallow. After refilling the big sailor's glass, he reached under the counter and came up with a battered biscuit tin into which he placed Toz's ten-shilling note and took out four shillings in change. Ignoring Toz's outstretched hand, he placed the coins down on the counter in front of Spider who deftly swept them up and handed them over to the youngster with a warm grin.

After returning the biscuit tin and bottle to their places, the surly proprietor shuffled off back to his chair. Throughout the entire performance, he had not uttered a single word to any of the five sailors.

'Well, he's a cheerful bastard if ever I've seen one,' Toz murmured as he pocketed the change.

'Yes. Somehow I don't think that he's any relation to old Akbar along the road,' George chuckled. He took a sip from his glass. 'Hmm, not bad at all though, and it is definitely an improvement on the stuff that Akbar likes to call beer anyway.'

'And that bloody rum,' quipped Toz, pulling a face, 'I mean, five fuckin' shillings for half-an-inch of coke!'

It may have been the drink, or possibly the effect of passive smoke inhalation from the hash pipes, but before long they found themselves giggling at the simplest of things. During the slouch, bottle, and tin routine, that was repeated with each purchase, they would go into fits of uncontrollable laughter and Fakhir's continuous silence only served to make things seem funnier for them.

There were a number of dark glances directed their way, and if they could have understood the angry mutterings which were becoming more frequent as the evening wore on, it would have given them some cause for concern.

When they left the bar shortly before midnight, cheerfully drunk and in high good humour, Olly's suggestion that it would be good fun to try riding the cow, still tied up outside, was greeted with wild enthusiasm and they all whooped and cheered when Spider produced a seaman's knife and deftly cut through the leather thong used to tether the animal.

With a little help, willingly provided by Peewee, Olly managed to climb astride the beast, but no matter how hard he squeezed with his knees, or kicked with his heels, the docile beast would not be moved. Toz tried pulling on the thong looped around its neck, but it was to no avail. The cow held its ground, refusing to budge an inch.

'Here, get out of the way, boy,' Spider said brusquely, still brandishing his knife. 'I know how to get the bloody thing moving.' Toz stood clear as Spider yelled, 'Hang on Olly,' and then cruelly stabbed the poor cow's rump with the spiked blade of the knife.

The beast let out a squeal of pain and took off along the street like a rocket. Taken completely by surprise, Olly almost fell off right away, but somehow he managed to keep a grip on the rough hair of the cow's neck and hung on for dear life.

'Yippee! Ride him, cowboy,' Spider whooped, spinning his cap after them. He turned to the others who were all laughing helplessly. 'What's the betting he doesn't make it to the end of the street then?' he asked, joining in with the laughter.

'No bets, Spider, look,' George said, wiping his streaming eyes with one hand and pointing with the other.

Spider looked back and saw that Olly had in fact already lost his seat but was still clinging grimly to the leather thong. He was now being dragged along with his ankles trailing in the dirt, throwing up a cloud of dust behind him.

Peewee sank to his knees, gasping, 'I haven't seen anything so funny in all my life.' Tears ran down his face and his ribs ached painfully as he struggled to regain control himself.

'Thar she blows!' Toz yelled as Olly finally let go and crashed to the ground. Free of its burden, the panic-stricken animal thundered off down the desert road and disappeared into the night.

Fakhir had come outside to investigate the ruckus and was just in time to witness the last few seconds of the spectacle. He didn't seem to be in the slightest bit amused. The cow was the highly treasured possession of one of his patrons and it was to this person that he now directed a rapid torrent of angry sounding Arabic through the open door of his bar.

Sobering quickly, George spoke urgently to the others. 'Come on, lads, there's going to be some aggro starting any minute now. Let's grab Olly and leg it out of here a bit sharpish.'

They ran to where Olly was sitting cross-legged in the dust. Apart from a slightly grazed elbow that he was examining and rubbing ruefully, he appeared unhurt, and as his friends rushed up he got to his feet nimbly enough. 'What's up?' he asked uneasily, looking back to where a crowd of Arabs were gathering outside the bar.

'Not a lot mate,' George panted. 'The locals are just about to re-enact the massacre at Khartoum, that's all.'

'Yeah, only this time, they've decided to put you in the starring role of General Gordon,' added Spider. He was staring grimly at the hostile crowd led by Fakhir that had now begun walking purposefully towards them. 'You lot had better start running,' he said. 'I'll stay here and kick some arse for a while.'

'Don't be an idiot all your life,' George said grimly, grabbing Webb by the arm. 'Come on he urged, we'd better get moving.'

'Not until I've sounded the retreat, cap'n,' Spider insisted theatrically. Shrugging off George's hand he drew himself up to his full height and placing a thumb at either side of his temple, waggled his fingers at the oncoming horde and blew them a very wet and loud raspberry.

George was tugging at his arm again. 'No more sodding about, Spider, please. For God's sake let's get moving.'

'Alright, mate, I'm coming now,' Spider chuckled, pleased with himself.

Concerned as he was, even George could not suppress a grin at Webb's comic antics.

As they turned to run, Peewee pointed ahead and yelled, 'Look, lads, there's a car! It looks like our bloody taxi.'

The vehicle was indeed the old Chevrolet, and as it slowed to pick them up, they were relieved to see the welcome face of Omar smiling out of the side window. They lost no time in bundling themselves into the vehicle, with George crying, 'Twenty shillings, twenty shillings, we'll give you twenty shillings if you get us out of here before that lot reach us.'

The arrival of the taxi only served to inflame the anger of the crowd who were now screaming hysterically and running at speed towards them.

Omar wasted no time in shoving the gear stick forward but was rewarded with a grinding shriek of protest from the gearbox and the stick juddered in his grip as the gears failed to engage. Unperturbed, the Arab nimbly double-declutched and rammed his foot hard down on the accelerator at the same time twisting the steering wheel, slewing the heavy vehicle in a violent turn. As the rear wheels spun and fought for grip on the loose surface Fakhir and those at the front of the crowd were close enough to receive the full force of a thick shower of sand and grit, leaving them shaking their fists, screaming and cursing as the car sped away.

A mile or so along the road, the driver slowed to avoid the cow which came trotting towards them on its way back to the village. The sailors waved and cheered wildly as the animal plodded past with an air of indignant indifference.

After the laughter had subsided, they sat back quietly, Spider and Olly sitting next to Omar on the front bench seat smoking cigarettes as the taxi motored along. A short period of reflective silence ensued that was eventually broken by Spider. 'Oh shit!' he suddenly burst out, twisting round to look at George and the two boys sitting in the rear. 'Sorry, guys, we're going to have to turn round and go back again. Just for a few minutes, that's all.'

'What!' Olly Green spluttered, almost choking on a lungful of cigarette smoke. 'Have you gone completely insane? Old Fakhir and his chums back there want to flay us alive.'

Spider coughed and said, 'No, I'm being bloody sensible for once. When you went off on that cow, I slung my hat after you. Then, what with George doing his Richard the Third impression; twenty shillings, twenty shillings for a fucking taxi,' he mimicked, 'I didn't have time to pick it up. I'll be right in the shit again if I go back onboard out of uniform.'

There was a very brief silence while the others digested this, and it fell to George to make a decision. 'Okay,' he said at last. Seeing as I don't fancy getting locked away in some dodgy Arabian love-dungeon for the rest of my life…' He removed his own hat and offered it to Webb. 'Fill your boots, mate - whose cap do you want? Take your bloody pick!'

14

Crossing the line

SQUEEGY LIPS HAD FALLEN in love and he was a changed man. This at least, was in his opinion.

It had happened to him during the afternoon in Aden which he had spent wandering around the Crescent and its dingy neighbouring streets, exploring the duty-free shops on his own.

It was nothing sordid such as falling for the prettiest girl in the local brothel, nor was it the result of a chance encounter with the beautiful daughter of some wealthy Arab prince. This was something entirely new to him, something that he could respect and become immensely proud of. Squeegy Lips had fallen in love with the art of photography.

He had already bought several small rabbits. A cheap but attractively lacquered combination cigarette case and lighter, a similarly lacquered powder compact for his wife and a carving of a family of elephants marching trunk to tail over what was supposed to be a typical jungle bridge.

The shopkeeper had given every assurance that the object had been hand carved from a single tusk of ivory, but Squeegy had observed that it bounced a couple of times when the man's young assistant had accidentally dropped it during wrapping so he held certain reservations as to the authenticity or compound material of the "object d'art". However, it looked good, and he thought it would look even better among the other curios that he had accumulated over the years, most of which were on permanent show in the living room of his married quarter, back in Devonport.

He was making his way back to the main road in search of a taxi when his attention was attracted by the backdrop of photographs behind a dazzling display of equipment in the window of a small shop.

Many of the photographs were of exotic locations around the world that he had visited in the past. In particular, it was a picture taken of the famous harbour at Rio de Janeiro overlooked by Sugar Loaf Mountain and Corcovado Peak with the huge statue of Jesus atop it that had caused him something akin to an epiphany. He was intrigued, not only because the picture happened to be a good one, but that it had just occurred to him that he had been there and could have taken that photograph himself, as well as many of the others that surrounded it.

'Alfred Jolly, you're a bloody great idiot,' he told himself aloud. 'The wonders of the world have been revealed before your eyes and yet you never really noticed them!'

He thought of his six-month-old son who would be getting on for a year-and-a-half by the time he got home again. What am I going to have to show him when he's old enough to understand what his daddy does for a living? Nothing. That's right, nothing. Well from now on, things are going to be very different.

He thought about his wife, Maggie, who before moving to live with him in Devonport had never been outside of the small Somerset market town where she had been born. How many times have I tried to answer her questions? What was it like in Bermuda, Alf? Come on Alf, tell me about Naples, is the Mediterranean Sea as blue as it looks in films at the pictures? Well, in the future I won't just tell her, I'll be able to show her, and our little Alfred, lots of pictures as well. Pictures that I have taken myself!

Overwhelmed by this sudden and uncharacteristic wave of emotion he entered the shop and treated himself to a belated Christmas present, an expensive Yashica camera, together with a long-range telephoto lens and a dozen rolls of colour film.

The equipment had set him back forty-seven pounds sterling, a considerable sum amounting to nearly three weeks' pay. However, he consoled himself with the thought that the set of three pairs of underpants that his wife had bought for him did not constitute a proper Christmas present. Besides, it was for a very good cause after all and he knew that it would have cost him more than double if he had bought it back home in England.

The ship was now on the second day of her passage to Mombasa and he had already used up four rolls of film. Three rolls had gone on taking shots of anyone or anything aboard the ship that he could get to stand still for long enough, and the fourth film had just been devoted entirely to photographing the replenishment-at-sea of more fuel oil and stores.

The men working on the deck of the supply ship on the port side had been far too busy to notice him, but the deck hands aboard the tanker to starboard were most obliging and gave him a great deal of encouragement by waiving gaily and adopting obscene or effeminate poses.

The signalmen were already disparaging of the yeoman's new hobby. 'Those bastards down there on the tanker must think that we're all a shower of brown hatters up here,' Peewee complained to Toz and Steve Tredrea. They were leaning over the port bulkhead, staring morosely down at the barrels, boxes, and packing crates that were piling up on the flight deck around the forward aircraft lift.

Although Peewee had spoken quietly enough, Toz turned to take a cautious look, but the yeoman was still preoccupied, standing on the starboard sponson. He had reloaded his camera and was already busily snapping away with the next roll of film. Satisfied that they would not be overheard, he said, 'Well you can't really blame them if they do, can you? I mean, what would you think if every time you looked round, a big fat ugly matelot was taking a picture of you - in your shorts as well!'

Steve Tredrea chuckled. 'That's just what's been happening to me,' he said. 'The bastard must have taken about thirty photos of me since we left Aden. Christ knows what he's going to do with them if they all come out.'

'Maybe he fancies you, Tredders,' chortled Toz, giving Peewee a wink.

'Perhaps he's planning to line the inside of his locker with them,' Peewee quipped with a smirk.

What the three juniors and the rest of the department had not realised was that Squeegy Lips was not yet attempting to take any serious photographs. He was merely practising. Although he had studied the instruction booklet carefully, the camera was still a very complicated piece of equipment to him. However, he was determined to master the art of using it correctly in time for the Crossing the Line ceremony that was scheduled to take place the following day. Then, HMS *Ark Royal* would enter the Southern Hemisphere for the first time when she steamed across the equinoctial line, the imaginary great circle around the earth that is commonly referred to as the Equator.

While the yeoman's increasing fanaticism was viewed both critically and cynically by the signalmen, some good had come out of it as George Allen pointed out at supper that evening.

'At least it's kept him off our backs lately, and with a bit of luck it should do for quite a while yet. I've heard that he's booked a seat on the safari bus trip when we're in Mombasa, so luckily we'll be rid of him for a whole week.'

'What!' Tom Collins slammed his knife and fork down savagely onto his tin plate. 'Shit! I've got a seat booked on that trip as well.' He glared across the table at George. 'Thanks a lot, mate, I don't say. You've really made my bloody day you have.

'Oh dear, what an absolute awful shame,' Peewee Hunt joined in with mock sympathy. 'I do think poor old Tom might be having second thoughts about his trip to the jungle, eh lads?' he said, grinning round at the others.

There was a loud chorus of "Arr" at this, to which Collins replied with a succession of obscenities before fiercely attacking his food again. Amidst the general banter Peewee did not notice the curious, almost sad smile which had flickered briefly across George Allen's face. The older signalman had just realised that his young friend was beginning to grow up. Six weeks ago, he mused, young Peewee would never have dared to take the rise out of Tom like that.

When the ship hove-to forty miles off the East African coast at latitude zero degrees in order to pay homage to their Royal Majesties Neptunus Rex and his queen, the glorious Amphitrite, JTO Hunt had no idea what lay in store for him.

"Crossing the line" was a very necessary ceremony designed to appease King Neptune for the ship's trespass across his domain, and to obtain his blessing and permission to proceed further. Tradition demanded that a number of sacrifices in the form of newcomers to life at sea must be offered up to him.

The flight deck had been cleared of aircraft and suitably prepared for the occasion. A sturdy dais in the form of a wide wooden platform was erected in the shade of the island immediately below the flag deck, and it was from here that the royal couple would conduct their court. Guilty or innocent – for many of those who had crossed the line before were mistakenly dragged up before the court - the punishment was the same.

First, there came a trip to the demon barbers for a sadistic shave and a hellish haircut, and for this purpose, a plastic chair had been placed to one side of the empty packing crate that served as the king's throne.

Next was a visit to the royal family's insane doctor and his team of zealous and equally crazed assistants to undergo a thoroughly nightmarish intimate physical examination.

Finally, the wretched victims were manhandled into a ducking chair that tipped backwards to deliver them into the shallows of the murky pool in which the Royal Bears disported gleefully in delicious anticipation of the imminent arrival of their hapless prey.

The flight deck and the upper deck area aft of the funnel were crammed with goofers, eager to witness the bizarre punishments meted out, and from the relatively less crowded space of the flag deck, a number of signalmen, including Peewee and Toz, watched the proceedings in comfortable amusement.

The royal guards, frightening, inhuman-like creatures, were constantly dragging a trail of screaming, pleading, and often sobbing defendants through the densely packed crowd of unsympathetic spectators who willingly assisted in hurling their terrified offerings onto the stage.

As Peewee was enjoying the spectacle, he felt an urgent tap on his shoulder from behind. He looked round casually, expecting to find one of his colleagues with a message of some kind. Instead, to his horror he found that the flag deck had been invaded by a horde of the weird submarine creatures from below.

Although he knew that they were merely hideously costumed members of the crew, they still appeared quite menacing. As they took hold of him, his desperate cries for help and terror-stricken mumbles of protest went in vain. He tried to fight free but it was useless. The revolting creatures were everywhere, their slimy bodies greased with cooking oil, and it was impossible to get a grip upon them.

As he was bundled through the hatchway and borne down the ladder, he became aware that he was not the only captive to be taken from the flag deck. Toz, it seemed, was offering a good deal of resistance for Peewee could hear him grunting and swearing, his Yorkshire accent far broader than usual. He must have been exercising some of his boxing skills too, for there were several loud fleshy cracks accompanied by gasps of pain from the familiar voice of one of the creatures. It transpired later that Toz had hit Sub Lieutenant Havers who was heard to say, 'I say, take it easy, old chap. It's only a bit fun you know.'

Fortunately for Toz, the young officer took the indiscretion in the spirit of the moment or it might have gone seriously wrong for him, almost certainly resulting in a court martial.

For the next ten minutes, Peewee suffered a nightmarish ordeal. As he was borne through the roaring crowd on the flight deck, securely held by his arms and legs, he desperately tried to relax and bring his spinning mind under control.

Suddenly he was up on the dais and seized by more guards then roughly manhandled into a kneeling position before the king and queen.

Somehow, he managed to summon up enough presence of mind to smile weakly as the Royal Clerk read out a list of preposterous charges against him.

Neptune himself, a titan creature of unarguably regal bearing, sported a filthy green beard of matted seaweed and wore a crown that had been formed from an old catering sized tin of pilchards. He smiled wickedly as he playfully prodded the boy with his sceptre, a rolled up Chinese umbrella known as a Wan-Chai Burberry.

The Queen, sitting demurely at his side, was tastefully attired in a cheeky off-the-shoulder affair that was an inspired creation of the Royal Dressmaker. Robustly constructed from tarred hessian the gown was set off by Her Majesty's choice of footwear, a glittering pair of sequinned sea boots that had been deliberately chosen to show off the delicate and graceful lines of her muscular legs. These had been suitably shaved and varnished for the occasion and were encased in provocatively tarty fish net stockings - made out of real fish net. She seemed oblivious to the chaos around her and sat quietly studying her reflexion in a hand mirror, teasing and combing her luxuriant flaxen tresses. The ensemble might have failed to quicken the pulse of a Milanese or Parisian designer of *haute couture* but it had the desired effect on the hundreds of excited sailors who thronged the spectacle. Shouts such as, 'Fifty kippers for a quick one,' 'Get `em out ya trout,' and, 'Two days tot for a flash of yer bot,' were haughtily responded to in regal fashion, when occasionally, this dazzling beauty, the King's consort, would look up from the mirror and treat her doting subjects to a dignified right royal, two-fingered wave.

Without warning, Peewee found himself on the move again, propelled backwards across the platform and thrust into the barber's chair. Instantly a large bucket filled with multi-coloured slime was fitted over his head and he almost gagged as he gasped for air. Mercifully, the bucket was soon removed and he was allowed to claw the muck away from his eyes, nostrils, and open mouth.

The barbers went berserk with their arsenal of giant combs, razors and scissors, and tipped more buckets of fouler smelling slime over him until the guards decided that he was now decent enough to be examined by the doctors.

The royal guards bore him across the platform and slapped him gasping and twitching like a landed fish onto the makeshift operating table where he was instantly set upon by a number of maniacal white-coated men, unidentifiable behind their surgical masks.

Once again it was the slime treatment. This time administered through gigantic hypodermic syringes that probed, found, and filled every nook and cranny of his body with the awful stuff.

Suddenly he was in a chair again, this time facing the island with his back to the crowd and the fearsome bears that splashed noisily below. Then the chair tipped violently backwards. The grey paintwork of the island spun away to be replaced by the watery blue cloudless sky and the upside down grinning faces of the spectators on the flight deck.

'Bastard, bastard! Oh, you bloody bastard,' he screamed as he went over. With his arms flailing and legs kicking uselessly, he slid from the chair and hurtled gracelessly into the salty water of the royal bear's pool.

It had not been King Neptune or any particular member of the royal cortege to whom his screams had been directed. As the ducking chair had tilted backwards, he had caught sight of Squeegy Lips high above on the flag deck. The yeoman had been perfectly poised, camera adjusted and lined up, ready and waiting.

'It's one thing,' Peewee later grumbled to Toz who had suffered the same fate, 'to be made to look stupid in front of all those people. But there was no need for Squeegy Lips to make a bloody photographic record of it!'

15

Mombasa

THE PORT OF KENYA at Mombasa was approached through a wide estuary that after a mile or so was reduced dramatically to a narrow channel. At the inward end of the channel there were several nasty twists and turns that had to be negotiated in order to gain entrance to the dockside. However, as the harbour was too shallow to accommodate *Ark Royal*, the captain was spared this hair raising navigational ordeal and the carrier anchored in the deep-water channel just outside the harbour entrance.

As it happened, the ship could not have been better placed. On one side, just ten minutes away by ship's boat and even less by one of the numerous 'K' Boat water taxis was a tiny wooden landing stage. From here there was a regular taxi service to and from the town which operated around the clock.

On the other bank, and just as easily reached, was the Royal Navy Liaison Officer's residence. It was a charming white-painted, plantation-style house, standing in several acres of exotically landscaped gardens with Coconut palms, Flame, Pawpaw and Mango trees. Many beautiful flowering shrubs and bushes were strategically dotted about. These were laid out across an immaculate manicured carpet of emerald green grassy lawn that sloped gently down towards the water where it was fronted by a spotless strip of glistening white sandy beach. The beach was very popular with the officers of visiting warships as it was enclosed with a steel meshed shark net and could be bathed from in safety. Kilindini harbour was notorious for the voracious sharks that infested it. Tiger sharks, Bull sharks and Makos were common and constantly patrolled the waters in search of offal dumped overboard or any other juicy titbits that might come their way. The *Carcharodon Carcharias,* or Great White shark, was also known to make the occasional visit.

As luck would have it, Knotty Ash and Tubbs McEwan's team of watchkeepers were on duty on the day of arrival. Normally this meant a great deal of extra work for the MSO as there was always a flood of welcoming signals and telegrams that had been sent ahead of the ship to the local signal station, in this case, to the Wireless Office of the Naval Liaison Officer. The less important routine signals were usually withheld from transmission, instead being kept for physical collection as "Hand Messages". These often consisted of long-winded stores signals listing hundreds of mundane items that had been, or were about to be, despatched from the United Kingdom.

It was surprising therefore when Knotty Ash and his men turned up to take over for the first dog watch at 1600 that Tubbs McEwan and his team were all on the flag deck engaged in far less industrious activities.

Tubbs was studying the "goings on" ashore on the NLO's beach through a pair of binoculars, while George Allen and Spider Webb were gazing wistfully across the short expanse of water on the other side to where a liberty boat had just deposited some thirty eager shore-goers onto the landing stage.

Toz, clad only in a pair of white shorts which he had rolled up high around his thighs to expose as much of his legs to the sun as possible, was stretched full-length on the deck and appeared to be sound asleep. However, he opened one eye and squinted up at the relief watch as they stepped out of the hatch combing into the bright East African sunlight.

'What's up, Tubbs?' Knotty enquired of his friend and opposite number. 'Nothing to do in the office, or have you left it all for us again as usual?'

Tubbs McEwan lowered the glasses and turned to face Knotty Ash. 'Cheeky sod!' he snorted indignantly. 'When we took over this afternoon there were twenty-seven signals to be typed. Twenty-seven,' he repeated, 'Plus a load of party invitations for the Ruperts. Anyway, they've all been dealt with now and the office is up to date. Talking of Ruperts,' he went on, still using one of the slang terms for an officer, 'the naval liaison officer has made a request for us to keep an eye on his grounds. Apparently there's been an intruder lurking about recently and he hopes that we might be able to spot and nail him.'

Ash looked across at the beach that was dotted with a large number of bathers. 'An intruder eh! How does he expect us to spot him amongst that bloody lot?'

'I think he was referring to night time, mate,' McEwan explained. 'That lot over there are mostly our Ruperts. They've been pissing it up all afternoon and I've got to say, some of the women are a big doggo but if you look carefully there are some cracking bits of essence among them.' He offered Knotty the binoculars, 'Here, have a gander and see how the other half lives.'

'That's bloody typical that is,' Olly Green griped. 'The first day in and the pigs are at it already. Cocktails and crumpet! Why don't we get invitations like they do, that's what I'd like to know.'

'It's because we're just a shower of shit, that's why,' Tubbs McEwan told him bluntly as he jumped back up to join Knotty Ash on the sponson. The leading hand had steadied the binoculars on top of the ten-inch signalling projector and what he saw through them caused him to whistle softly through his teeth. Almost right away he had caught sight of the SCO, Lieutenant Commander Buckfawn who appeared to be enjoying the company of a stunning looking bikini-clad blonde.

'Wow,' he breathed softly. 'Old Fuckborne has trapped himself a nice bit of talent, the rampant old bugger. She is *absolutely* essence and looks young enough to be his daughter!'

'Dirty lucky bastard, more like,' McEwan said, chuckling at Knotty's colourful corruption of the officer's name. 'She's been playing about with him all afternoon. Right little raver if you ask me.'

'Playing with him?' George Allen jumped up and elbowed himself into a position between the two leading signalmen. 'I don't know about that,' he went on. 'The last time I looked they were both going berserk in the oggin. I thought they were drowning at first, but Spider reckoned they were just getting their jollies by having it off with each other.'

Toz came lithely to his feet and joined them at the side of the sponson. 'It's a pity Squeegy isn't here with his camera,' he said. 'With that telephoto lens he's got, he could have taken some great action shots to send home to his missus.'

Everyone chuckled and Olly Green said, 'Come on, Knotty, let's have a butchers, I've got a lazy lob-on twitching away down here you know.'

'Well in that case, you shouldn't look or you'll end up having to take yourself in hand,' the leading hand told him sternly, but handed over the glasses with a smile.

The group broke up when Tubbs went below taking George and Spider with him. Tom Collins followed Ash into the MSO leaving Olly up on the sponson happily entertaining himself with the binoculars.

Toz didn't seem to be in much of a hurry to get out of the sun and stayed on the flag deck for a while chatting to Peewee. Their conversation revolved mainly around Mombasa, wondering what sort of a run ashore it would turn out to be.

'What time do you reckon we should go ashore tomorrow?' Peewee asked eventually.

Toz shook his head slowly, undecided. 'I don't know really,' he answered uncertainly. 'Seeing as I've got the middle watch tonight and the forenoon in the morning, I think I might just crash out during the afternoon. I don't want to be knackered as well as pissed tomorrow night.'

'That's probably a good idea,' Peewee agreed. 'I'm thinking about going ashore for a quiet look round during the day because I've got watchkeepers leave from 0900. I'll aim to get back for about five o'clock though and give you a shake, just to make sure you get up. Then we can have a shit, shower, shave, shampoo, supper and steam ashore about six-thirty. How does that sound?'

'Sounds bloody great to me, and talking of supper, I'm going down for mine right now. He gave Peewee an impish grin before adding, 'That's if you can manage things up here without me of course.'

'Cheeky sod,' Peewee replied sourly. 'Anyway, with you out of the way I can enjoy the show on the beach in private. Now that Olly's disappeared into the office, I can have the binoculars all to myself. You never know, I might even spot the phantom lurker lurking about in the undergrowth.'

Toz laughed as he moved towards the ladder. 'If he's been spying on that lot over there all day, he's probably gone home suffering with wanker's whiplash by now.'

'Dirty minded bugger,' Peewee called after him as his friend went down the ladder.'

'Takes one to know one,' Toz's voice drifted up faintly from below.

Tubbs McEwan and his team were all back promptly at 1800 for the last dogwatch and after a certain amount of persuasion, Toz managed to talk Peewee into relieving him half an hour early for the next watch change. The main dining hall had been transformed into a cinema for the showing of the Rodgers and Hammerstein film *South Pacific* that evening, and Toz wanted to make sure that he would be able to get a good seat. For his part, he reciprocated by returning to relieve Peewee an hour earlier at 2300 bringing a gift of a warm but greasy egg banjo with him.

Peewee munched gratefully on the unexpected treat and was looking forward to an early night when Toz called out sharply.

'Hey up, get the binoculars, quick. I think I saw someone moving over there!' He was pointing towards the grounds of the Naval Liaison Officer's residence.

Peewee grabbed the binoculars and leapt onto the sponson next to his friend. Toz snatched the binoculars from him and peered into the darkness on the shore. The beach party had long since moved inside and the grounds, like the beach, were now deserted.

Toz studied the patch of ground where he was sure that he had seen movement, but whatever it was that had caught his eye seemed to have disappeared. He was just beginning to think that he must have been mistaken when Peewee hissed urgently into his ear.

'I think I can see him, mate. A bit further away from where you're looking. Quick, let me have the glasses before I lose him again.' Toz passed them over and Peewee quickly focused them on the spot where he was absolutely certain he had seen something or someone move.

At first he could make out nothing but some large bushes in the foreground of a neat line of palm trees. Then he saw it again. A definite flash of movement reflected in the pale light of the high moon.

'Got him!' he breathed gently. Lowering the binoculars he turned and stared at Toz. 'I think we've found the phantom lurker mate. Over there in the bushes,' he said, sounding deadly serious.

Toz sounded positive when he agreed and said, 'Right then, it's decision time. Better tell Knotty and see what he wants to do about it.'

'That sounds like a sensible decision to me,' Peewee replied. 'You go and tell him while I keep a lookout. Seeing as I know exactly where he is, I don't want to risk losing sight of him.'

The leading hand reacted immediately but cautiously. His first thought was to curse the fact that he had given Tom Collins a stand-off from the evening watch as he was due to be on the safari trip that was leaving at 0730 the next morning.

To cover himself he had rung down to the mess and ordered Clive Appleby who had answered the phone to go to the PO's mess and rouse the Duty Communications Yeoman to inform him of the unfolding situation on the flag deck.

Next, he telephoned the officer of the watch on the quarterdeck to advise him that the flag deck watch had spotted an intruder in the NLO's grounds.

He further advised the officer that the signalmen were standing by to illuminate the grounds with a twenty-inch signal projector if necessary.

The officer of the watch reacted immediately and promptly assumed command of the situation. Within minutes he had turned out the six-man duty watch of the Royal Marines who wasted no time in applying camouflage paint to their hands and faces. After being issued with their L1A1 self-loading rifles they attended a hurried briefing and were then rushed ashore in one of the local water taxis. The Kenyan boatman was so excited at being involved in the drama that he only charged the marines one shilling per head for the trip which was half the normal tariff.

By order of the officer of the watch, the telephone line from the MSO to the quarterdeck was kept open as the official link for the operation. Via this, he was to be kept fully informed of any developments noted by the flag deck watch.

To this end, Peewee who was still watching through the binoculars would call 'Intruder still visible' at intervals of about thirty seconds to Toz who stood at the open door of the MSO. Toz would relay these words to Olly Green manning the telephone who in turn would pass them on to the bosun's mate at the other end. The bosun's mate would then call 'Intruder still visible, sir' to the officer of the watch who had taken up an observation position with his telescope at the starboard rail.

LTO Ash had been instructed to have the twenty-inch projector switched on without further orders as soon as the commandos were in position.

'By in position,' the OOW had explained, 'I mean as soon as they are within twenty-feet of the target, or as near to that as you can judge.'

As soon as the marines reached the beach, Knotty took over with the binoculars ordering Peewee to line up the powerful projector, and Toz to stand by at the on switch. Once ashore, the Royal Marines quickly reached their target area where ghostlike, they used the cover of the plentiful vegetation to spread out and encircle the spot before closing in, moving with deadly silence.

'Stand by, lads,' Knotty murmured. His hands were sweating badly and he had to keep shifting his grip on the binoculars.

'I hope to God those bootnecks don't leap up and scare the shit out of a piece of paper that's got caught in the bushes,' Toz muttered nervously.

He was echoing all of their misgivings. It had been a good twenty minutes since the first sighting and now the three of them were praying that the whole exercise would not turn into an embarrassing fiasco.

'Here we go then, lads,' Knotty grunted at last. The marines are in position so let's treat the bastard to a display of traditional British seaside illuminations. Stand by at the light... Stand by... Illuminate!'

The Royal Navy twenty-inch projector is designed for signalling in Morse code at a distance of up to twenty miles in bright sunlight. The strength of its light is calculated in candlepower estimated at forty-five million candles, give or take a couple of hundred. When Toz threw the switch and Peewee squeezed the trigger, a solid beam of light slammed into the bushes like a rocket-propelled fist.

The commandos were instantly up and running, the need for silence ended. Screaming like a horde of banshees' they converged upon their prey.

Tom Blowers, the duty yeoman, arrived on the flag deck exactly as Ash spun round and shouted, 'Turn that bloody light off now! Quick!'

'Do it!' Blowers screamed. The yeoman had no idea what was going on but he instinctively backed up the leading hand.

Peewee instantly swung the lamp upward, shooting the beam high into the night sky while Toz fumbled the power switch back into the off position.

With the light extinguished, the two boys looked worriedly at Ash who had collapsed to his knees on the sponson. His head had cracked against the metal bulkhead and his body was visibly shaking as Blowers and the juniors stared down at him.

'What is it, Hooky, are you all right?' the yeoman demanded anxiously. When Ash failed to answer, Blowers voice became more urgent as he tried again. 'For God's sake, man, what on earth did you see over there?'

The leading hand made a feeble gesture of apology towards the yeoman with one hand but he was clearly unable to answer as his body convulsed again, seized by a violent and uncontrollable fit of hysterical laughter.

Peewee glanced uneasily at Toz who shrugged and continued to stare dumbly at the LTO.

It was two long minutes before Ash recovered enough to answer and even then he was still finding it difficult to speak properly.

'Bloody hell,' he wheezed as he struggled into a sitting position with his legs dangling over the sponson. For a few moments he just sat there sucking in great lungfuls of air, coughing spasmodically.

Eventually, when he looked up at the boys, his eyes and cheeks were wet with tears. He switched his gaze to the yeoman and tried to speak but he was obviously still having difficulty in doing so. Suddenly he began shaking his head as if trying to clear it and he shrugged helplessly before blurting out, 'It was Buckfawn, the SCO...' he paused to take another deep breath which seemed to steady him and finally the rest of the words came pouring out, 'how the bloody hell could we have known that the bastard intruder would turn out to be our own boss, the SCO, shagging that dolly bird. You should have seen their faces when the marines... oooh!...'

Overwhelmed by another spasm the leading hand collapsed again, rolling sideways across the sponson. His body writhed and shook as he laughed and sobbed helplessly, fighting to dispel the scene that had been so brilliantly lit up for him in the projector's beam of light. It was a tableau that he knew would remain etched into his memory until the day he died.

16

Rita and the Island of happiness

DECIDING THAT IT WOULD be prudent to put as much distance between himself and the Signal Communications Officer, Peewee took advantage of his watchkeepers leave and went ashore at 0900 on the first liberty boat.

There were a couple of dozen other men in the boat and the incident of the previous night seemed to be the main topic of conversation.

If only they knew that I was the twenty-inch operator, he thought to himself with quiet amusement. He knew that he had done the right thing by getting away, especially after overhearing a steward giving his version of another embarrassing moment for the SCO.

The steward had been on duty in the wardroom at breakfast and was comically explaining to anyone who cared to listen, how the communications officer had been sitting red-faced among a number of fellow officers, none of them bothering to hide their smiles. When the executive commander had walked in and openly complimented him on the efficiency of his flag deck staff, Buckfawn had been treated to a spontaneous round of applause led by the grinning Captain of Royal Marines.

The journey into Kilindini took less than ten minutes and when Peewee got out of the taxi beneath the massive arch of concrete elephant tusks which spanned the bottom of the main road, he was so pleasantly surprised at the very reasonable fare that he gave the driver an extra sixpence as a tip.

159

Unlike Aden where the ancient and the modern are thrust crudely into one, the island of Mombasa had a dividing line drawn firmly between the two.

On the eastern side was the medieval port, dominated by the cluttered and densely populated old Arab town. It had seen little change in the three hundred years since the Portuguese had been driven out, and it was still used exclusively by the traditional Arab dhow traffic.

On the other side, Kilindini port with its huge cranes, container sheds, and deep-water berths was said to be the finest harbour along the entire length of the East African coast.

The recently developed town may have looked very modern, but Peewee, looking upwards along the wide and gently rising main thoroughfare was not disappointed. Mombasa may only have been a tiny island, an infinitesimal speck on the edge of a vast continent, but to him it was still Africa. He was not going to allow any amount of modernisation to spoil it for him and besides, while coming ashore in the boat he had heard some of the older hands referring to the place as "Raha" which in Swahili meant, *island of happiness*, and he was keen to find out why for himself.

He began moving uphill, walking slowly and taking time to peer into the shop windows, each an Aladdin's cave filled with exotic merchandise. Gold, silver, brass, and copper trinkets, ivory and wooden carvings, and brilliantly coloured finger paintings were crammed into every available square-inch of window space.

Some shops displayed shocking things such as stools, coffee tables, and doorstoppers made from the stumps of elephant's legs and feet. The severed hands of Gorillas were also on sale, some of them shown holding sweets, jewellery, and toiletries such as gaily-coloured bars of soap in order to demonstrate their versatility. Peewee was particularly disgusted by one of these displayed to demonstrate its use as an ashtray.

By mid-day, he had seen and walked far enough. The streets were rapidly filling with people, many of them Japanese, German, and American tourists from the cruise ships, but members of his own ship's company were also becoming more frequent.

The sun had thoroughly established its presence, reflecting a steamy heat from the walls and windows making the air uncomfortable to move around in.

He was exploring a side street off the upper end of the main road when he stumbled across the Rainbow Bar. It was a place whose dubious merits he had heard discussed noisily and favourably by a group of drunken naval airmen returning from shore in the very early hours of the morning.

The Rainbow was the largest bar that he had been in so far and it was furnished in much the same way as the Trocadero in Gibraltar. It was obviously a place that catered for the fast-drinking seamen rather than tourists, but at that time of the day, the few customers were outnumbered by the hostesses. Most of these were dressed alike in short, brightly patterned frocks, and many shared the same tribal hairstyle, criss-crossed with furrows that showed through to the scalp.

The few men in the room were easily recognisable as merchant seamen, but the boy knew that before long the place would become crowded with uniformed sailors from the *Ark Royal*.

After buying a bottle of chilled Tusker beer from the bar, he found an empty table next to a large open window from where he could enjoy the passing scene outside but was soon forced to move to a cooler spot as the heat coming through the window was becoming unbearable.

As he stood up a female voice called, 'Hey, Chico, come over here and sit with me.'

He looked round to see a pretty African girl with a glossy mane of sleek black hair smiling at him as she patted the seat of a vacant chair at her table. She was not very old, probably about the same age as him, he thought, but the memory of Aden was still fresh in his mind. Not wishing to be reeled in again he shook his head and moved away to another table.

Undeterred, the girl got up and followed him. When he sat down again she sat uninvited in the chair opposite, resting her arms on the table smiling confidently.

'OK. If you won't sit with Rita, then Rita sit with you. You don't mind eh?'

Feeling uncomfortable and a little annoyed at her persistence, he stared defiantly across the table and said, 'Look here, I'm not buying you any drinks if that's what you're after.'

The girl lifted her shoulders in a delicate shrug. 'That's okay, Chico, I don't mind. But you can still talk with Rita. Yes?'

The young sailor relaxed a little at that and smiled back at her. 'Alright, you win. I'll talk to you, but stop calling me Chico. My name is Peewee.'

The girl giggled softly. 'You got funny name, but I still call you Chico. Rita always call nice young boy, Chico.'

It was the boy's turn to shrug. 'Oh well, call me Chico then if you want to. I don't suppose it makes any difference.' He picked up the beer bottle and emptied the remains of the beer into his glass.

The girl was on her feet in an instant. 'You finish your beer! Rita fetch some more for you. Before he could object, she scooped up the empty bottle and was on her way to the bar.

While she was gone he pondered his course of action, and by the time she returned, he was prepared. He had removed all the loose change from his pocket, eight shillings and fourpence, and placed it in the centre of the table.

'Hey Chico, that too much money!' The girl stared at him in surprise. 'Tusker only two shillings a bottle. You very rich or something?' She picked up two of the shilling pieces and pushed the rest back towards him.

Peewee didn't touch the money but looked up at her and said, 'No, I'm definitely not rich. I just wanted you to know that that's all the money I've got.'

Rita eyed him doubtfully for a long moment. 'You got no paper money Chico?' she asked eventually.

'I'm afraid not, love,' he lied, nodding sadly at the small pile of change. 'That's the lot, all six and fourpence of it. When that's gone I'm broke.'

The girl continued to stare at him for a few moments, still unsure, but then her face broke into a sunny smile and she sat down again. 'You don't have to worry, Chico, you got enough for three more beers.'

The young sailor looked surprised. 'I thought that you would want a drink as well. A rum, or something like that,' he added cautiously, somewhat taken aback.

Rita laughed and shook her head. 'You want to buy me some rum? No Chico, Rita only drink Tusker. But you don't have much money so I buy my own beer.'

Peewee was even more taken aback. He had been expecting one of the shiny faced barmen to appear at any moment with a bill asking for payment at a hugely inflated price for the bottle that the girl had brought back for herself. He pushed the money back into the middle of the table and said gallantly, 'Well, if you really want to sit here and talk to me, and you're not expecting me to buy you expensive drinks, you must allow me to buy you at least one bottle of beer. I've got plenty of money back onboard my ship, you know.'

The girl shrugged and got up again. 'Okay, Chico. You buy me one beer now but next time I buy for you. Taking another two shillings from the dwindling pile on the table, she went back to the bar leaving him shaking his head wonderingly after her.

True to her word Rita bought the next round, and eventually, when Peewee's remaining money had gone, she insisted on paying for another although this time she went without, herself.

During the two hours or so they had been together they had talked a great deal. Rita had hopes of going to England one day and her questions about London, and Liverpool in particular of all places, were endless. It transpired that one of her many sisters, a girl who had also worked at the Rainbow Bar, had met and married a Nigerian seaman of British

163

nationality. He had taken her back to England to live with his parents in Liverpool.

For his part, Peewee asked her all the usual things. What was a girl as bright as her doing in a place like this when she could easily get a job in a shop or office etcetera. No doubt Rita had been asked the same sort of questions many times before, but she answered the boy willingly and frankly.

It seemed that the best-paid and most comfortable jobs went almost without exception to the Asian girls. There were several opportunities open to girls of Rita's class. For instance, she could earn as much as three pounds a week labouring for ten hours a day in the cement factory at Bamburi. There were also jobs to be had in the dockyards, either here on the island at Kilindini, or over on the mainland at Kipevu where the work was equally hard and the pay equally low.

In the end, Peewee had to agree that her current occupation was sadly the best of a number of evils. At least she was able to make a good living by local standards and after all, there were so many visitors to the bar that she was able to pick-and-choose her own customers.

A little later on, another girl came up to their table and spoke to Rita in rapid Swahili. Rita replied to her in the same tongue, and then smiled apologetically at the boy. 'This my friend, Judy,' she told him. 'We share a room together and now we have to go home for a break. No more work for us until tonight.'

Peewee nodded. 'That's all right, I understand.' He looked up at the other girl who might have been Rita's twin sister but for the difference in hairstyle. 'Judy, how do you say thank you in your language?' he asked her.

The girl's face lit up with a sunny smile. 'Asante,' she giggled.

Peewee shot her a grateful smile in return then looked back across the table. 'Asante, Rita,' he said politely.

Rita gave her friend an expressive glance and received an understanding nod in reply. Discreetly, Judy then slipped away leaving Rita and Peewee alone.

'What you do now, Chico? You go back to your ship?' asked Rita, a soft expression on her young face.

'Yes, I suppose so. I'll have to go back onboard to get some more money anyway.' He felt a sudden pang of guilt saying this, for nestling in his pocket were four East African twenty-shilling notes. However, having misled the girl this far, he couldn't think of anything else that he could say.

Rita sat quietly for a moment, staring into her long empty glass. When she looked up again there was a determined look on her open honest face.' Chico, I go now in taxi with Judy. I would like it very much if you come with me. Tonight I can lend you some money to buy drink – you can pay me back tomorrow – okay?'

Peewee stared at her, astounded. Of all the sea stories that he'd heard told, he had never heard of one quite like this. He was conscious of his face burning hotly when he answered, 'I'd love to, Rita, but I really do have to go back to the ship.'

The girl looked hurt. 'You don't like Rita, Chico?'

He shook his head. 'No, honestly, it's not that. It's just that I promised my friend that I would go back onboard to meet up with him. It wouldn't be fair to let him down.'

Rita brightened. 'But if you don't go, your friend will come here anyway! All sailors come to Rainbow Bar at night. You come home with me Chico,' she urged. I bring you back to meet your friend tonight. Maybe I fix him up with nice girl like Judy, he pleased at that, yes?'

Peewee thought about this for a moment, wondering what Toz would expect him to do under the circumstances.

It didn't take him long to decide. 'Alright, Rita,' he said decisively, adding for the second time that afternoon, 'You win.'

The girls' apartment was in an older part of the town. There wasn't much to it, just a tiny kitchen, an even tinier shower room cum- toilet and a reasonably large bed/sitting room with two double beds, each covered by a spotless white sheet and positioned against either wall.

The room itself was clean and tidy, but sparsely furnished. A small wooden table stood beneath the solitary window, littered with bottles, jars, tubes and other paraphernalia that women find essential for daily survival.

There was no sign of a wardrobe or cupboard, but a number of neatly ironed cotton dresses hung on a rail that had been fixed to the wall facing the beds.

As there was only one chair, a rickety and uncomfortable looking thing made of bamboo, Peewee remained standing. He felt clumsy and out of place in his uniform while Judy busied herself in the kitchen making coffee, and Rita fussed around in an unnecessary attempt to make the room more presentable to her guest.

When Judy brought the coffee, Rita took Peewee's hand and sat down on her bed pulling him down to sit next to her. Judy made herself comfortable on the one opposite and the two girls began chatting away cheerfully in Swahili. Still feeling out of place and more than a little out of his depth, the young sailor sipped his drink slowly and said nothing.

It was the first time in his young life that he had been in such an intimate situation and he was in truth very nervous and apprehensive. He was certain that the girl had not invited him home simply to offer him a cup of coffee and he was not sure if he would be able to cope with the situation if, or when, it might arise. His only sexual experiences so far had not been happy ones, being those that had happened to him since joining the *Ark Royal* barely two months ago.

He did not have long to wait before finding out. As soon as she had finished her coffee, Judy stood up and quite unperturbed by his presence, began to remove her dress.

Peewee blushed and averted his eyes, but Rita took his hand again, squeezing it warmly.

'Don't be shy, Chico! Plenty men see Judy undress. It's okay if you look, I don't mind. Anyway, we undress now as well. I want good long time in bed before we go back to the bar.'

She got up off the bed still holding his hand and half pulled him to his feet. Judy was already naked and Rita surprised him when she pulled the thin dress over her head to reveal that she had been wearing nothing else at all underneath.

Slowly, he began undressing himself, still blushing and embarrassed at the unabashed looks of open curiosity that the girls were giving him. However curious or not, his biological make up was functioning correctly. When he removed his underpants, his erect penis swung up and jutted out proudly bringing girlish giggles of astonishment and admiration from them both.

'Hey, Chico,' Judy laughed throatily, 'You got good one there. I think you give Rita very good time today.'

Peewee smiled bashfully, replying, 'You're not at all bad yourself, love.'

He had meant it too. Although he had never seen a naked woman in the flesh before, his natural instinct assured him that Judy and Rita were two very desirable women. Both of them were young with extremely desirable, slender, supple, and soft-skinned bodies. Rita's smooth skin was without blemish, as was Judy's but for an unsightly large and ripened abscess that adjoined, and dwarfed, the nipple on her left breast

He had no way of knowing that the girls saw him in a similar light. The twelve months he had spent in basic training had seen to that. HMS *Ganges*, the Royal Navy's foremost training school for boys had a fearsome reputation for its unmercifully strict and harsh discipline. It was however, a reputation equally renowned for its tortuous physical regime. A *Ganges* boy might easily cover three thousand miles on foot during his training year. Most of them "at the double". By the time he had graduated from the establishment, he had developed a very fit, lean and hard, muscular body.

Had he been able to understand their conversation over coffee he would have been pleasantly surprised and delighted to learn that he was seen as a far better prize than most of the clients that they regularly brought home from the Rainbow Bar despite the fact that on this occasion, he apparently had no money!

A curtain wire ran end to end through the centre of the room and was suspended just below the ceiling. The curtain was tied back next to the kitchen door and Rita undid this now, drawing it far enough to effectively divide the room in two. 'Okay, Judy,' she chuckled mischievously, 'You see enough now. Time you go to your bed and leave Chico for me.'

Judy giggled again and with a final joke at the boy's expense, she ducked under the curtain into her own side of the room.

Once in bed, the girl brushed the boy's clumsy attempts at foreplay aside. It was clear from both her verbal and physical demands that she was eager to get on with it and would not be able to wait for long. When the moment finally came, it was as he had feared all along, his inexperience that let him down.

Rita was lying on her back, her slim legs draped over the kneeling boy's shoulders. She had been using her hands to guide him, but now sensing that he was almost there, she let go and clutched at the sheet with her fingers, preparing herself for his entry. Gasping heavily and soaked in sweat, the boy pushed and strained. Although he could feel her opening a little, his penis was beginning to hurt, and he realised with a feeling of shame and frustration that he was not going to be able to penetrate much further.

Rita must have realised this too for she suddenly straightened her legs across his shoulders, her taught thigh muscles squeezing his neck in a warm scissor grip. 'Stop, Chico, wait,' she hissed urgently. 'You go wrong place for Rita. That no good without special cream. Why you don't tell me you want to go this way before?'

The boy froze and instantly pulled away from her as she relaxed her grip and allowed her legs to slide gently from his shoulders.

Peewee ran the back of his hand across his sweating forehead. 'I'm so sorry, Rita. It's just that I've never…' he stammered, then blurted out, 'It's my first time! I've never been with a girl before!'

'Hey,' Rita sat up a little using her elbows for leverage, eyes wide at the revelation. 'Chico,' she said softly, smiling tenderly, 'Why you don't tell Rita you a cherry boy?'

From the other side of the curtain came a muffled peal of laughter that only served to worsen his embarrassment. He looked down at the young African girl and mumbled another apology.

Genuine tears sprang to the girl's eyes as she reached up and pulled him down onto her, holding him tightly in a passionate embrace. 'Oh Chico, Chico,' she cried softly, smothering his face with wet kisses. 'You stay with Rita. I will teach you. I teach you everything about girls.'

True to her word, the girl taught the boy as much as was possible during the rest of the afternoon and early evening, even losing her glossy black hair in the process. The boy didn't care that it had been a wig and probably wouldn't have noticed if she had been completely bald. He was happy. He was on Raha, the *island of happiness* - and he was no longer a cherry boy.

17

Rainbow's end

THE EVENING TURNED OUT to be just as memorable for the young sailor. On their return to the bar, Judy had lost no time in spreading the news of Rita's conquest with a "cherry boy" among the other girls. From then on, wherever he looked there was a shiny black face beaming in his direction. Worse still, many of his shipmates who now crowded the place must also have heard for he caught several of them grinning or winking in his direction.

Rita was more attentive than ever and she had bought him his first two drinks. He had politely turned down her offer to lend him money, explaining that when his friends arrived he would be able to borrow from them.

As she was officially at work, the girl had to leave him from time to time and he was sitting alone when Toz arrived in the company of several of his friends and messmates, George Allen, Knotty Ash and a couple of sparkers among them.

Toz feigned a show of annoyance as they crowded round the table and sorted out their seats. 'You're a reliable sod I don't say,' he complained without preamble, while the others grumbled that they had wasted hours of valuable drinking time while scouring the city in search of him.

It was all meant in fun though, and when Peewee explained how he had been so unexpectedly detained ashore they congratulated him in traditional masculine manner.

'You lucky, dirty little bastard,' Tubbs McEwan said grinning broadly. 'What's it like, no longer being a virgin then?'

Knotty squeezed Peewee's leg and leered evilly into his face. 'Yeah, come on then, tell us what it feels like!'

The boy flushed. 'Sore,' he answered simply, pushing Knotty's hand away and joining in with the laughter.

'Hey, Chico! You and your friends want some beer?' Peewee looked up to see a large, older girl smiling down at him.

It was Tubbs who answered with a big smile, 'Yes please, my dear. Young Chico here is celebrating, so we'll have six bottles of cold Tusker right away.'

The girl repeated the order and flashed Peewee another dazzling white-toothed smile before moving away.

'That's not her is it?' Taff Jones enquired, hooking a thumb after her. 'She seems to fancy you all right, boyo. Looks a bit doggo though!

Peewee shook his head. 'No thank you. That's definitely not her. I just seem to be the object of everyone's attention in here tonight, that's all.'

'Can't think why,' George Allen offered dryly.

'I can,' Taff said with a smirk. 'It's because the girl has told all her mates about his tiny todger.'

'Pay no attention, he's just jealous,' Bungy Williams told Peewee through the laughter.

'Seriously though, what is she like?' George asked, nodding in the direction of two enormous girls sitting with some sailors at a nearby table. If she's anything like those two over there, I reckon you deserve a medal.'

Tubbs McEwan chuckled. 'Personally, if a girl wanted to buy all my drinks for me and take me home afterwards for a free afternoon of nooky I wouldn't give a monkey's doodah what she looked like.' He shrugged, 'I mean, you don't look at the mantelpiece when you're stoking the fire do you?'

'Very true, Tubbs,' Knotty agreed, nodding sagely, 'but you can't stoke the fire properly if your poker's not long enough, can you?'

While Tubbs was trying to think of a suitable reply, the girl returned with a tin tray that was loaded with eight bottles of Tusker. Tubbs was about to remind her that he had only ordered six when Rita and Judy appeared at the table, each dragging a chair up with them.

'Oh, hello,' Tubbs said, looking surprised as he pulled out his wallet. 'It looks like we've got company lads, and not at all bad looking at that!'

Peewee stood up and moved his chair to make room for Rita, while Knotty and Taff edged theirs apart to admit Judy.

'So, Chico, your friends come at last. I told you all sailor come to this bar. Now you got some money, yes.'

Conscious of everyone staring at him with amused expectancy, the boy introduced the two girls to his friends who greeted them warmly.

Tubbs gave the hovering hostess enough money to pay for all the drinks but she surprised him by only taking enough for the six he had ordered.

'Rita already pay for two beers,' she told him, putting the correct change in front of him.

Tubbs made a weak protest insisting that he didn't mind paying for the lot but Rita said, 'No, it's okay, you can buy more drinks later.'

Tubbs shrugged and pocketed the change. 'That's fine by me,' he said, 'It won't be my round again for a while yet anyway.'

The pleasant atmosphere developed another flavour as a band struck up, filling the place with a raw, ethnic style of jazz music. Some of the hostesses pulled sailors to their feet and the dance floor was quickly packed with dancing couples. It was a colourful sight, tanned-skinned sailors in their white tropical uniforms gyrating wildly with the black-skinned girls in their short gaily-printed cotton dresses.

All of a sudden, a terrific cheer went up from across the room and everyone turned and looked to where two sailors had climbed onto a pair of tables that had been shoved together to form an makeshift stage. As the crowd around them began clapping and shouting, they began to remove their uniforms in a comical parody of striptease artists.

Peewee and Toz were particularly amused to see that one of the men was Milligan, the naval airman who shared their sleeping quarters in the bunkspace.

'Hey up, lads,' Knotty shouted, 'The Irish lot are going for it. Looks like we're about to get the dance of the flamers!'

Peewee and Toz grinned at each other in eager anticipation of what was to come. They had heard of it many times, but had yet to witness, the legendary *Dance of the Flaming Arseholes.*

Except for their bell-bottom trousers and underpants that in accordance with the rules of the dance had been dropped around their ankles, the pair were now entirely naked.

Milligan's partner, a tall red-haired Irishman with the surname of Cassidy had been in the Fleet Air Arm for more than ten years. For most of that time he had been known by the nickname of "Hopalong" until the recent visit to Aden where he had succumbed to a debilitating attack of diarrhoea that had laid him low for a full week. He was now being cheered by the newly given nickname of "Trotalong" which unfortunately for him seemed to have stuck.

Milligan was enjoying himself. His skinny, heavily tattooed arms described circles in the air as he moved his sweating body in a ridiculous caricature of a belly dancer. Urged on by the crowd he turned a full circle on the table, thrusting and jerking the lower half of his body in crudely suggestive movements.

'Hold 'em down, you Zulu warrior; hold 'em down, you Zulu Chief, chief, chief, chief,' the crowd sang and chanted with delight. The cheering rose to a crescendo as each man finally bent over to be seized around the neck by eager hands reaching out from in front. They were then held firmly in the braced position, grimacing as a stiffly rolled-up newspaper was inserted firmly, and none-to-gently, into each man's anus. Someone shouted, 'Just the roll of the ship lads,' which was immediately followed by a chorus of, 'More like a roll of Lino!' There were cries of 'Give 'em a light,' and 'Get the bleedin' matches out,' and the noise of the crowd soared to another level as both rolls of paper burst into flames.

'Ally ally zumbar, zumbar zumbar, ally ally zumbar, zumbar zay,' the throng sang merrily as the pair, their heads finally released, leapt up and down like madmen. Miraculously, hampered as they were by the clothing around their ankles, neither man lost his balance, nor the roll of paper that blazed away at his rear.

The spectacle was soon over. In accordance with the ritual, before they could sustain any serious burns both men were drenched with scores of pints of beer that effectively put out the flames.

From then on, things became even more chaotic as the crowd split into several large groups, each trying to outdo the others as some of those among them performed their particular party piece.

Several different songs were being sung at the same time, each group of singers striving to out-sing the others. Beer was flung everywhere but all in fun. The men of the Royal Navy were simply enjoying a good run ashore.

By this time, Taff Jones had disappeared with the girl who had been sitting next to him, and Tubbs McEwan seemed to have had a change of heart. He was now getting along famously with the big pockmarked girl who was called Alice.

George and Toz were still on their own having successfully resisted the advances of a number of girls throughout the evening. Toz was going through a period of homesickness, not so much for his family as for his girlfriend. He had written to her that afternoon, asking her to become engaged to him. He and George were now in a deep meaningful but drunken discussion concerning the pros and cons of early marriage.

It was well after midnight and the revelry was still in full swing when Rita and Judy decided that they would like to leave, and so after exchanging farewells with those still sitting around the table, Peewee, and Knotty who had discreetly negotiated a financial arrangement with Judy, left the bar in the company of the two girls. Back at the girls' apartment, the formalities of the afternoon were dispensed with. None of them were in the mood for drinking coffee or making small talk and they didn't even bother to turn on the light. Rita was naked and helping Peewee out of his clothes even before Judy had disappeared through the curtain towing Knotty along with her.

As Rita pulled him down onto the bed, something began to tug at Peewee's memory. He knew that it was something important, something he had meant to tell one of his friends, but whatever it was, Rita was not giving him time to dwell on it. Anxious to continue the lessons that she had begun in the afternoon she was upon him at once, her hands and lips exploring the most intimate parts of his body. The boy did not get much sleep that night but after what little he had been allowed, he awoke coughing and choking, and spitting out vile tasting pieces of something foul, from his mouth.

'What's the matter, Chico, you not like sweets?'

He sat up and glared at Rita who was sitting cross-legged on the bed next to him. Daylight was flooding into the room through the tiny window and he saw that she was holding a saucer-sized dish in which was heaped a pile of tiny glistening objects.

'Jesus Christ! What are they?' he coughed, spitting out another piece of the awful stuff. The Lord's name was about to be taken in vain a number of times that morning.

'They are just fish eyes. I boil them in sugar and water for you.' She held the dish out. 'You like some more?'

'Fishes eyeballs! No thank you,' he said firmly, averting his gaze and brushing her hand away. 'Is that what was in my mouth?'

Rita chuckled softly. 'You asleep with your mouth open so I think I wake you up with nice surprise.'

Peewee groaned. 'You certainly did that alright.' He glanced up at the window. 'Christ, it looks pretty bright out there. Have you got any idea what the time is?'

'I wake you up at seven o'clock,' Rita answered promptly.

'Seven! Bloody Hell. I'd better get my mate up a bit sharpish then. We're supposed to be back onboard by eight.' He swung his legs off the bed and stood up unsteadily, grabbing hold of the curtain for support.

'Christ,' he muttered, 'I must still be drunk. 'He waited until the moment of dizziness passed, then called softly through the curtain. 'Knotty... Knotty. Wake up mate. It's gone seven and we've got to get back to the ship.'

At first there was no reply, but after a few seconds as he was about to call again, he heard the sound of bed springs creaking followed by a gruff noise that was half cough and half grunt.

Satisfied that Ash was making a move, he was about to turn round to look for his clothes when Rita came up silently behind him and wrapped her arms tightly around him.

For a long moment she stayed there, gently massaging his buttocks with her rough pubic hair and pressing her warm breasts into his back. He clasped his hands over hers, enjoying the sensation she was causing and feeling himself responding naturally. Rita pulled one of her hands free and reached down to give his interested penis a firm but gentle squeeze.

'No time now, Chico, you must go back to your ship,' she sighed, reluctantly pulling free of him. 'You wake your friend again while I make some coffee.

'He was on the point of giving Knotty another call when a loud cry of 'Lord Jesus Christ,' followed by a drawn out groan of, 'Ohh no...,' came from behind the curtain.

Hurriedly he pulled the curtain aside and found Knotty kneeling at the side of the bed. He was shaking his head from side to side, moaning softly. 'Knotty, are you alright, mate? What's the matter?' he enquired anxiously.

Slowly, Knotty raised his head and looked up at him. His skin looked grey and there was a terrible expression on his face as he rolled his eyes towards the inert form of the girl on the bed.

Peewee stared down at her, uncomprehending at first. Then he saw what it was that had so shocked Knotty and he felt the blood drain from his face.

Judy was still asleep. She was lying on top of the bed covered only up to her thighs by the white sheet. One arm was draped across her stomach, the other lay out flung across the mattress.

It was at her left breast that both of them were staring. The large abscess that had looked so ripe the previous day was now a withered piece of mottled black skin surrounding a tiny dark red core.

Knotty turned to face back to Peewee, his face strained. 'I thought it was her nipple.' He sounded almost apologetic. 'I've been sucking away on the bastard thing all bloody night!'

Peewee grimaced and forced himself to swallow the bile that had formed in his mouth. 'Oh Christ, Knotty,' he groaned as the memory came flooding back. 'I'm so sorry, mate. I meant to warn you about that last night!'

18

A way sea boat's crew

THE TEN-DAY "FLAG SHOWING" visit to Mombasa had been a success and many thought of it as an enjoyable holiday. Everyone aboard the ship agreed that it had been a "bloody good run."

For the men, apart from the attractions of places such as the Rainbow Bar, there had been free rail trips to the capital, Nairobi, and several outings to the Tsavo National Park where the wildlife of darkest Africa was viewed in comfort and safety through the windows of an air-conditioned safari bus.

For the officers there had been an endless succession of society invitations; luncheon, dinner and cocktail parties at foreign embassies and the homes of the rich and influential The Cold War was intensifying, and such parties were very often used as polite and discreet battlegrounds, where it was hoped that the combination of attractive female company together with unlimited amounts of expensive alcohol freely provided might loosen a few unwary tongues. The officers and men were constantly reminded of their duty to report any unusual conversations or actions that might be construed as suspicious.

As a consequence a steady trickle of such reports found their way into the main signal office for encryption before being forwarded to GCHQ, the government communication headquarters in Cheltenham, for analysis, as well as to the MOD, (Ministry of Defence) in London.

Peewee and the other juniors were encouraged to process these as it provided a perfect opportunity for them to improve their standards of ability at operating the Top Secret KL7 encryption machine. The juniors often found the intimacy detailed in the candid reports, highly amusing.

One report containing the Spanish words, "Bahia de Cochinos," made the duty watch in the MSO chuckle when they found that translated, the words meant "Bay of Pigs." As a wardroom steward had submitted it, they initially suspected it to be a veiled reference to the on-going Bacchanalian revelries taking place across the water on the NLO's beach where many of the ship's officers, commonly referred to as "Pigs", were in frequent attendance. The MSO staff casually wondered what the analysts themselves would make of the steward's report.

The Naval Liaison Officer's beach parties, though, remained ever popular and continued to take place every day. The flag deck watch had maintained a keen visual lookout, but despite their vigilance they had not observed any obvious intruders. They had not spotted Lieutenant Commander Buckfawn again either. The SCO was about the only ship's officer for whom the NLO's parties seemed to have lost their appeal.

Even Squeegy Lips was happy. After two days on safari in Kenya the trip had culminated in an excursion across the border into Tanganyika.

Here he had spent an enjoyable week at the Kibo Hotel, five-thousand-feet up on the slopes of Mount Kilimanjaro. Even Collins who had gone on the trip, had no complaints to make about him. Apparently, the yeoman had been up at a very early hour each morning in order to climb a little higher to take as many shots as possible of the sun rising over the snow-covered slopes. Collins had spent most of his time in the hotel bar and had seen little of him.

Toz was also very happy. He had been ashore several times and had taken advantage of some of the freely provided local excursions, but apart from the first night in the Rainbow Bar he had not been drinking to excess. He had received a letter back from his girlfriend on the last day in harbour. She had accepted his proposal of engagement.

Steve Tredrea on the other hand was not so happy. The same post had brought him a letter from his girlfriend in which she told him that she had found someone else. In the short Dear John she had told him not to bother writing to her again and asked him to return her photograph.

George Allen carried out a whirlwind tour of the mess decks and returned with a thick wodge of unwanted photographs of ex-girlfriends that had been understandingly donated by other members of the Dear John Club.

Tredrea had brightened considerably since George had given him the pack along with the suggestion that he send them all to his ex-girlfriend with the inclusion of a short note. "Sorry, can't remember which one is you. Please take yours and return the rest."

Peewee Hunt was experiencing mixed feelings. Over the ten days, he had seen a great deal of Rita and the two of them had become extremely close. He was in fact suffering from his first taste of lovesickness. Although he hadn't yet discovered it, he was also suffering from his first dose of venereal disease.

On the morning of sailing, both banks of the channel were crowded with well-wishers, white and black, turned out together to wave their farewells.

A troop of boy scouts had taken up a prime position on a sparse, grey coral hummock overlooking the channel exit. Two of the boys were supporting a large banner bearing the words, BON VOYAGE HMS ARK ROYAL. As the ship passed at its closest point, the troop came raggedly to attention and their white scoutmaster fired a one-gun salute. In deference to his rank, the captain was entitled to a seven-gun salute, usually fired from an ancient cannon or a modern saluting gun. In this case he had to settle for a single shot from a starting pistol. Quite unperturbed, the captain had turned to the SCO with a smile and the words, *'Semper aliquid novi Africam adferre*, according to Plato, eh signals?'

'Quite so sir,' Buckfawn had replied dutifully. The navigating officer shot the SCO a friendly smile. He had also recognised the ancient Latin quotation that translated as, "Africa always brings us something new."

The scouts had been rewarded with a hearty cheer from the sailors lining the flight deck that had been quelled by a stern, 'Silence on the upper deck,' issued over the command broadcast system by an authoritative voice from the bridge.

Five minutes later the aircraft carrier was out into the estuary, settling onto the first leg of her four-and-a-half-thousand mile journey across the Indian Ocean, bound for Singapore.

If anybody aboard the aircraft carrier needed reminding that the holiday was over, they did not have to wait long. Barely three hours later and just fifty miles off the coast of East Africa the aircraft carrier made her prearranged rendezvous with three Royal Fleet Auxiliary vessels, *Tidesurge, Fort Duquesne* and *Resurgent* - an oiler, an air supply ship and an ammunition supply ship respectively, along with the Destroyers HMS *Chichester* and *Cavalier* who were to be her escorts. Between them, they would carry out a full week of trial exercises before rendezvousing with other British warships including the smaller aircraft carrier HMS *Centaur* and a number of warships from SEATO, the South East Asia Treaty Organisation. The SEATO contribution would include vessels from Pakistan and the United States of America, and as the large-scale naval exercise progressed ever eastward across the waves, ships of the Australian, New Zealand, Thailand, and the Philippine navies would also become engaged.

Aboard *Ark Royal* the days of sunbathing and flight deck sports were over. Everyone was afforded the opportunity to prove that he had a job to do - his reason for being there. The known skivers and even the "scientific loafers," those who had developed the knack of managing to look busy when in fact they were not, were driven into pulling their weight as the aircraft carrier and her consorts went through an exhaustive round-the-clock programme of exercises that for *Ark Royal*, included a great number of potentially dangerous night-flying sorties.

During this period some uninvited and unwelcome visitors that had taken up permanent residence aboard the ship made life a misery for the exhausted men as they attempted to snatch a quick meal in the forward main dining hall where food was now being served twenty-four hours a day.

Cockroaches! The few disgusting creepy-crawly creatures that had succeeded in smuggling aboard, either during the ship's passage through the Suez Canal, or while at Aden had rapidly multiplied. They were now in evidence as an infestation throughout the ship but were particularly manifest in and around the main dining hall.

Being *thigmatropic*, cockroaches love to feel pressure on three sides of their body, and the deckhead, the ceiling over the dining hall, provided all the warm and moist cracks and crevices in which they thrived. During every take-off, the port or starboard steam catapult's launching shuttle screeched and whined as it raced along its trough in the flight deck, accelerating the plane it towed from nought to one hundred and sixty-five miles per hour in two seconds. This was followed by a sickeningly loud, deck shuddering thud as the tapered spears attached to the pistons that towed the shuttle slammed to an abrupt halt as they plunged into the water brake at the end of the track.

The result, every time, was that hundreds of the revolting things were violently dislodged from their cosy little nooks and crannies. They rained down to land on plates of food and into mugs of tea, as well as upon the men seated in the hall below. Despite the stress and pressure of working a constant four hours on and four hours off – in some cases, just two hours off – the sailors bore this with the blunt stoicism that is typical of the men of Her Majesty's Royal Navy. It was not long before these insect showers inspired the men to greet them with boisterous choruses from well-known songs, the words of which were suitably altered. *Boiled Beef and Cockies*, *Life Is Just a Bowl of Cockies*, and *Cockies from Heaven*, were particularly popular.

Night and day the exercise ground on, and while the greater part of the training operation was given over to both day and night time flying there was still plenty of time to spare for gunnery practice and to close-up at action stations for long hours at a time.

There were many replenishments-at-sea with the auxiliary vessels, some out of necessity but the majority of them just for exercise. Whenever the captain found a dull moment, he would slip in a quick "Man Overboard" drill, and, just for good measure, make the Chief Engineering Officer's day by ordering a mock emergency steering breakdown.

Sadly, the week did not pass without another tragedy. It happened on the fifth day out from Mombasa during the first dogwatch.

For JTO Hunt it had been relatively quiet on the flag deck. There had been the usual hoisting and lowering of flying signals and an occasional exchange of messages by flashing light between the carrier and other ships. Apart from this he had spent most of the watch idly enjoying the spectacle of the *Scimitars* diving and strafing the splash target towed on a five-hundred metre steel-wire-cable astern of the ship.

Repeatedly the aircraft dived, nearly always from the same point in the sky. From his vantage point on the starboard sponson, the junior would try to predict whether each aircraft would score a hit. He had become quite an expert at this and judging by the height and angle of approach, he was able to guess with a remarkable degree of accuracy just how close to the target the pilot would deliver his rockets.

At about half past five, Knotty Ash came out of the office in search of some fresh air. Cramped after the confinement at his desk he stood just outside the door, stretching his legs and flexing his shoulder muscles. After a few moments, he walked across and joined the boy up on the sponson.

'How are they getting on?' he asked, squinting up into the sky.

'Not bad,' Peewee replied without looking round. 'They've had more hits than misses anyway.' He was carefully studying the approach of the next aircraft. 'He's going to miss though,' he went on, pointing to the fast approaching blue grey speck in the sky. 'He's coming in far too high and he's left it a bit too late to get a good diving angle.'

'Really! Hmm, clever little bastard aren't you.'

Peewee glanced round but if any sarcasm was intended there was no trace of it on the face of the leading hand. 'Well you get quite good at it when you've been out here long enough,' he said, returning his gaze upwards.

'I can't even see the bloody thing yet,' Ash murmured. 'It's a bit bright out here after you've been in the office for a while.' He peered over the boy's shoulder, shading his eyes with one hand. 'Ah, yes, I've got him now. You reckon he'll miss the target then!'

'Yeah. He's left it far too late,' Peewee said, nodding. He chuckled. 'That means a bollocking for him from Flyco.'

Knotty Ash reached for the binoculars dangling by their cord from the handle of the twenty-inch projector. 'I think you might be wrong,' he said as he stared at the warplane through the glasses. 'Look at the bastard now - he's coming straight down at it!'

Fascinated, they watched with baited breath as the *Scimitar* screamed down at an angle almost perpendicular to the target.

Whoosh. The heavy wood and metal target rocked and bucked violently and the surrounding water erupted in a cloud of seething foam as the rockets found their mark.

'Bull's-eye!' yelled Ash, studying the target through the binoculars.

Hunt remained transfixed to the *Scimitar* that was still descending at terrific speed. Although the angle of the dive was broadening all the time, the gap between the aircraft and the sea was narrowing far more quickly and the boys hushed 'He's not going to make it, Knotty,' was drowned by the urgent voice that bellowed from the command system.

'Emergency. Emergency. Away sea boat's crew. This is not an exercise. Repeat. This is not...'

The last part of the broadcast was lost as the *Scimitar* entered the water and disintegrated instantly with a single ear-splitting explosion. An intense blinding-white glare hung briefly above the surface before being engulfed and doused by a roaring column of dirty grey water that rose some fifty-feet into the air.

'Pull yourself together, lad. Here's your gear. Now get down and into the sea boat at the double.'

185

Still shocked and reeling from the noise of the explosion, the boy mechanically accepted the portable radio set and the pair of semaphore flags that the leading hand was thrusting at him. His legs felt like jelly and he fell as much as he scrambled down the ladders to the starboard boat deck.

Within minutes of reaching the flat greasy slick that marked the point of entry into the sea, the pilot's fate had been determined beyond any doubt. As the coxswain made his first pass, a sharp-eyed junior seaman perched up front in the bow cried out suddenly. With the aid of a boat hook he managed to recover a small piece of a reddish brown-coloured blubbery substance which the medical attendant in the boat immediately identified as a piece of human lung tissue.

When the young signalman relayed the news of this find to the ship, he received a hesitant acknowledgment from Communications Yeoman Blowers who had been summoned up-top and was now manning the portable radio on the starboard bridge wing.

There was a short pause before Blower's voice crackled back through the headphones. 'Request medical attendant confirm your last.'

The boy stared dazedly at the medic who was crouching on the deck-boards in the small space between the coxswain and himself. 'They want to know if you can confirm that it's... er, what you say it is.'

The medic looked indignant as he nodded furiously. 'I've cleaned the blood and guts out of enough operating theatres to recognise a piece of lung when I see it,' he replied testily. Nevertheless, he lifted up the polythene bag that now contained the grisly item and studied it again before nodding assertively. 'It's definitely lung tell them,' he said quite firmly.

After a further two hours of fruitless searching and with daylight fading, the boat was ordered to return to the ship.

Peewee Hunt had hardly acknowledged the order when the young seaman in the bows started yelling and pointing to a brightly coloured object bobbing up and down in the water about two boat-lengths away.

'It's a flying helmet,' the lad shouted excitedly. 'It must have only just come to the top or we'd have spotted it before.'

They all stared with strained and anxious faces as the coxswain manoeuvred cautiously alongside the fluorescent-orange helmet.

The junior seaman hooked his plimsolled feet around the thwart and leaned out as far as he could, but the helmet bobbed past just out of reach of his stretching fingers.

'Steady as you go 'swain,' the boy cried. 'She's drifting back port side towards you!'

The coxswain slammed the gears into reverse and gave the boat just enough port helm to bring the stern end a little closer, and Hunt gripped the gunwale tightly. His eyes were glued to the helmet that was now only inches away from him in the water.

'Grab the bloody thing then, lad,' the coxswain called sharply. 'If we miss it now I'll have to go round again.'

Galvanised into action, the boy lunged down and grabbed the helmet easily with both hands. Lifting it out of the water was an entirely different matter. The helmet seemed incredibly heavy and it was all he could do to maintain his grip on its smooth, oil-slicked surface.

'Give us a hand someone, or I'll lose it,' he gasped.

Another pair of hands reached down past his face and took a grip under the rim. 'All right, son, I've got it as well.' Peewee recognised the voice of the medical attendant. Between them, they hoisted the sodden flying helmet inboard and lowered it gently, upside down, onto the decking of the boat.

The coxswain stared down into the helmet. His nut-brown weather-beaten face had turned deathly white. 'Dear God. Just look at it!'

'No wonder it was so heavy.' Even the medic's voice had taken on a strange note. 'That must be most of his body compressed in there. The force of the explosion must have squeezed him right into it!'

'Jesus Christ. It looks just like a Christmas pudding!' one of the seamen said idiotically.

As the medic kneeled down and hunched forward to peer more closely at the hideous looking mess inside the helmet, Peewee Hunt sagged back against the gunwale. A tremendous roaring sound was filling his head and he was finding it increasingly difficult to breathe. He could feel the hard edge of the gunwale digging into his buttocks. His eyes were still open but the boat, and the men in it, had become indistinct shadowy shapes that were rapidly being swallowed up by a dense, blood-red mist.

The last thing that he heard before he passed out completely, was the matter of fact voice of the medical attendant saying, 'For Chrissakes, someone haul him back inboard before he goes over the side or we'll be farting about out here all bloody night!'

19

Revenge – a dish best served...

'WELL, WELL. LOOK WHO we've got here now. Our little shell-shocked hero has returned. Had a pleasant holiday have we?'

The expression on Yeoman Jolly's face matched the sneer in his voice, but it was completely wasted on Peewee Hunt. After an absence of three days spent confined to bed in the sick bay, he had just returned to duty on the flag deck. The delighted grins on the faces of the others who had stopped work to welcome him back more than compensated for the yeoman's sour greeting.

'Nice to have you back again, mate,' George Allen said, ignoring the scowl that Squeegy Lips directed at him.

'Cheers, George,' Peewee nodded, at the same time flashing a returning smile to Toz who was grinning sunnily at him from the port sponson. Even the usually churlish Tom Collins was smiling pleasantly, as if pleased to see him.

'I suppose you realise, that thanks to your clever bit of skiving out of the rest of the exercise, we've all had to graft that much harder to cover your bloody share, Hunt,' Jolly grumbled.

'Oh! Well, Yeo, you've got such a good team of men that I'm sure everyone managed without me all right,' Peewee replied smugly. He held out a piece of folded paper. 'I've been given this chit by the Senior Medical Officer. I think you ought to read it.'

'What's that?' The yeoman snatched the note from the boy and fumbled it open with his thick, awkward fingers. Everyone stood around, waiting in silence while he studied the wording on the official medical document.

'Seven days' light duties!' Jolly roared, crumpling the paper in his fist.

'You've had three days on your back already! Christ Almighty. I don't know what this bloody mob is coming to. They'll be expecting us to change your sodding nappies next.'

'Just a minute, Yeoman,' George Allen spoke up strongly. 'Shock can be a pretty dangerous thing you know.'

'Shut your trap, Allen,' Jolly snapped, his tone ugly. 'Shock my arse. I'll tell you this, Hunt. You'll be in for an even bigger shock when the chief yeoman hears about this, just you wait and see.' He swept the boy aside and lumbered towards the ladder. 'Get back to work you bloody lot. And that includes you, Hunt,' was his parting shot.

'Bastard,' George muttered after the yeoman had disappeared.

'I'll drink to that, mate,' Toz said joining them. 'The trouble is, he's probably right about the chief. I don't expect he'll be too pleased when he sees your sick note.'

Peewee gave them a cheery grin. 'I wouldn't worry too much about the chief. Him and Blowers came to visit me in the sick bay last night. The chief said that if the doctor didn't order it, that he would personally put me on light duties for a week. He spent most of the time telling me about blokes he'd seen suffering from shell-shock during the war, and told me that passing out in the sea boat was really nothing to be ashamed of.'

A slow grin spread across George's face. 'Good old chief,' he chuckled. 'It looks like it's Squeegy's turn for a bit of a shock.' He put an arm around Toz's shoulders and drew him away from Peewee. 'Come on, mate,' he sniffed theatrically. 'Some of us have got work to do.'

Late that night as they lay side by side in their bunks, Clive Appleby carried on a mainly one-way conversation in an attempt to gratify himself with the junior. 'That bastard Jolly has got no sense of right and wrong,' had been his main theme. Every now and then he would slip in a sentence such as, 'At least you know you've got a good friend here,' and, 'You know I'll always watch out for you, mate,' each time reaching out to squeeze the boy's arm or shoulder to endorse the point.

Peewee knew where Appleby was coming from. Satisfied that all around them were soundly asleep, he gently prodded the older man with his fingers. 'Clive,' he whispered. 'Clive, are you still awake?'

The signalman's hand closed gently around the boy's wrist. 'What d'you want?' he whispered back.

Peewee moved his face closer to the centre of the bunks. 'I don't know if you're interested or not, but I've got a massive hard-on!'

Appleby quietly wriggled onto his side so that he was almost face-to-face with the youngster. 'We'd better do something about it then,' he murmured softly, sliding his arm inside the boy's blanket.

Peewee allowed Appleby to fondle him for a few moments and then placed his hand over the signalman's, squeezing it in a way that suggested he had had enough.

'What's the matter? I thought you wanted it,' Appleby whispered thickly.

'I can do that for myself, I wondered if you wanted to do something a bit nicer for me,' he replied in a suggestive whisper.

Appleby made no reply but the boy could feel the vibration as the signalman wriggled down inside his own bunk. A moment later he felt the bedclothes lift as Appleby ducked his head inside. Fighting back his revulsion, the boy forced himself to relax. During his time in the ship's hospital, he had spent many hours reflecting over the few short months since he had joined the *Ark Royal* and in particular, what Appleby had done to him during his first week onboard. Determined to go through with the whole sordid act, he lay back inwardly squirming and left the obsessed Appleby to finish what he had started.

In the morning, the first thing that the boy did was report to the sick bay for an embarrassing medical inspection. The fresh yellow discharge that stained his underwear was enough to provide the sick berth attendant with a diagnosis that confirmed to the boy something that he had been worried about for some time.

After leaving the sick bay he made his way down to the mess to report his predicament to LTO Robson. Appleby was there, busily mopping the deck and studiously avoiding him.

After the junior had finished speaking, Robson threw back his head and laughed loudly. 'Guess what, lads, this dirty little bastard has only gone and got himself a raging dose of the clap. The yellow peril on patrol in the pants and all!'

The boy smiled levelly across at Clive Appleby who had ceased his industrious activity. He stood frozen to the spot, face white as a sheet. He never made another advance on Peewee Hunt again.

20

A thief in the night

AFTER MORE THAN A month at sea, much of the time spent with the ship's company closed-up at action stations, HMS *Ark Royal* arrived in Singapore and docked alongside Number 8 berth in the Royal Naval Dockyard at Sembawang.

On the morning of her arrival there was a terrific uproar taking place in the signalmen's side of the communications mess. During the night a number of the men's lockers had been broken into and a great deal of money and various small items of personal value had been stolen.

One or two of the victims were listlessly sorting through their belongings, resigned to the fact that their money had gone. They knew from experience that any chance of finding the thief and recovering it was slight.

There were others who were not taking it so calmly. Tom Collins in particular was in a terrible rage. He angrily demanded some form of action from the leading hand of the mess.

'It's that bastard Spider who's been at it again, Robbie,' he complained heatedly. 'Get the bloody regulators down here to search his fucking locker.'

'All right, Tom, calm down a bit,' Robson soothed. 'You're not the only mess member who's been robbed you know.'

'I know I'm not,' Collins replied caustically, 'But that's not the point is it? There's only one thieving bastard in this mess and we all know who that is, don't we?'

'That's enough of that kind of talk,' Robson told him sharply. 'And that goes for everyone else as well,' he added, glaring at the sullen faces around him. 'I didn't go ashore in Aden and I only went ashore once in Mombasa. I've been saving up for a bloody good time here in Singers, where I really know my way around. I've also had over forty quid nicked so I don't feel too happy about it either. Still, just because Spider's been done for it once before, it doesn't automatically make him guilty this time.' 'We'll just have to hang-fire and let the regulating staff do their bit.'

Collins slumped onto an empty bunk and scowled down angrily at the deck. 'I'm sorry Leading Hand,' he said sulkily, 'You don't have to spin us that kind of shit, and besides, the Crushers won't find fuck-all. You know it's him, just as well as the rest of us.'

It was just at that moment when Spider Webb appeared in the mess. If he had heard anything of what Collins or anybody else had been saying about him he gave no indication of it. After opening his locker and taking out his washing gear, he made straight for the bathroom, leaving the locker door standing wide open. Even after he had passed out of earshot, no one, not even Collins, seemed inclined to mention his name further.

After Robson's report to the Regulating Office an official search was ordered and immediately carried out. With the entire mess present, it was conducted thoroughly and enthusiastically by a Regulating Petty Officer assisted by two Leading Regulators, one of them Spider's old friend, Pussy Catte. From their point of view the search was not in vain.

In Olly Green's locker, an illicit hoard of four cans of beer was uncovered. These were duly confiscated and Green was subsequently charged for having them in his possession.

Two envelopes crammed with pornographic photographs were discovered in Clive Appleby's locker. These were also confiscated and Appleby found himself lined up outside the Regulating Office along with Olly Green. Fortunately for Appleby, the photographs were not of a homosexual nature or he would certainly have faced a court martial.

As soon as they had finished with the lockers the regulators started on the men's bedding. Before long, the mess became strewn with a tangled litter of sheets, blankets, pillows, emptied hammocks, and dozens of startled scurrying cockroaches that had been disturbed during the search. Still nothing came to light except for a wider selection of obscene literature and some badly stained mattress covers.

Eventually a small army of Men Under Punishment were brought down to the mess. Armed with an assortment of tools such as pliers, spanners, and screwdrivers, and under the supervision of the regulators, they unscrewed the inspection covers from the plumbing and wiring trunkings, electrical junction boxes, and even dismantled and removed whole sections of the air-conditioning system.

No conceivable hiding place was left unsearched. The conscript searchers became filthy in the process but nothing was found except for a tiny scrap of crusty, yellowed paper, discovered lying in the years of accumulated dust and grime that had settled in the half-inch, cockroach infested gap between a section of the air conditioning and the deckhead.

Although it was somewhat faded, the cartoon depiction of a bald headed man with a long nose peering over a wall and the message, "Kilroy was here – 1953" was still clearly legible. The RPO concluded that it had probably been placed there during *Ark Royal*'s original fitting-out.

Toz nudged Peewee. 'Seen that before. It was carved into a wooden loo seat in the heads of our mess in Duncan Division at *Ganges*, only I'm sure it said 1958. I must have looked at it loads of times when I was having a pee. Sat on it a lot, too,' he ended, sounding almost wistful.

Toz had uttered this information in a hushed voice, not wishing to be overheard by the RPO. Peewee was a little taken aback at his friend's revelation. In the toilet block of Keppel 5 mess in *Ganges*, the toilets had been without the luxury of any seats at all.

After they had finished with the mess, the MUPs were dismissed, but the search moved on to the cavernous bunkspace where more regulating staff were already waiting to assist. In order to ensure that each man's bedding was correctly searched, strictly in accordance with the rules laid down in Queens Regulations and Admiralty Instructions, all members of the ship's crew who occupied bunks in the huge compartment were rounded up and ordered to attend the search as witnesses. It meant something of an upheaval to many, especially to those men who were off-watch, as they were obliged to take over from those on duty who were summoned to attend the search. It also meant that if the culprit was discovered, he would have been so under the suddenly hostile eyes of his friends and messmates. As with the system for appointing sentries for men held in the cells, this was another piece of fiendishly subtle naval discipline.

Despite Spider Webb's well known past record, the regulator who tore his bunk apart did so with no more relish than he did those belonging to the others. Spider's bunk was found to be clean - if only in the legal sense of the word.

More pornography was discovered inside Clive Appleby's pillowcase, and, stuffed well out of sight within Pip Piper's bunk, was a small elderly teddy bear with one glass eye. The junior was obliged to undergo an embarrassing interrogation before a gathering band of amused spectators from other departments.

Toz Tozer's bunk was the last to be searched. Knowing that this was the regulators last chance of success, a hushed silence fell over both the signalmen and the watchers-on.

The search was made by Leading Regulator "Anchor Face" Frow who was well known for his by-the-book adherence to duty. It was this pedantic nature coupled to the fact that he was entirely intoxicated with the power his position afforded him that had earned him the derogatory nickname. Any stickler of this type was generally referred to as anchor faced. Like the majority of those who served in the regulating branch of the service, he was possessed of a bad attitude and despised by all who had suffered the misfortune of crossing his path over the years. He took his time, systematically removing the sheets and blankets one by one, giving each a thorough shaking before moving on to the next. Toz's pillow case was carefully stripped away and the pillow squeezed and prodded in search of any unusual lumps. Finally, the thin canvas-covered mattress was hauled off the bunk. As it fell to the deck, it took with it a large, well-padded manila envelope that Toz had obviously concealed there for some reason.

Frow let out a sharp gasp of triumph as he bent down to seize it. He straightened up holding one corner of the envelope gingerly between finger and thumb as if it was the tail of a dead rat. A hard gleam of satisfaction shone in his eyes as he stared menacingly at Toz. 'Right then, lad. What's all this about, eh?'

The silence in the bunkspace was eerie, seeming to crackle with electricity as everyone waited for the boy's reply. Ashen-faced, Toz stared back woodenly, saying nothing.

Frow shrugged, and there was an air of smugness about him as he said, 'Well we'll all just have to take a look together then, won't we?'

Ignoring the fact that the envelope was unsealed, and the flap was simply tucked in, Frow tore it open and scattered the contents haphazardly into a loose pile on the deck.

The spell was broken and the silence was shattered by the immediate change of mood from the onlookers. There were loud cries of anger and the language used might have melted the chaplain's ears had he been present.

Toz spoke at last. 'Satisfied, Leading Regulator?' he enquired thickly. Leading Regulator Frow stepped back, mouth agape and speechless as Toz knelt down to retrieve the neatly bound bundles of letters and assorted family photographs that lay strewn amongst the wreckage of his bedding.

Throughout the Royal Navy there is an unwritten rule that such items are deemed sacred. Personal letters and photographs were taboo.

In the minds of every man present, Frow had committed sacrilege. As he beat a hasty retreat from the compartment a loud voice yelled, 'Gimme a four letter word that rhymes with Frow!'

'Cunt!' More than a hundred voices shouted their answer in unison.

197

21

Singapore

SINGAPORE ISLAND IS ABOUT one and a half times the size of the Isle of Wight and remarkably similar in shape. The journey from the naval base at Sembawang in the north to the city in the south was not far when measured in miles, but it was very often a long and tedious one when counted in time.

The road was not in a good state of repair and vehicles were further slowed by the crowded villages dotted along the route through which drivers had to pick their way with a great deal of care.

Today, hampered by a sudden downpour of torrential rain that reduced the taxi driver's visibility to almost nil, the trip to the city was a particularly long and dreary one. Peewee and his friends George and Toz could not have cared less. They were glad to be ashore and away from the oppressive atmosphere of the mess following the thefts and the resulting action taken by the regulating staff.

George was very happy. Being one of the unlucky ones who had his money stolen, he had not expected to be going ashore until the next payday.

Now, thanks to the many friends who had rallied round and chipped in with a little of their own, he now had nearly thirty Singapore dollars, about four pounds in English money, to get by with.

As the taxi entered the saturated outskirts of the city, the rain stopped as suddenly as it had begun. Within minutes, the brilliant afternoon sun was raising clouds of steam from the roofs, roads, and pavements. By the time they reached the Britannia Club the city streets and pavements were already bone dry.

On climbing out of the air-conditioned Mercedes taxi the humidity hit them like a physical blow. By the time they had run the motley gauntlet of pimps, prostitutes, porn dealers and diverse street hawkers clamouring for business outside the entrance to the club, the three of them were sweating profusely.

The doorman, an immense and impressive looking Sikh who sported a tangled bushy grey beard, welcomed them with a friendly smile. In impeccable English he politely suggested that the shaded comfort of the terraced cafeteria at the rear of the club would be to their liking. George, who had been to the club before, led the way.

The Britannia Club was a redbrick, early colonial building standing in a substantial amount of ground space on the corner of Bukit Timah Road. It was a credit to the NAAFI and boasted a host of amenities. There was a superb restaurant, a beer and dance hall and even an elegant cocktail lounge. For the more competitive visitors there were several games rooms where billiards, snooker, and table tennis were extremely popular. On the upper floors were a number of pleasant, airy rooms which could be rented cheaply by the night or for longer periods by servicemen enjoying a few days of local station leave.

Directly across the road on the opposite corner was the world famous Raffles Hotel. Because of this, the staff at "The Brit" worked especially hard to please their military clientele. A NAAFI Club it may have been but the staff refused to be bettered by their imperious rivals, and consequently they were often tipped more generously as a result.

Shaded by a wide balcony and overlooking the open-air Olympic-sized swimming pool, beyond which, set in a couple of acres of landscaped greenery, were tennis and badminton courts, two putting greens and a cricket pitch, the terraced cafeteria was indeed a pleasant spot.

Being a midweek afternoon there were few locally stationed service personnel around (most would be at work), but there was no shortage of females, mostly service wives, dotted around the pool area basking in the sun. The pool was alive with happy, boisterous children, safely watched over by at least three lifeguards while their mothers worked on their tans.

Their enjoyment of the afternoon was considerably heightened when a well-endowed teenage girl lost her bikini top at the start of a swallow dive. She had been showing off her impressive diving skills for some time and to her credit she did not let any embarrassment spoil her performance. With commendable aplomb she rose into the air, proudly displaying her tautly stretched young breasts for a tantalising moment, before jack-knifing and entering the water with hardly a ripple. The three friends were unable to resist leading the other delighted spectators in a little patter of applause when she broke surface at the far side of the pool.

At six o'clock, the main bar opened and there was a general exodus from the cafeteria. Iced coffee, milkshakes and lemon tea were pleasant enough between bar hours but they became merely also-rans when compared with a cold pint of Tiger beer.

The bar, eighty feet of polished mahogany counter, was in a vast, wood-panelled room that at an earlier time had once been an eloquent banqueting hall. Within minutes of opening it was normally seething with men taking the advantage of filling themselves up with superb ice-cold Tiger beer at forty-five cents a pint before moving out to explore the local fleshpots. In the city bars a small bottle of Tiger could cost anything from two dollars upwards. That evening though, apart from a small number of men from the *Ark Royal* and other ships, and a handful of soldiers in civilian dress, the place was unusually empty.

George put it down to a number of reasons but in particular to one fact. There was a floodlit rugby match between the British and Australian navy taking place at HMS *Terror* that evening.

Nevertheless, they would probably have stayed much longer and enjoyed a few more cheap pints had it not been for the arrival of Olly Green and Tom Collins.

Had Olly been by himself they would certainly have teamed up. However, Collins, despite the fact that Olly had loaned him twenty dollars, was still sullenly mourning the loss of his money. He was in an ugly and dangerous mood and made no attempt at friendly conversation. He sat down and glared around at his surroundings, often scowling fiercely in the direction of the two juniors. Whenever he did speak, it was generally to utter yet another dire threat against "That bastard Spider". After exchanging a round of drinks George and the boys made their excuse and left the club in search of lighter entertainment elsewhere in the city.

'Christ! I'm bloody glad to be clear of that miserable bugger,' Toz said, once they had fought clear of the crowd of evil peddlers outside the club.

'Same goes for me,' Peewee said, nodding in agreement. 'Did you see the way he kept looking at me and Toz, George? I thought he was going to get up and have a go at one of us at any minute.'

George chuckled. 'I wouldn't be surprised if he does end up having a go at someone the mood he's in. Olly's welcome to him as far as I'm concerned.'

'Yeah, stuff him,' Toz agreed. 'Anyway,' he brightened. 'Where to now? We've still got a few hours of freedom to use up.'

'Yes, come on, George. You're supposed to be the expert around here, remember?' Peewee said.

'Well...' George mused, 'There's the New World. It's a kind of fun-fair that's a bit different to what you two are probably used to. Or we can try out a couple of local bars, and maybe round the evening off with a trip down Bugis Street?'

'Fun-fair!' Peewee stared at George. He had poor memories of the one at Felixstowe where he had been once or twice on a rare Saturday afternoon leave period whilst at *Ganges*. 'Please tell us you're joking, mate.'

'He must be,' Toz agreed. 'The other idea sounds better to me.' He looked at George. 'You were joking about the fun-fair weren't you?'

'No, I wasn't actually,' he told them, smiling. 'The last time I was out here in Singers, the New World was reckoned to be one of the best runs out. They even had a crazy looking ape-man sort of creature on display in a cage who was supposed to be the original Wild Man of Borneo - if you could believe it.'

Peewee looked cautiously at Toz. 'Well... I don't know,' he said hesitantly.

'Right then!' Toz said positively. 'Let's have a show of hands on it. All those in favour of the fun-fair...' Only George lifted his hand. 'Okay then, now, all those in favour of bars, brothels and Bugis Street...'

'Oh well,' George capitulated gracefully. 'I suppose we can always go to the fair some other time.

The Singapore trishaw is a larger three-wheeled version of the traditional rickshaw and it is unquestionably the cheapest and most convenient means of moving about the city. The drivers have an encyclopaedic knowledge of the countless short cuts through the narrow, reeking back streets that were barred to taxis. They also have an intimate knowledge of all the dubious places of interest to visiting seamen and supplement their meagre earnings with commission paid to them by the proprietors of such establishments.

Two of the bars they were taken to turned out to be nothing more than the reception rooms of brothels where a client could enjoy a complimentary bottle of cold Tiger while waiting for one of the girls to become available. Others were simply more luxurious and far more expensive versions of Akbar's at Little Aden, except that the hostesses were classier, and far more brazen in their offers of personal services.

Peewee was the only one to become tempted at any stage. In the Lucky Dollar Saloon he was hopelessly unable to resist the company of an astonishingly beautiful Eurasian girl who had introduced herself as Lucy.

Even George and Toz were impressed enough to buy her a drink, but Peewee was completely reckless. In less than an hour Lucy had sweetly cajoled him into buying her at least half-a-dozen expensive green-coloured sickly looking drinks. He finally came to his senses when, after whispering a furtive, 'How much?' into her dainty ear, she replied with the bland statement, 'Short-time cost one hundred dollar. Long-time cost two hundred dollar. All night cost five hundred dollar, but for you, I give special price. Only four hundred fifty dollar.'

'You should have asked her if she'd let you have it on easy-terms, mate,' Toz joked when they walked out into the street a few minutes later.

George chuckled. 'Yeah, ten per cent down and the rest over the next five years. Mind you,' he said more seriously, glancing sideways at Peewee, 'Knowing your luck you'd probably end up catching another dose!'

The boy grimaced at the painful reminder. It was less than forty-eight hours since the MO had discharged him as fit and cleared of the farewell gift that Rita had given him. 'I'll tell you what though,' he said, grinning impishly at his friends, 'Because she's so gorgeous I reckon she'd be worth it! If I had four hundred and fifty bucks I'd be in there like a shot.'

Toz surprised him by nodding enthusiastically and saying, 'Too bloody right, mate! Even I would be prepared to risk a dose for the pleasure of an all-night in with juicy Lucy.'

Peewee turned and gave the Lucky Dollar a wistful glance. 'Do you still reckon it's worth going on to this Bugis Street place, George?' he asked hopefully. 'After all, the time is getting on a bit. We could go back and finish the evening off in there,' he said, hooking a thumb in the direction of the bar.

George chuckled softly and said, 'It'll be worth it, mate. Believe me, it will be worth it.'

To give Bugis Street some shred of respectability, it could be honestly described as a late-night street market. That was the first impression formed by Peewee and Toz when they climbed out of the trishaw at the Victoria Street end where it was filled with the brilliantly lit stalls of hundreds of cheapjack traders.

Bugis Street was the place to go in Singapore, especially in the late evening when it really began living up to its infamous reputation. Frequented as much by tourists as by servicemen, it was an exotic hotchpotch of sights, sounds and smells, a smoky mixture of sweat, beer, perfumed incense, burning charcoal and spicy cooking from dozens of food and drink stalls.

Apart from refreshments, most of the traders seemed to specialise in cheap jewellery and watches or novel and portable electrical goods from Japan. There were also a good number of record stalls, each blaring out a continuous cacophony of Western and Oriental music.

George and Peewee looked on with amusement as Toz haggled comically in pidgin English with one of the traders. Eventually reaching an agreement, he left the stall proudly displaying a brand new automatic Seiko watch with a gleaming stainless steel bracelet. 'Just take a look at this,' he said smugly, holding out his wrist before their admiring eyes. 'Over thirty quid's worth back home, that is. I got it for twenty bucks and my old one in part exchange.'

'That's a bit of a bargain then,' Peewee said, looking impressed. 'You paid less than three quid for your Ben Hur back in Gibraltar, if I remember correctly.'

I know, mate,' Toz said, looking pleased. 'Apparently Seiko have got some sort of promotion going on and their agents over there,' he nodded in the direction of the stall, 'are authorised to give as much as they like in part exchange.' He beamed at them both. 'I reckon I struck lucky there, lads.'

'He's an official Seiko agent then, is he?' George asked, eyeing the roguish looking Chinese behind the stall dubiously.

Toz looked hurt. 'Of course he is,' he said indignantly. 'He wouldn't have said so if he wasn't, would he?'

George suppressed a laugh. 'No, of course not,' he agreed amiably.' Anyway,' he added, wrapping an arm around Toz's shoulders, 'If you've finished your shopping for the night, I suggest we wander on down the street or we won't have much time for a drink.'

Once they were clear of the market area, the warm air became even hotter, fuelled by the heat that radiated from the dozens of charcoal braziers. Powerful cooking smells assailed their nostrils strongly but it was not unpleasant. Peewee soon found his mouth watering at the delicious aromas wafting from the giant iron woks of the food stalls. They were in constant use, and along with the smells came also the sounds of hissing, spitting, grilling meats.

This part of the street was crammed with rickety tables surrounded by stools and chairs. Even old packing crates, or indeed anything that could be used to sit on. There was no apparent division between those belonging to one owner or another. When the three sailors eventually seated themselves around a vacant table, they had no idea as to which stall they had offered their custom.

There were small, ragged children everywhere. Most of them were the luckier ones who worked for the stall owners, dashing about taking orders and delivering steaming plates of food to the tables. The others, less fortunate, pimped, begged or stole to help their poverty-stricken families.

A young boy took their order for three bottles of beer almost immediately, but within seconds, another smiling boy of about fourteen was at their table. When George told him that they were already being served, the boy shook his head and said, 'You like jig-a-jig my little sister? She velly clean girl and give you good time for five dollar each.'

'Peewee and Toz stared aghast, but George smiled gently past the boy at the prettily dressed but pitifully thin little girl who hovered in the background watching them hopefully. Taking a coin from his pocket he held it up between finger and thumb. Without hesitation the girl rushed in and snatched the coin eagerly, then turned and scampered away as fast as her skinny legs would carry her. The boy didn't even stop to say a word of thanks and took after her like a rocket.

'Bloody hell,' Toz breathed, shaking his head in disbelief. 'Fancy having to go on the game at that age! Poor kid. She couldn't have been much older than about nine or ten.'

'Oh, I doubt very much if she was actually on the game,' George said. 'It's probably more of a clever confidence trick really. The idea is that you see the poor little mite all sorrowful and hungry so that you take pity on her.

They know that grown men would not be interested in the offer of sex. Well most grown men that is, because there are some weirdo's in this world. Anyway, if you're green enough you end up giving them some money out of pity.'

'Like you just did,' Peewee reminded him.

George chuckled. 'Yes, like I just did. I bet those two make as much between them on a good night as we do in a week.'

The street was now beginning to liven up and becoming more crowded by the minute. When they had first arrived, the balance seemed to be in favour of the casually well-dressed tourists, but more uniformed men were arriving all the time.

A crowd of drunken Australian sailors sitting some distance away were undoubtedly having a good time. Judging by their raucous behaviour and the bawdy victory song they were singing, it was a safe bet that the Royal Navy had lost the rugby match earlier that evening.

One of their cheerleaders, youngish-looking but completely bald, seemed somehow familiar to Peewee, but as he had never met any Australians he shrugged it off as just one of those things.

As well as street hawkers, many prostitutes were now weaving between the tables. Few of them seemed to find any willing clients, but it was not surprising as most of them were very drab and sexually uninviting creatures. Both Peewee and Toz remarked on this after being approached by a haggard looking woman who smiled sloppily at them through a mouthful of badly-stained teeth.

'Well you can't expect to find girls like Lucy in a place like this,' George told them. 'Bugis Street is the end of the line for most of them. They're either too ugly to get a bar job, or else they've been kicked out of one because they're getting a bit past it.'

'You can say that again,' Toz agreed as he turned his face to avoid giving any sign that might be mistaken for encouragement to a particularly unwholesome woman who was wending her way in their direction. George and Peewee did the same and they all let out a sigh of relief after she had passed them by.

Peewee suddenly found his eye caught by a very attractive Chinese girl. She was lounging on the corner of one of the dark, stinking alleyways that ran off the street. 'Take a look over there lads,' he said. 'How about that for a rose amongst the thorns?'

George just smiled and nodded agreeably, but Toz drew in his breath sharply. 'Dear oh dear oh dear! She is absolutely essence. What was it you were saying about all the girls down here? I mean, there's not much wrong with that one over there. She's an absolute cracker.'

George grinned back at him unoffended. 'I can't be expected to get it right every time,' he said. 'Anyway, for all we know she might be the daughter of one of the stall owners.'

The girl certainly stood out from the other shabby women in the street. To begin with she was much younger, probably in her late teens, but it was the provocative way in which she was dressed that set her apart. With her saucy beret, shoulder bag, and striped nautical tee shirt set off by the vivid-red mini-skirt that exposed a tantalising length of her slender legs, she might have just stepped out of the Montmartre district of Paris.

When Toz moved his chair round to get a better look the girl caught sight of him. Smiling seductively, she held up the fingers of one hand as if to signify the number five. Next, she curled the fingers of both hands, placing them in front of her lips as if holding an invisible trumpet and mimed an unmistakably sexual offer.

'Christ Toz! Did you see that? I think she's offering you a gobble for five dollars!'

At that moment, their attention was diverted by a tremendous commotion rising up from amongst the crowd of Australian sailors. The bald-headed man was standing on top of one of the tables and was in the act of removing his trousers.

'Here we go then,' Toz laughed merrily. 'We're about to get the dance of the flaming arseholes again.'

Although that was obviously the man's intention, it did not seem to be going down too well with the others.

'Get yer kecks back on yer Pommi poofter,' a rough voice shouted.

'Yeah, too true, Blue,' yelled another. 'We've seen too many English arseholes already tonight.'

Someone hurled a plate of fried rice that struck the bald man squarely in the chest which acted as a signal for everyone else to follow suit. Within seconds, the man was plastered with a greasy mixture of beer, soup, curry sauce, rice and noodles. Fortunately for him, none of the plates aimed at his head made contact but flew past to land among the laughing spectators sprawled around the surrounding tables.

The spectacle came to an abrupt end when one of the Australians jerked the table savagely from under the man's feet. There was a comical flailing of arms as he fought uselessly to regain his balance. As if in slow motion, he tilted further and further backwards before he fell, crashing down between the table and chairs.

Another of his companions feigned a great show of concern and emptied a bottle of beer over the man's bald skull as if in an attempt to revive him.

Miraculously unhurt, the man leapt to his feet, hauled up his trousers and bolted into the crowd, ducking and dodging to avoid the plates and bottles that followed him.

While everyone else was still laughing Peewee suddenly leapt to his feet and began yelling excitedly. 'Olly, Olly, over here, mate, over here!'

The man was running at a tangent to their table, but hearing the boy's voice, stopped and looked round. A wave of relief swept over his face as he caught sight of Peewee and the others.

Peewee glanced down at George and Toz. 'It's Olly Green,' he told them needlessly. 'I would've recognised him earlier except for his new haircut.'

His friends had stopped laughing and were now staring incredulously at the bedraggled figure that came limping towards them.

Olly was in a dreadful state. His white front and trousers were soaked with brown stains, and odd bits of rice and vegetable matter were sticking to him everywhere. He had lost his cap and there was a nasty looking bruise showing above his right eye. 'Cheers,' he said with a weak smile before collapsing onto the chair that Peewee offered him.

'Where's Tom? And how on earth did you manage to get mixed up with that Aussie lot?' George greeted him.

'Collins! Don't talk to me about that bastard.' Olly gave a short, snickering laugh. 'He shot through on me just after you lot left the Brit. Reckoned he was going back onboard to sort Spider out. Ha! That'll be the day. He might be an angry bastard, but he has more sense than to try that. Anyway, it's the last time I'll lend him any money. I could have done with that twenty bucks myself. I'm dead skint now.'

'It's just as well that Peewee spotted you then,' said Toz. 'I must admit that you look totally different with your head shaved like that.'

'Are you trying to suggest that I look stupid or something, Tozer?' Olly retorted somewhat heatedly.

'No of course he's not,' Peewee put in quickly. 'Actually, I reckon it looks pretty good, Olly. You've got just the right sort of face for it. I mean, it would look pretty silly on most people, wouldn't it?'

While Olly was trying to work out whether the boy was offering a genuine compliment or otherwise, George, who had been keeping a wary eye on the Australians further down the street, said urgently, 'Listen, I don't want to worry anybody, but the Aussies keep staring this way. It might be a good idea if we head off back to the main road and find a taxi.'

'That's the best idea I've heard tonight,' Olly Green agreed. 'I don't trust those crazy colonial buggers any further than I could throw them. Most of them are from that Aussie carrier *Melbourne* and they're bad enough, but there are a couple of nutters from the *Vendetta* - typical destroyer types - shot away to fuck. Just because they won a bloody rugby match, they turn into a bunch of psychos. One minute they're all matey; the next they want to kick your bloody head in. Fuck knows what they would have been like if they'd lost. If that idiot Collins hadn't shot through and left me on my own, I'd never have got involved with them.' He chuckled ruefully as he tried to adjust his soggy clothing in a vain attempt to make himself look more presentable.

As they got up and moved off towards Victoria Street, the Australian sailors yelled and hooted in derision but thankfully made no effort to follow them. Peewee looked around, hoping to catch another glimpse of the young Chinese prostitute, but she was nowhere to be seen. Oh well, he promised himself, you will just have to come back here again before we sail for Oz.

22

Knickerless Nicola

AS THE MEN, ESPECIALLY those who were on their first visit to the Far East, became more familiar with the facilities and entertainment to be found at hand in and around the Royal Naval Base, visits to the city became less frequent.

There was a very good and agreeably priced cinema in the dockyard that was open seven nights a week showing reasonably up-to-date films. In addition, within the naval barracks, HMS *Terror*, there was the Armada Club, a very lively place run by the NAAFI where the beer was even cheaper than at the Britannia Club.

The Armada was full on most nights of the week, especially if there was a game of rugby, hockey or football going on. With its huge outside seated veranda, drinkers could enjoy a prime view of events taking place on the floodlit sports field.

Just a short distance away was a newly built dance hall where visiting sailors could dance with the daughters - and occasionally the wives – of those servicemen who were permanently based on the island.

Also within the grounds were squash, tennis and badminton courts, a superb open-air gymnasium and swimming pool, all of which were hugely popular in the daytime. There was even a professionally acclaimed golf course lying snugly landscaped between the dockyard and the barracks.

These facilities were so well augmented by the restaurants, cafes and ice cream parlours, plus gift shops and services such as cobblers, launderers, dry cleaners and tailors, that it was no wonder that the men of the Far East Fleet thought of HMS *Terror* as their exclusive country club rather than a Royal Navy barracks.

At midnight, when the Armada Club closed, many of the men made their way to Sembawang Village, a sprawling bag shanty situated immediately outside the main dockyard gate. Here a sailor could find almost everything that Singapore City had to offer albeit on a smaller scale. The drinks in the bars were cheaper and there were plenty of roadside food stalls that did a roaring trade. These were especially busy in the early hours when the sailors returned to their ships armed with gigantic fried king prawn banjos or a container of Mah Mee soup to sustain them during the long walk through the dockyard. Strongly seasoned with freshly ground spices and densely packed with garlic and onion, this shrimp and noodle speciality had the effect of keeping everyone, friends and enemies alike, at bay for the following twenty-four hours or longer.

Sembawang's greatest disadvantage was the limited choice of girls which meant there was the probability of a higher risk of infection by diverse variations of venereal disease.

Peewee Hunt had spent most of his off-duty leave without travelling any further than these places, and it was not until the last day of their stay that he made a return trip to the city. This time he went alone and as it was also the monthly payday he had plenty of money to spend. A little over one hundred Singapore dollars which amounted to around thirteen pounds in sterling. Despite this, he was sensible enough to opt for the much longer ride on one of the routine Royal Navy service buses from the dockyard rather than spending twelve dollars on a taxi. The journey by bus was slow, hot and uncomfortable, but it had the benefit of being free.

Naturally enough, once in the city he made his first stop the Britannia Club where he enjoyed a pleasant and leisurely meal in the restaurant before moving on to the bar in search of a drink.

The bar was much busier than it had been on his first visit and Peewee recognised many faces from the *Ark Royal* though none that he knew personally or particularly well. After finishing a pint of ice-cold Tiger, he drifted out of the bar and made his way out into the street.

The pimps and hawkers outside the club were as active and eager as ever and this time, without the security of his friends, the boy found it more difficult to ignore one or two of the more persistent ones. He had nearly made it clear of the throng when he found himself suddenly grabbed by the arm and tugged sharply sideways. It was by a Chinese man who then lashed out a savage kick in the direction of a skinny Indian youth who had been hovering closely behind the young sailor, jabbering angrily at him at the same time.

The youth scowled unpleasantly and spat a defiant globule of phlegm onto the pavement before melting back into the crowd.

'Fuckin' India bastard try takee you wallet,' explained the Chinese, smiling so broadly that Peewee thought that the tightly stretched parchment-like skin of his face was in danger of splitting open.

'Well, er, thanks,' he mumbled. He was at a loss as to what to say next but it seemed that nothing was necessary as the man was already leading him towards one of the many taxis lined up in the road, asking a stream of questions as they went.

'Okay, where you go now? You wanna go special good bar? You wanna go jiggy-jig small boy, nice girl? I know all best place in Singapore. You wanna go Bugis Street? You tellee me, I takee.'

Guessing that it was not going to be an easy matter to shake off the taxi driver after the incident with the pickpocket, the boy thought frantically for a suitable reply. His intention had been to have a bit of a walk around the city before moving on to Bugis Street later but now he found himself caught in a dilemma. He realised he would have to let the man take him somewhere.

'Oh well, I suppose Bugis Street will do,' he succumbed with reluctance.

The taxi had hardly pulled away from the kerb before the driver launched into another sales pitch. 'Velly early for Bugis Street,' he told the boy. 'No good gel, no good boy, no good bar. You likee Bugis Street later. I take you good place now, you trust me, okay.'

'No, I'd rather go to Bugis Street now please. I've got to meet my friends there,' the boy lied unconvincingly.

'Okay, you say, so I takee you Bugis Street.' There was a brief silence and the young sailor was just beginning to feel that he had won when the driver began again, this time speaking in a throaty, conspirationally low voice.

'Hey, you likee nice gel for fucky eh? Velly young gel, velly clean.'

Despite his reluctance, the boy was unable to ignore the tingling of interest taking place between his legs. He realised with a mild sense of shock that it was becoming an all-too familiar occurrence.

'Well... how young and how much?' he enquired guardedly.

The Chinese flashed a quick sideways grin. His top row of teeth were all gold the boy noticed. 'Velly young gel. Mebbe fifteen, sisteen, no more.'

'Yes, but how much? How many dollars?' Peewee asked again.

The driver briefly took both hands off the wheel and gave a slight shrug. 'It up to you how much you like. You go for short-time, fifteen, twenty dollar. You likee long-time, mebbe thirty, forty dollar.'

Peewee hadn't realised that he'd been holding his breath. He sighed loudly letting the air rush through his lips. 'Okay,' he said, 'I'll go for short-time.'

Ten minutes later, after manoeuvring through a maze of squalid side streets, the taxi emerged onto Beach Road and turned left. After another two hundred yards or so, the car suddenly swung left again to pass through a high-walled gateway into a pebbled courtyard beyond.

A large colonial-style house overlooked the courtyard and Peewee experienced a sudden shock as he realised that this was it. He had never visited a brothel before and he had been conjuring up images of a seedy-looking wooden shack with sagging walls and a rusting tin roof. There was not even a red light in evidence as far as he could see.

The driver led him across the courtyard and up an impressive, but worn looking, flight of stone steps. Here he gave a series of smart raps on the solid looking double doors. As they stood waiting, Peewee noticed a tiny lizard scamper up the stone recess and disappear inside a small crack in a corner of the lintel. He also noticed that the white paint on the doors was peeling badly.

The doors were opened by an ancient Chinese woman who exchanged some brief words with the taxi driver before shooing him away and ushering the boy inside, pulling the doors to and locking them behind her.

Peewee found himself in a wide, dimly lit hallway that reeked with the smell of burning incense. A clump of joss sticks glowed dully from an ornate holder that hung beneath an unframed painting of the Laughing Buddha.

'Okay, you come.' The boy followed as the old woman shuffled along the corridor and turned right through a heavily beaded curtain into a slightly better lit, large, square room. This seemed to be some sort of reception or waiting room for there were several bamboo armchairs arranged around a glass-topped table on which were scattered a pile of magazines and newspapers. An ancient refrigerator stood in a corner of the room, and after seeing that the boy was seated, the woman opened it and produced a small bottle of Tiger beer. Snapping the lid off the bottle, she said, 'Okay, you dlinkee beer while I go fetch gel.'

Peewee nodded a thank you and accepted the bottle gratefully. Up until then he hadn't realised how dry his mouth and throat had become.

As the wizened old woman shuffled back out through the curtain, the boy sucked the beer from the bottle too quickly, creating too much froth. He was too thirsty to care though and took another large gulp without waiting for the foam to settle. Consequently he was still coughing and spluttering when the Chinese madam returned, bringing with her a slightly plump but reasonably attractive Malayan woman wearing a sarong. She looked to be in her late-twenties or older.

'You likee this one?' The old woman cocked her head enquiringly. The woman smiled broadly, exposing one or two gold teeth, and rubbed the flat of her hand in a suggestive circular motion over the lower part of her abdomen.

Once again the boy felt himself beginning to stir. 'Yes, alright,' he managed to say croakily. He didn't know quite what else he could say and he was sure it would be pointless to bring up the fact that he had been expecting a girl more his own age.

'You go short-time or long-time?' was the madam's next question.

'Oh, er, well short-time I suppose,' the boy replied huskily. He was beginning to feel embarrassed by the formality of it and all he wanted to do was get on with the job and get out of the place as soon as possible.

'You gimme thirty dollar,' demanded the crone, holding out a skinny, claw-like hand.

Peewee pulled out his wallet and carefully removed three ten dollar notes, regretting more and more by the second that he had allowed himself to get into this situation.

With the bargain thus sealed, the Malayan woman took the young sailor's hand, led him out of the room and further along the dark corridor.

They passed two closed doors on the right and turned into a third that was open.

The room was scented with the smell of burning sandalwood incense and was devoid of all furniture except for a low, hard looking bed and a tin bucket that was half filled with crumpled tissue paper. There were no windows and the walls on either side of the bed appeared to be simple plywood partitions. From the other side of the partition that must have been the second room they had passed came some muffled, primitive masculine grunts.

The woman slipped out of her sarong and was already lying on the bed, legs apart and knees in the air before the boy had undressed himself. As soon as she caught sight of his erect penis, she rolled over and reached under the bed, coming back up with a jar of Vaseline in her hand. Beckoning to him to join her on the bed she smeared a generous portion of the lubricant over his penis before applying an equally generous amount to her vagina. Next, after wiping her hands with tissue paper she replaced the jar under the bed, exchanging it for a box of matches and a hand-rolled cigarette. When the cigarette was alight to her satisfaction she resumed her original position on the bed and slapped her belly in an unmistakable "get on with it" gesture.

It was all over in less than two minutes. The prostitute had puffed away quietly throughout the act without showing the slightest trace of emotion at all. After they had both wiped off the jelly with tissues the tin bucket was just about full.

Five minutes later, disillusioned and feeling disgusted with himself, Peewee climbed back into the waiting taxi, tersely telling the driver to take him to Bugis Street. The driver set off without a word and didn't speak again until they arrived at Bugis Street, and that was only to ask for twenty dollars for service, fare and waiting time.

The taxi driver had been right about Bugis Street. It was too early. There were a few European faces dotted around the tables among the food tables. Tourists by the look of them, Peewee guessed.

Apart from himself there were no other uniformed figures to be seen. Even the market stretching along Victoria Street did not seem to have got going, and the narrow walkways between the stalls were all but devoid of patrons.

Glancing at his watch, he was mildly surprised to find that it had only just turned seven o'clock. He remembered that it had only been about half-past -six when he had left the Britannia Club and been practically hijacked into going to the brothel. 'Bloody short-time,' he muttered to himself, 'I should sodding well say it was!'

While trying to think about where to go or what to do next he sat down at one of the empty tables in the street and ordered a bottle of Tiger from the shiny-faced young Indian boy who appeared immediately to serve him.

The beer was so cold that its flavour had been lost and Peewee could only sip at it gently. He had almost made up his mind to find a trishaw to take him to the Lucky Dollar Saloon, where he hoped he might make the acquaintance of Lucy again, when he was startled by a sultry feminine voice speaking to him from behind.

'Hello, would you mind if I join you for a drink?'

Spinning round, the boy's heart missed several beats as he recognised the beautiful Chinese girl in the French outfit from his earlier visit to the street standing behind him.

'Er... no, of course not,' he stammered.

'Thank you,' the girl smiled, exposing a neat set of ivory white teeth. 'I'll have the same as you then if you don't mind.'

Peewee attempted a mature smile. 'A bottle of Tiger then. I'll get it right away.'

The small Indian boy was already at the table with a bottle and glass, his smooth, satiny face beaming at the unexpected extra custom.

The girl seated herself at the other side of the table and struck a coquettish pose with her chin resting upon the fingers of her left hand. She was regarding Peewee with a smile that could have been interpreted as one of amusement, speculation or genuine interest.

The boy was convinced it was the latter. Boy oh boy, she is a real cracker, he thought to himself, returning the smile and trying not to stare too obviously at the tantalising white triangle of underwear that had become exposed when the girl negligently crossed one slender golden-skinned leg over the other.

The girl poured some beer and raised her glass. 'Thank you for the drink...' She paused before adding with a shy smile, 'Sorry, I not know your name.'

'Alan,' he blurted out feeling a little foolish. He was about to add, 'My friends all call me Peewee,' when instinct warned him that his nickname might sound a bit silly to such a beautifully poised young girl.

'That is nice,' the girl replied. 'Alan. Yes, I think you got a very nice name. My name is Nicola. I hope you like it too.' Her voice was quite soft and low and although not word-perfect, her command of the English language appeared to be far superior to that of the Singaporeans he had met so far.

He smiled bashfully across the table. 'I think it is a very lovely name,' he managed, and then felt his face start to burn as, idiotically, he asked, 'Does it mean something special in Chinese?'

The girl's hands flew to cover her lips as she giggled her reply. 'No, Nicola is not even a Chinese name. My father was French officer and he gave me French name when I was born.' Astutely noting the boy's embarrassment she sought to ease his discomfort by saying, 'It's okay, Alan, I have proper Chinese name of course, from my mother. She call me a very special name.' Teasingly she waggled a delicate finger. 'Maybe I tell you, but only if we become friends. Now, Alan, you tell me how long you stay in Singapore.'

'I've been here just over three weeks. In fact we are sailing tomorrow, so this is my last day here,' the boy told her.

'Three weeks!' The girl's large almond-shaped eyes widened. 'How come we not meet before?' Before he could reply, the girl waggled the finger again, this time in admonishment. 'I know. You already met some beautiful girl who taking care of you. I think she is much better looking than me,' she finished contritely.

'No, no, not at all,' Peewee found himself responding. It had become his turn to offer reassurance. Besides, a lively group of uniformed soldiers had just sat down at the next table and he found himself drawing confidence from the nearby presence of fellow servicemen. 'I haven't been out with any girls at all, and anyway, even if I had, you would still be the prettiest girl that I've seen here.' Nicola smiled demurely and sipped gracefully at her drink as he added, 'In fact I think that you are the most beautiful girl that I've ever met in my life.'

A raucous laugh suddenly went up amongst the neighbouring soldiers. Glancing round Peewee realised at once that he and the girl were their source of amusement. One, a lance corporal, winked lecherously and shouted, 'Get in there, lad. Word is that your ship is going tomorrow. Last storm in a port and all that,' he finished, giving the boy a thumbs up.

221

Jealous bastards, Peewee thought as he turned back to Nicola, surprised to find a rather worried expression on her face.

'Alan, if you wish to go and drink with them I will not mind.'

The young sailor gave a quick shake of his head. 'No, of course not. I don't even know them. I'd much rather stay with you if that's okay?'

Nicola still looked concerned. 'Alan,' she began, looking at him with an expression that suggested she was about to burst into tears, 'I must tell you about myself. You have only just come to Singapore and because you are from a ship you are going away already.' She cast an angry glance in the direction of the soldiers. 'Those ones,' she continued, 'are here for long time in Singapore. They see me in Bugis Street many times and they know what I do. Sometimes they make me feel very ashamed,' she finished, lowering her head and staring down into her lap.

During the relatively short time that had elapsed since leaving Plymouth, Peewee Hunt had learned a great deal along the way, and at that moment he was experiencing a surge of confidence. Reaching across the table he took the fingers of her right hand in his and gently said, 'It's quite alright, I understand.'

Nicola pulled her fingers free of the boy's hand and sat back in her chair. 'No!' she replied vehemently. 'You do not understand.' Picking up her glass, she downed the contents in one swallow and made as if to stand up and leave.

'Nicola, listen to me,' Peewee said urgently. 'I really do understand. I know that you are a prostitute and that is why those squaddie bastards over there are laughing at us.' He leaned forward and grasped her hand again, this time more firmly. 'Just ignore them,' he said, then shrugged and added in a milder tone, 'They're only jealous because you're with me and not them, that's all.'

Nicola began to relax a little. 'Okay, Alan,' she admitted with the trace of a smile beginning to return, 'So you already know about me. Do you still think I am your most beautiful girl?' She paused briefly then continued, 'Many men say this to me, but I can tell when they are lying. Just like you I think.'

It was the sailor's turn to feign anger. 'All right,' he said, letting go of her hand, 'If that's what you think then you might as well go and chat up some other bloke. I really meant it when I said that you are the most beautiful girl that I've ever met in my life. Just because you're a prostitute doesn't change that. I'll tell you something else as well. If my mates were here right now, I'd be really proud to introduce you to them.' He gave a quick jerk of his head in the direction of the soldiers. 'They're not like that lot you know. You would like my friends. They're matelots,' he finished proudly.

Nicola's face shone with happiness as she reached across and took back his hand in both of hers. 'Alan, no man has ever said such kind things to me before.' She let go again and looked down at the table as she finished quietly, 'Except for older men who drink too much beer and want a good time but don't want to pay for me.'

Peewee was hooked. 'Nicola,' he said, smiling gently. 'I am not drunk and if it would help you to get away from this place,' he spread his arms and hands in a gesture that took in most of the street, 'I would give you my whole year's pay if I could.' Even as he spoke, the boy realised that the throbbing erection he was suddenly experiencing was responsible for the direction that the words spilling off his tongue were taking, so he stopped talking and they both sat quietly for a moment. They could hear the soldiers laughing and joking amongst themselves, no longer interested in the boy and girl.

Nicola spoke first. 'Look, Alan,' she said, pausing briefly before continuing, 'I make my money from rich tourists, the fat Germans and Yankees who come here at night. Tonight I must look for such men, but now, when it is so early...' She gave a dainty shrug, leaving the implied suggestion hanging boldly in the moist warm air between them.

It was an emotive moment. The young sailor's throat had gone dry and his voice was husky and a little shaky as he stared back at the girl and said, 'I don't think I've got enough money to afford someone as special as you.'

Nicola smiled, shaking her head gently. 'Alan, this time you don't understand. I want to make love with you. Not for money, just from love.' She stood up suddenly, holding out her hand to the boy. 'Please will you come with me? It is not far to the place where I stay.'

Peewee found himself on his feet following in her wake as she picked her way through the maze of chairs and tables. If the group of soldiers made any comments at their departure, they went unheard by the sixteen-year-old sailor who was too busy contemplating his good luck. You've done it again without paying for it you lucky bugger, he was thinking, smiling inwardly as he went after the girl.

Nicola had been telling the truth when she had said that she didn't live far away. As they reached the end of the road at the junction of Bugis and Victoria Street, she took his hand and led him around the corner turning almost immediately into a dingy corridor. The alleyway was narrow and slimy, and stank of rotting garbage and stale urine.

Feeling him holding back the girl tugged firmly on his hand. 'Don't worry, Alan,' she said reassuringly, 'We are here now.' Letting go of him she turned and pushed open a door that was set into the damp wall of the passageway just a few footsteps in from the pavement. The boy's legs were trembling as he followed her inside and up a steep flight of worn concrete steps where they emerged onto a small landing with just two doors, one leading off to the left and the other to the right.

Nicola produced a key and inserted it into the lock of the left-hand door. Pausing to flash him a happy smile she opened the door and said, 'This is my home, Alan. Please come inside and be my welcome guest.'

Peewee followed her into a room that was surprisingly large and cheaply but adequately furnished and laid out. There was a mirrored dressing table, a tall but narrow wooden wardrobe and a small wicker armchair. Dominating a large corner of the room was a very low double-sized bed that was neatly made up with prettily encased pillows and a pastel-pink coverlet.

An open box of tissues, together with a clean ashtray, sat upon the polished surface of an occasional table next to the bed. Underneath the bed was a raffia basket that the boy was pleased and relieved to see was empty.

Still looking around, he saw that there were a number of shelves fixed to the walls at varying heights. For the most part these were dotted with plastic pots of assorted sizes containing clusters of brightly coloured silk flowers.

There were also several framed pictures and Peewee was surprised when he realised that, without exception, they all contained the front covers of women's expensive glossy fashion magazines.

Nicola laughed lightly as she observed the sailor taking in the details of her room. 'You like my place, Alan? It is pretty - like me you think?'

'Yes, definitely,' he replied, nodding, 'I think it's very nice.'

Nicola gestured to an opening at the far end of the room. 'When you need to go pee-pee you can go in there,' adding in almost the same breath, 'It is also my kitchen. After, I will make us some coffee or Chinese tea, if you like.' She moved to stand directly in front of him, her eyes looking searchingly into his for a moment, then took his head in her hands and kissed him fiercely, her tongue urgently probing his mouth, her teeth biting almost painfully on his lips. A stale mixture of soy and garlic came off her breath that at another time might have repulsed him. At this time, being kissed for the first time like this since Mombasa, he could not have cared less.

By the time he became aware that he was being forced over backwards and found himself tumbling onto the bed, Nicola was in complete command.

Straddling him, she kissed and nibbled his face, ears, and neck. In a state of near ecstasy, the boy relaxed and lay back groaning softly, completely at the mercy of the skilled attentions of the girl.

225

As suddenly as she had begun, Nicola stopped and quickly raised herself into a kneeling position next to him. There was a wanton expression on her flushed face as she said, 'I think you are a wonderful big man, Alan.' Pressing her hand lightly against the swelling in his white bell-bottom trousers she purred, 'Oh yes you are – all the time I knew it.'

Her hands became busy at his belt buckle and the tight button of his waistband. A soft but joyous sound escaped her lips as she slowly unzipped him and allowed the front of his trousers to spring apart exposing the bulging Y- fronts within.

Still lying on his back and cradling his head in his hands, the boy assisted Nicola's efforts to remove his trousers by alternately raising each of his knees, before straightening the required leg and arching his back sufficiently enough to allow her to tug his uniform white front over his head. Then, he saw with incredible clarity that she had simultaneously managed to wriggle out of the red mini-skirt and kick off her shoes at the same time.

Her tee shirt flew off next and the boy was in heaven as she bent down to press her firm but soft warm breasts against the hot skin of his chest. Her lips found his neck again and kissed their way along until they were nuzzling an ear. He felt her soft hand pressing down on his navel, then moving in a southerly direction to take possession of his manhood in a grip that suggested it was some long-lost property now returned to her.

The boy levered himself into a sitting position and wrapped his arms around her. Softly he kissed her neck and shoulders, allowing one hand to wander up and down the warmth of her spine and finely muscled back. They remained like this for a few moments, savouring each other's company until the girl disentangled herself and pulled free from the embrace.

Surprised but not disconcerted, the sailor lay back and gazed up at Nicola who was now standing upright at the side of the bed. Lifting her hands she played carelessly with the dusky nipples that stood out so appealingly against the light golden colour of her skin. 'Are these not beautiful?' she enquired teasingly.

Raising himself up onto an elbow Peewee groaned, 'Nicola, they are gorgeous, but please come back here,' then collapsed back onto the bed sighing loudly.

Positioning herself on one knee the girl stretched seductively over him and took hold of his penis again. 'Now I think it is time for washing this big bad dragon,' she said with a throaty chuckle, at the same time giving the throbbing member a firm squeeze.

'Wash it!' the boy exclaimed sounding mildly shocked. 'It's alright, really it is,' he told her quickly. 'It hasn't got anything wrong with it, honest.'

Nicola chuckled again. 'I know that,' she said soothingly, but I want to kiss him and so I like to wash him first if you do not mind.'

Peewee allowed himself to relax again. 'Actually, I think I might enjoy it very much,' he gave in with a smile.

He watched her as she walked towards the kitchen, enjoying the show with immense pleasure as the two softly rounded swellings scantily concealed within the silky fabric of her panties vied with each other for his attention. 'Mmm,' he murmured softly as she passed out of view, 'George and Toz, you are not going to believe this when I tell you.'

When the girl returned she was carrying a small bowl of fragrantly scented water on a tray, together with a pink face-flannel and matching hand towel. The boy could hardly control his excitement as she set about washing his genitals gently but thoroughly with the tepid water, afterwards dabbing and patting him dry with the towel, and he was grateful for the short respite that was granted to him when she returned the redundant articles to the kitchen. She was back in less than a minute, kneeling beside him on the bed as before. Then, beginning with his eyes, nose, and lips she slowly kissed her way down his body coming to a halt at his lower abdomen with her warm cheek brushing softly against his burning upright member. The boy writhed on the bed groaning with pleasure, his fingers clawing at the mattress as she took him fully into her mouth. The room and the bed on which he lay no longer existed as he found himself floating in the weightless void of a universe that was at once sweet and cloying and totally silent.

From out of the silence, a strident voice was suddenly crying. 'No, no, stop, wait, wait for a moment,' and then he was back on the bed, eyes wide open, sheepishly realising that it was he who had been doing the shouting.

Nicola was smiling down at him, her eyes shining. 'I think that you are enjoying it very much, yes?'

Something resembling a growl left his lips as he reached for her shoulders, pulling her over and under him as he rolled into the dominant position. Now it was her turn to be on the receiving end. He felt totally calm and under control as he said, 'Nicola, that was absolutely fantastic. Now I'm going to give you something that you will never forget either.'

Copying her tactics he kissed his way down from her forehead to her breasts then hooked his fingers into the delicate lace panties and tugged down firmly. He was a little disappointed when Nicola shouted, 'No, please, no,' and began squirming and kicking her legs about.

By then it was too late for her to stop him. The panties were already pulled down to her knees and Peewee found himself staring uncomprehendingly at a small, underdeveloped but unmistakable set of male genitalia.

Totally shocked and utterly speechless he was still staring in disbelief when he realised that Nicola was crying uncontrollably.

Cocooned within the pink bedcover, Nicola remained hidden but could be heard babbling a stream of sobbing apologies and excuses which simply fell upon the deaf ears of the stunned young sailor as he dressed rapidly and hurriedly made his way out of the room and down the stairs into the alley.

Once in the street he walked away quickly, retracing his steps towards Bugis Street. He felt quite sick and was intent only on finding a taxi or a trishaw to get away from the area as soon as possible.

As he turned the corner his heart sank at the sight of the burly figure striding towards him. Inwardly cursing his luck, he managed a weak smile in reply to the one that beamed at him from the face of Spider Webb.

23

Said the spider to the fly

HAD IT NOT BEEN for the chance encounter with Webb, there would have been no doubt that Peewee Hunt would have hired a taxi to take him out of the city and back to his ship at the Sembawang naval base.

Telling himself that he'd had a shit run ashore and still cursing his bad luck at the fluke of timing that had brought him into contact with Spider, he was now deeply regretting that he had turned down George and Toz's invitation to join up with Olly and Knotty for a farewell session at the Armada Club.

He had politely tried to detach himself from Webb, using the excuse that he wanted to get back in time to have a last drink with the others, but his imposing messmate would have none of it.

'Stuff those bastards,' were his exact words. 'Your oppos Tozer and Allen are alright, but the rest of them are a bunch of two-faced fuckers who still think that I'm the bastard who stole their money. As far as I'm concerned they can all swivel on this,' he had finished, extending the middle finger of his right hand.

'Well, what do you want to do now?' Peewee asked, realising that he was stuck with Webb. 'It's still a bit early for round here. We could go to the Britannia Club for a couple of beers if you like. Or we could head off back to Sembawang and finish the night off in the village.' he rounded off, wistfully hoping that Spider might go for the latter suggestion. In his heart, he was still desperate to get away from the Bugis Street area, and preferably out of the city altogether.

'I've got a much better idea,' Spider replied with a wicked grin. 'I've heard you and your mates going on about some tasty little party who works in a bar and charges a fortune for a fuck. You never know, but I reckon with your baby-face and my film-star looks we might just be able to sweet-talk her into giving us a bit of discount for a threesome.'

The boy groaned inwardly but privately admitted to himself that it was not the worst of suggestions. Despite being unable to shake off the sense of feeling trapped for the third time that evening, he shrugged and replied, 'Yes, why not. The girl's called Lucy and she works at the Lucky Dollar Saloon. I don't know about getting any discount out of her, but it'll be a good laugh trying,' he finished, managing to summon up a small chuckle.

They soon found a vacant taxi and climbed into the back where they were greeted in the usual manner.

'Okay, where you wanna go? You wanna go jig-a-jig with nice gel for good time?' the driver called over his shoulder.

'Right first time, John,' Spider replied. 'But nowhere that you want to take us. What's the name of that place again?' he asked, giving the boy a nudge.

'The Lucky Dollar,' Peewee told the driver, surprising himself by adding in a louder voice, 'And make it quick. Me and my mate are thirsty.' He leaned back into the leather seat feeling oddly pleased with himself. Well sod it, he was thinking. If you can't beat them, join them. At the same time he was telling himself that at least things couldn't possibly get any worse after his earlier experiences that evening.

The Lucky Dollar Saloon was not particularly busy when the pair arrived, but after a quick glance around Peewee was disappointed to see that Lucy was happily ensconced among a mixed-bunch of seamen who he did not recognise, even though their hats displayed *Ark Royal* cap ribbons.

She looked as attractive as ever and it heartened him considerably when she flashed him a smile of recognition as he and Spider sat down at a vacant corner table.

Webb gave the boy a sly wink. 'So that's the party, is it?' he chortled. 'No wonder you and your oppos kept going on about her. She's a bit of alright if I say so myself. Not like these two, eh,' he added, rolling his eyes in the direction of two dreary looking girls who appeared to be making a beeline towards them. 'For Christ's sake, don't buy them any drinks or we'll be lumbered with them all night.'

The girls tried their best and worked hard on the two sailors for quite a while, but without success. No drinks bought for them meant no money for them either. The girls worked strictly on a commission basis only. The bar paid a commission on every expensive drink that the girls could wheedle out of the customers. In turn, the girls paid the bar a percentage of the money they earned on the sale of their sexual favours.

One of the girls finally gave up and returned to a stool at the bar. The other, arguably the more attractive of the two who had introduced herself as Thelma, persisted for a while longer, hoping to crack the defence of the less-experienced boy sailor at least.

In fact, she had very nearly succeeded. Peewee was on the verge of giving in and offering to buy the girl a drink when Spider, who had been becoming more disgruntled by the minute, suddenly perked up and rapped the table with his knuckles to gain the boy's attention. 'Hey up, lad,' he called across the table, 'Look what the cat's dragged in!'

Peewee, seated with his back to the entrance looked round and was mildly surprised but pleased to see that Tom Collins had entered the bar. He was expecting to see George and the others follow him in, but was disappointed as it soon became apparent that Collins was on his own.

'Go on then, give him a shout,' Webb went on, adding in a grumble, 'Not that he's a good mate, but seeing as he's here he might as well join us.'

As Collins looked around, something resembling a sneer spread across his face as his eyes registered the slight form of the youngster. The sneer vanished in an instant when he spotted Spider Webb sitting on the other side of the table.

It looked as if Collins was about to walk straight out again without speaking to them when Webb's coarse shout stopped him. 'Where d'you think you're going Collins? There's two of your messmates over here, so come and have a drink with us.'

Collins looked nervous as he came over to the table, and there was a shaky looking smile on his face as he stuttered, 'I'd really love to Spider, honest I would, but I'm looking for George and the others. I thought that they might be here, but obviously they're not. They've probably gone to the Britannia Club so I'm going to have a look for them there.' He made as if to move back towards the door when Spider pulled him up again.

'Hang on a minute, Collins, don't give us that crap. They're all on the piss at the Armada Club. You should know that because you were supposed to be there with them.'

Collins looked harassed. 'What? Oh, yes, of course. I couldn't find them at the Armada so I thought they might have changed their minds at the last minute.' He stopped at that, seemingly short of anything else to say.

Spider snorted then gave a low chuckle. 'Well then you miserable bastard, you might as well stay and have a drink with us after all. The three of us can have a look round for the others a bit later on.' He turned to the girl, Thelma. 'Fetch us three more beers, love, and get a nice drink for yourself as well.' His face creased into a villainous grin as he jabbed a finger at Collins and added, 'He's paying by the way.'

While the delighted girl went off to the bar, Peewee tried to lighten the atmosphere. Spider had lapsed into silence and Collins, who was now sitting down, appeared distinctly uncomfortable and uneasy.

'Well, Tom,' the boy began, I don't know about you but I'm looking forward to getting back to sea tomorrow. We've only got a couple of weeks of exercises and then we're off to Australia. Can't be bad eh?'

Getting no response, he tried again, this time with Webb. 'What about you, Spider? Do you reckon that Aussie-land will be a good run then? George has been there before and he says it's absolutely brilliant.'

Webb ignored the boy but grunted a thank you as Thelma arrived with the drinks. The boy's heart skipped when he saw that she had also brought Lucy with her.

'Hello, darling, you come to see Lucy again?' she piped in her lilting, musical voice.

Peewee grinned happily and was about to make an appropriate reply when the girl made straight for Tom Collins and plumped herself down on his lap.

'Bloody hell, lad,' Spider burst out, looking at Peewee, puzzled. 'I thought she was supposed to be friendly with you!'

The boy could barely disguise the disappointment in his voice as he replied, 'So did I, but it seems she knows Tom a lot better than me by the looks of it.'

Sitting on Collins' lap with an arm curled around his neck, Lucy smiled at Peewee good-naturedly. 'Of course I remember you, cherry boy, but when you come here before you got no money.' She ran her fingers possessively through Collins' hair and planted a wet kiss on his face before carrying on. 'This number one special man for Lucy. He got plenty money. He come here three times and pay me full price for very long-time, so I much happy now he come see me again.'

The air-conditioning system might have gone into overdrive as the temperature in the bar suddenly plummeted during the course of the exchange.

Thelma was looking worried as Lucy gave an uneasy laugh. They could tell from the ugly expression on Webb's face that something was seriously wrong.

'Money!' Webb's snarl sounded menacing. 'What fucking money is she talking about Collins?' His voice rose, and he sounded dangerously angry as he tore into the ashen-faced sailor. 'There's only one way that you could have got hold of that kind of money, and that's by nicking it from your messmates, you thieving bastard!'

If Collins had any answers or excuses he was given no time to provide them. Webb was already on his feet, sending the table and everything on it crashing sideways.

Lucy began to scream hysterically as she went over backwards with Collins under the weight of Webb's charging body.

Muttering, 'And that's for my mate, George,' Peewee managed to slide a well-aimed toecap between Collins' legs before steering himself clear of the melee, in no doubt that Spider could manage quite well by himself.

Chaos reigned as women screamed and some of the other men from the *Ark Royal* tried in vain to intervene and save Collins from the savage beating that he was receiving. One or two of them suffered painful backhanded slaps from Webb in the process.

It was fortunate for Collins that a military police patrol happened to be nearby and had responded to the bar owner's urgent whistle blowing in time to save him from the very real possibility of being beaten to death.

Webb was formally arrested and taken away by the MPs. An army medic attended to Collins as he lay sprawled on the filthy bar room floor. Eventually, his badly mauled body was placed on a stretcher to be taken by ambulance to the British Military Hospital.

Peewee Hunt and the other sailors were detained for questioning before being herded, under guard, onto an army bus. They were then ferried to the Fleet Regulating Office at *Terror* barracks and held throughout the night for questioning and statement taking by some seriously anchor faced regulators. An RPO accompanied by Leading Regular Frow were there to represent *Ark Royal*. Frow was in his element.

In the end, after several long hours they were informed that they would not be detained in Singapore when their ship sailed in the morning. The Fleet Master-at-Arms was satisfied that their written statements would suffice for future proceedings and they were returned to the *Ark Royal* under the escort of the RPO and Frow, just as dawn was breaking over the dockyard.

Neither Webb nor Collins were seen aboard the ship again. Webb was detained in the cells at HMS *Terror* to await court martial proceedings while Collins remained in hospital for a number of days before being discharged into the care of the sick-bay staff at HMS *Terror* naval barracks. The surgeons had done what they could, but they had been unable to save the sight of his right eye. He would remain at the barracks until required to give evidence at the court martial.

Peewee Hunt had been forced to endure a succession of grillings from the SCO, the Chief Communications Yeoman, and of course, his messmates. The ultimate fate of Webb and Collins became the hot topic for debate as the ship cleared the Malacca Strait and steered a south-easterly course towards the operational area in the Java Sea.

'Well it's just what we all predicted when we heard that he was coming back,' Knotty Ash intoned. 'It'll definitely be services no longer required this time.'

'Yeah, but how unfair,' protested Tubbs McEwan. 'Collins blamed Spider right from the start after our lockers were robbed and it was him who'd done it all the time. The bastard deserved what he got, and more, in my opinion,' he concluded to a chorus of agreement.

'I bet Collins doesn't get done for his thieving though,' Olly Green muttered bleakly. 'The regulating bastards will be so chuffed to have nailed Spider again, they won't want any mitigating circumstances to get in their way.'

'You're damn right there,' spat McEwan. 'The trifling fact that he's guilty as sin won't be of any help to him.'

'Personally, I think we're better off being shot of the pair of them,' Robbie Robson put in sensibly. 'Spider was a nasty bastard and Collins was a miserable one.'

'Was this Spider bloke as bad as everything we've heard?' Smudge Smith enquired. Smith, a wiry Liverpudlian with prematurely receding hair was one of two signalmen on loan to the department from the MSO in Singapore dockyard. He had brought with him the gift of a cardboard box containing a dozen or so green praying mantises that he had captured and collected in the luxuriant grassy areas of the naval base. Sharing them out between his new shipmates, he explained that they should be allowed to roam free in their personal lockers as they loved to eat cockroaches. This turned out to be quite true. Smudge's mantises gorged on their insect relatives, especially the softer shelled new-borns, and within a matter of days the lockers were cleared of the vile creatures and the mantises had all noticeably put on weight. Following their success, they were often let loose in the mess, and although they did their best and definitely made a difference, at the end of the day the mantises were outnumbered by at least two or three hundred to one. Lovingly cherished by their owners, they made remarkably interesting pets and were given fun names. Peewee called his the *Green Gobbler*, while Toz's was simply called *Manty*.

The other newcomer, a tall black man with an athletic build and a strong Birmingham accent, was one of those rare individuals who had not been given a Royal Navy nickname. Born and raised in Birmingham, the devoutly Christian parents of TO2 Hall had unwittingly seen to that. At his Christening he had been baptized and named Kingdom. Traditionally superstitious, no Royal Navy seaman, past, present or future would ever be inclined to play about with the name of someone called Kingdom Hall.

Olly Green gave a grim chuckle. 'Believe me, of that there is no doubt,' he told the new arrivals, adding, 'and Robbie is absolutely right, we're better off without him. And that bastard Collins.'

Signals were eventually received regarding the fate of Webb and Collins. Some fourteen days had elapsed since leaving Singapore and with an exhausting exercise period behind them that had been marred by the loss of a *Fairey Gannet* and its pilot, the carrier was steaming into the Indian Ocean at a leisurely and economical eighteen knots when the first signal arrived. It informed the captain and crew that Webb had been found guilty on charges relating to the, prejudice of good order and naval discipline, and had been sentenced to two years in Colchester Military Prison, to be followed by a dishonourable discharge from the Royal Navy.

A further signal advised that Collins had been flown back to the United Kingdom to join HMS *Victory* barracks in Portsmouth from where he was also to be discharged from the service on medical grounds.

Two days out from Fremantle, much to the amusement of George, Toz, and their new friend Kingdom Hall who had replaced Collins in Knotty Ash's watch, Peewee Hunt took up weight training as a hobby.

At about the same time Yeoman Jolly's hobby suffered a setback. He had got into the habit of leaving his camera in the signals store beneath the mainmast where it would always be on-hand should the chance for an interesting shot occur.

Unfortunately for the unpopular yeoman, his camera had been "got at" by someone. It did not take very long for that "someone" to be very quickly blamed as the phantom watchkeeper. The film had been removed from the camera at the point where there were only two or three exposures remaining, and then replaced with a brand new roll. The diabolical perpetrator had then used the camera to take thirty or so pictures of the slop bucket before stopping at the number on the bezel that indicated where Squeegy Lips had taken his last photograph.

When the yeoman had taken his last shots and had the film developed, he was at first perplexed and then apoplectic. He had just three photographs of his own to add to his collection, plus more than thirty close-ups of the revolting slop bucket.

The culprit had tried to be artistic, as Chief Communications Yeoman Wilcox observed when Jolly complained to him. 'Well, if the phantom watchkeeper took these, I have to say that he obviously knows a thing or two about taking photographs,' the chief had said while studying them in the bright sunlight. 'I don't think they're all entirely bad, Yeoman. They've come out really well.' He smiled as he handed them back. 'Quite imaginative really, the way that they've been taken from so many different angles!'

24

A warm welcome down under

NOW IN THE GAGE Roads close to the mouth of the Swan River, the carrier slowed to pick up the harbour pilot, maintaining steerageway while the man was transferred from the launch that came alongside. Within minutes they were back under way and steering the short distance up towards the harbour at a speed and course now directed by the pilot.

A flotilla of small craft bedecked with strings of colourful bunting were on hand to greet them, horns hooting loudly as they closed the harbourage. At the entrance to the moles, the North Mole to port of the ship was swarming with flag-waving locals, all of them cheering a welcome as the mighty Ark slid majestically through into the inner deep-water harbour beyond.

Once through the moles the carrier quickly reduced speed, and with the assistance of the waiting tugboats slowly manoeuvred through a full one hundred and eighty degree turn. Finally, as she edged starboard side on into her berth alongside the crowded wharf, a brass band welcomed them with a spirited medley of nautical marches.

'Hands secure from harbour stations' was piped at noon, followed almost immediately by, 'Shore leave will commence at fourteen hundred hours.'

Yeoman Jolly soon put paid to any plans made by the four juniors for getting ashore so early. 'Hunt, Tozer, Piper and Tredrea,' he bellowed, as the rest of the signals staff were making their way below. 'The ship is open to visitors the day after tomorrow so I want you lot back up here straight after you've had your dinners. This whole area needs to be washed down

241

in readiness for painting, which you shower of shit will be doing all day tomorrow.'

'What a bastard,' Steve Tredrea moaned as they waited in the long queue outside the dining hall. It seemed that every man aboard was going ashore soon after eating.

'Yes, a right bastard. But more so for me and Peewee,' Toz grumbled. 'You and Pip are both in today's duty watches so you can't go ashore anyway, whereas...' he left the word hanging for emphasis before finishing, 'Me and Mister Muscles here were hoping to be trapping some gorgeous Aussie Sheilas this afternoon'.

Peewee grinned. It was only a few days since he had joined the weight-lifting enthusiasts who trained on the focsle so he was still subject to some mild teasing, especially from Toz who had said, 'You'll be joining the Ark's wrestling team next,' along with the tongue-in-cheek suggestion, 'I bet you'd be good at the Nagasaki knicker-lock.

'That's right,' he joined in. 'We were planning to show them the good-looking members of the department as soon as we could.'

'Yeah, and now they're going to have to wait for us until the flag deck's been washed down,' Toz sighed in mock despair.

'As Tredders said, what a bastard,' Pip Piper chuckled. 'Still, at least you'll both have nice clean hands, even if they'll look like they belong to a Chinese washerwoman.'

'It's not just our hands they'll be interested in though,' retorted Toz with a smirk, adding, 'Not if everything we've heard about Aussie girls turns out to be true.'

The friendly banter continued throughout their lunch break, and when they returned to the flag deck there was a dark scowl on the face of Yeoman Jolly and a surprise in store for Peewee Hunt.

'Ah, young Hunt, I've been waiting for you.' Yeoman Blowers glanced at his watch. 'The SCO wants to see you in his cabin. Ten minutes ago.'

Alarmed that he must be in some sort of trouble, he looked at the yeoman worriedly and asked, 'Do you know what he wants to see me about, Yeo?'

'That's for the SCO to tell you, Hunt,' Squeegy Lips snarled, still scowling.

Yeoman Blowers responded to the concerned look on the boy's face. 'Actually, you've been assigned for special duty.' He smiled, 'There's a shower of old hacks. That's newspaper reporters to the rest of you,' he explained, looking at the other juniors, 'And JTO Hunt here has been selected as the Press Liaison Officer's Assistant no less.' Turning his attention back to Peewee he continued, 'Sounds like a very cushy number to me so get below and report for your briefing before the SCO changes his mind.'

'Aye aye, Yeo,' the boy replied smartly. He headed for the ladder still looking bewildered but no longer worried.

On his return to the flag deck half an hour later, still somewhat dazed, the junior was surprised to find the flag deck deserted by all except Yeoman Blowers and Steve Tredrea who was part of the duty watch.

'All sorted and ready for tomorrow?' Blowers greeted him briskly.

'Yes, Yeo,' the boy replied. 'Lieutenant Spencer-Hudson is the press liaison officer and basically I'm going to be acting as his clerk - a bit of typing and lots of tea making I expect. I still can't work out why the SCO has chosen me for the job though. Surely one of the senior hands, a TO1 or a TO2 at least should have been given it.'

Tom Blowers chuckled. Apparently the SCO wanted someone with the deadly art of the gift of the gab, and between them, he and the chief decided that that person was you.'

'I still don't understand though, Yeo,' Hunt resisted stubbornly.

'Gift of the gab, lad. Gift of the gab. Don't you get it? The SCO, the Chief Communications Yeoman, and not to mention myself, are all still amazed that you are not still being held by the regulating staff in HMS *Terror*. The SCO thinks that the statement you gave about the scrap between Webb and Collins was inspired. If you had said just one thing out of place, just one sentence in answer to a regulating petty officer's question not happily received, you, my son, would not be onboard right now. The people from the press are likely to ask you a lot of questions. Some about the ship, and some about how it feels to be thousands of miles from home, etcetera etcetera.'

The yeoman stopped talking and looked at his watch again. 'Shit,' he mumbled. 'I've got to get below and change, I'm going ashore in forty-five minutes. Enjoy your leave this evening, Hunt,' he said as he turned away.

At the hatchway, he halted stiffly and spun around. 'Remember - gift of the gab, lad.' He winked and smiled broadly then went through the hatchway and disappeared below.

'So, what's all this about then?' demanded Steve Tredrea when the two of them were on their own. 'Sounds like a bit of favouritism if you ask me.'

Hunt felt suddenly angry. 'Do you want to do a swap with me then because that would suit me just fine? I tell you, I'm probably going to get a load of shit from everybody about this, especially from Squeegy.'

'Sorry, mate,' Tredrea apologised, sounding earnest. 'I shouldn't have said that.' He smiled and gestured around the flag deck. 'This will cheer you up a bit. Yeoman Blowers has overruled Squeegy.' He's secured us all from cleaning. Squeegy looked bloody livid but didn't dare argue. George and Toz are below getting ready. They're waiting for you so it looks like you'll still get ashore early if you get a shufty on.'

Peewee brightened. 'Good old Blowers,' he muttered, throwing an arm around Tredrea and slapping him on the back before making for the hatchway. 'Cheers for that, Tredders,' he called over his shoulder. 'See you tomorrow.'

As he raced down through the series of ladders and companionways to his mess, anxious to catch up with his friends who he had no doubt would already be ready and eager to get ashore, the young sailor pushed his worries to the back of his mind and focused on the prospects of his first run ashore in Australia. He already shared the view of most of the men onboard that this vast country was the nearest thing to home since leaving England, even though it was the furthest!

The three friends were ashore just before four in the afternoon and were soon aboard the modern commuter train which ran through the suburbs on the twelve mile journey from Fremantle to Perth. Arriving at their destination some thirty minutes later, the trio set off on foot for an investigative tour of the city.

'Bloody hell,' Toz complained almost three hours later. 'If you ask me, it seems pretty tame here. Not much sign of any nightlife coming up for later.' He glanced up and pointed to the lush green landscape of Kings Park rising above the city to the west. 'There's probably more going on up there than down here.'

'If you're into flora and fauna,' George shot back agreeably. 'I think it's pretty nice here though. Especially that London Court place. Some of those old buildings are fantastic and I've got to say that the whole place makes me think of home.'

'Me too,' Peewee joined in. 'In fact it reminds me of Cheltenham. My mum took me there to visit her sister when I was twelve. Years ago now.'

'Never been there, but I've heard that place is bloody boring as well,' Toz sniffed.

They had found their way into several pubs but none that offered much in the way of the good run ashore that they were looking for. Apart from one near the railway station where a couple of rough looking drunks had warned them to leave the local women alone, they had been greeted and welcomed with warmth in each place, but all were lacking in the right kind of atmosphere to suit the sailors.

'Well it's still pretty early,' Peewee said as they continued to trawl the streets, 'There's bound to be somewhere where we can all have some fun.'

Peewee's optimism appeared to be unfounded until much later when they were sitting drinking schooners of excellent ice cold beer from the locally acclaimed Swan Brewery. They were in a riverside pub comfortably seated on sturdy handcrafted chairs built out of reclaimed ship's timbers.

The table around which they sat was of similar construction and its polished, but scarred and battered surface bore testimony to many years of use. The legend, "Kilroy was here 1949" together with the long-nosed, bald headed man was carved into the wood. Toz idly traced the lettering with a fingertip while musing aloud, 'This Kilroy bloke gets around a bit, don't he?'

Peewee found the place fascinating. The walls were crammed with framed prints and paintings of nineteenth-century sailing ships. Most of them were of British men-of-war, ships of the line, but there were some very graphically illustrated prints. These were of whaling cutters chasing down and harpooning their prey, and of the mother ships, hauling the carcasses of once magnificent animals inboard. The prints, which could be considered historical documents, certainly offered stark support to the increasing, world-wide condemnation of the brutality of the whaling industry. One of the prints, entitled, "A Yankee Whaler", had been defaced with the words, "Yanks go home". Peewee suspected that it was a fairly recent addition, given that the print itself was dated 1863.

Again, the welcome had been warm, but to the landlord's dismay, just before ten-thirty as it was approaching closing time, the pub was suddenly invaded by a boisterous crowd of cheery men from the *Ark Royal*, Knotty Ash, Olly Green and Kingdom Hall among them. Unusually, for such an early time of night, Knotty appeared to be extremely drunk, but as Kingdom explained, the leading hand had allowed himself to become embroiled in a friendly discussion that had escalated into a heated argument concerning the last Ashes test between England and Australia. Kingdom told them that the drinks between Knotty and the proprietor of the Northbridge pub that they had barely escaped from unscathed, had been going down quicker than any wickets that had fallen on either side.

At closing time the landlord rang a bell and began crying out words of encouragement for everyone to drink up and move on. In an effort to rid himself of the unruly sailors more quickly, he had also shouted out more than once, 'Come on, lads, there are plenty of Corkies where you can have yourselves another drink.' George had been pressed at the bar in the rush when last orders was called, and although he had been unsuccessful in getting served in time, a barmaid had whispered into his ear what "Corkies" was all about and where it could be found.

Outside in the street, George explained to the others that Corkies was not the name of any particular establishment but a place that did not have a licence to sell alcohol. They were places licensed to make a charge for opening the bottles that their customers brought with them.

'I didn't understand everything she said but apparently there's one not far from here. There's also a sort of off-licence close to it where we can buy some bottles to take in.'

'That sounds a bit strange,' Kingdom Hall commented. 'I can't believe you can just take your own drinks into somewhere without paying.'

'That's the whole point of it though. You pay what they call corkage,' George told them, and went on to explain, 'When we go in, we have to hand over our bottles to the bloke behind the bar. He sticks one raffle ticket on each bottle and gives us the other one to use to identify us as the owner of the bottle with that number on. We pay a small price - about sixpence - to have the cork pulled out, or in our case, the top snapped off, and then we get the bottle back. It's that simp... Hey, steady on, mate!' He broke off as Knotty Ash suddenly cannoned into him before lurching off the pavement and stumbling into the road.

'It's alright, lads, I'll take care of him,' Olly Green called over his shoulder as he went after Ash who was now staggering drunkenly across the road. As he caught up with him he turned and shouted, 'Have fun boys. I probably will, getting this drunken idiot back onboard. If I can find us a taxi, that is.'

By this time, several other groups of sailors had emerged from the pub and some of these moved quickly to catch up with the pair. 'Hold on there you two,' someone cried, 'We're all going back to the ship, so let's give you a hand.'

'Well that's a relief,' George murmured gratefully as they watched the group heading away. 'I was about to suggest that we give this Corkies place a miss and help Olly out. He'll be alright now though with that lot looking after him.' He shook his head, adding, 'I just hope they get him over the gangway without any trouble.'

'I'm sure they'll be fine,' Kingdom said reassuringly. He looked at his watch. 'It's almost eleven and we've got to be back by two o'clock ourselves, so, if we're going to have another drink we'd best get a shufty on.'

'Sounds good to me,' Toz said.

'Me too,' Peewee agreed. 'Where is this place again, George?'

'Just follow the Pied Piper,' he replied with a smile and set off at a brisk pace, mentally following the directions given to him by the barmaid.

'This seems like a nice place,' Toz remarked. He and Peewee were looking around the premises at the predominantly young clientele of both sexes, spread about the unconventional assortment of tables, chairs, and well-used sofas that made up the furniture in the bohemian-styled place. George and Kingdom were checking-in the bottles they had bought en-route with the friendly young man behind the polished, hardwood counter.

'It's certainly different' Peewee mused. He was noting the mixture of artwork that adorned the walls. Old film posters, black and white as well as coloured, hung everywhere with geometrical and classical works of abstract art dotted among them. Set into a recess about six-feet wide was a dark wooden bookcase that was crammed with large encyclopaedias and other old hard-bound books. The whole place was set off by the bare floor that was painted in large glossy black and white squares, giving the appearance of a giant chessboard. The carefully arranged spotlighting in shades of red, orange, and green added a final relaxing touch of ambience.

'Here we go, boys, get your laughing tackle round these.' Kingdom Hall handed each of them a bottle of Swan. 'George has gone off to find the heads,' he told them, his eyes also taking in the offbeat flavour of the place. Looking down at the floor, he laughed, saying, 'They must have done this just for us.'

Looking at their puzzled faces, he laughed again. 'Black and white. Like you lot and me. It was meant to be a joke,' he ended lamely.

Toz chuckled, 'It's alright, mate, we got it. Very punny!'

'Hello hello, did I miss something funny?' George called, on his way back from the men's room. They were still chuckling as he came up and re-joined them.

'No. Definitely not, and as I'm outnumbered by you lot, let's go and find somewhere to sit.'

It was George's turn to look puzzled, but as Peewee and Toz merely shrugged their shoulders, he pulled a face and shrugged back.

'Suit yourselves,' he told them indifferently.

There were many smiles and warm words of welcome directed at them as they picked their way through the room where the four managed to find the only vacant table in the place, a scaled down refectory table that could seat six to eight people comfortably around it.

Surrounded by lively chatter and friendly laughter the sailors relaxed and worked their way steadily through their stock of beer, enjoying the relaxed atmosphere of the place more by the minute.

Their enjoyment was further increased at the arrival of two very attractive young girls, each carrying a bottle of wine and a glass. When they politely enquired if they could join the sailors, at their table, it being the only one left with spare seats, Kingdom was on his feet in an instant, standing smartly to attention as he gallantly invited them to sit down. 'Ladies, please make yourselves comfortable. It would be an honour if you would join us,' he said as smoothly as possible in his Birmingham accent.

After introductions had been exchanged, the girls seemed more than happy to engage in light-hearted conversation and banter with the sailors.

Emily, a petite girl whose long wavy red hair framed a pixy-like face that sparkled with a light dusting of freckles, proved to be the more talkative of the two. She looked radiant in a high-collared mandarin-style dress, richly embroidered in shades of green that went well with her hair.

Her friend, slightly taller and with a willowy figure, that Peewee found very sensual, was called Gillian. She wore her natural blonde hair in a bob and was wearing a simple knee-length, pale cream crocheted dress that emphasised the graceful contours of her slender form. Peewee thought that she looked adorable – absolutely essence.

'What do you two do for a living?' George casually enquired of the girls.

'Oh, we're both from Hollywood,' Emily replied, a smile on her face, eyes twinkling.

Toz's face lit up, 'Don't tell us that you're both Australian film stars! 'The lads back onboard will never believe us.'

'No, we're definitely not film stars,' Gillian sighed. She shot a sideways glance at Emily who was still smiling mischievously. 'We're both nurses from Hollywood hospital. Emily just loves winding tourists up with the name, don't you?' she finished, digging her friend sharply in the arm with her elbow.

'Well I'd hardly say that we're tourists,' George said lightly. 'We lowly members of Her Majesty's Royal Navy are not here by our own choice, you know.'

'Oh, but I'll tell you something,' Emily replied quite warmly. 'Us girls are quite glad you're here. The average Australian bloke believes that we come last in line behind...' She counted off from her fingers to emphasise her point, 'Cricket, rugby, beer and politics. You Pommies seem too have a lot more respect for women. At least you take the trouble to learn our names before trying to get us into bed.'

'Emily!' Gillian gasped, blushing. She appeared profoundly embarrassed by her friend's outburst.

'It's true though, Gill, isn't it,' Emily shrugged. 'I don't know about you but, personally I'm fed up with being called Sheila and regarded as a piece of raw meat.'

'Actually you've just reminded me of a joke that one of our mates told me while we were in Singapore,' Peewee broke in. He smiled at Gillian,

'Don't worry; it's not a rude one.' Hesitating, he looked to his friends for encouragement.

'Go on then, get on with it,' George smiled, making a point of looking at his watch. 'Don't take all night about it. We'll have to see these beers off and start making a move back quite soon.'

Taking a deep breath Peewee took the plunge. 'There was this pregnant Australian girl climbing over the parapet in the middle of Sydney Harbour Bridge when her ex-boyfriend spotted her. "Sheila," he cried out, "What in the name of a Dingo's doo dah do you think you're doing?" "I'm going to jump in and kill myself, that's what," she cried back. "And it's all your fault!" "S'truth Sheila, what do you want to go and do something like that for?" "Because you've made me pregnant and I know you'll never marry me. That's why." The bloke smiled and gave her a big wave before shouting, "Good on yer Sheila, I always said you were a real good sport!"'

To his great relief the joke had gone down well. Peals of laughter were coming from both of the girls and the reaction of his friends could not have been better. Kingdom Hall in particular was almost splitting his sides with laughter.

'Bloody hell mate, nice timing,' Toz coughed. 'Who told you that one then?'

Peewee smiled happily. 'Olly Green. The day after his run ashore with those Australian matelots back in Singers.'

George Grant also complimented his young friend and then reminded everyone that he had not been joking about the time. After a brief discussion and further checking of watches, they made a collective decision that they could afford another fifteen minutes to finish off the four remaining bottles in their stash behind the bar. While George and Toz went off to collect the beers, and to ask the barman to order a taxi, Kingdom chatted away with Emily. Peewee, still flushed with the success of his joke, attempted to impress Gillian further.

'It's a shame that you're not called Matilda. If you were I could sing the song to you,' he tried hopefully.

251

Gillian gave him a strange smile in reply. 'Obviously you know nothing about Australians. Unless it's some more jokes,' she said rather sternly.

Peewee felt slightly taken aback and could not understand what he had said that was wrong. He need not have worried, for as quickly as she had cooled, her warm smile had returned. 'Everyone who's not Australian seems to think that Matilda is, or was, some bushman's memory of an old romance with a dance hall girl or something like that.'

Peewee decided to tread cautiously. 'So, what was she really?' he asked carefully.

Gillian took a tiny sip of wine from her glass before replying, 'Neither.'

The boy was unable to ignore the feeling that he was being set up for something and decided to back away from the subject altogether. 'I'm sorry I mentioned it in the first place, but I just thought that Matilda must have been very important to someone once.'

'Stop winding the poor boy up,' Emily suddenly intervened. She was smiling broadly.

Gillian giggled deliciously as she decided to put him out of his misery. 'A Matilda isn't a girl at all, it's just a blanket. The kind that early Australian men carried around with them as they wandered about the country looking for work. 'Some of them still do out in the bush. It's something to snuggle down in at the end of a long hard day.' She shuddered at the sudden thought that had entered her head. 'I'd rather not go into the waltzing part of it!'

'The waltzing part of what?' Toz enquired as he and George passed round the last of their bottles.

'Gill's just been explaining what a Matilda is,' Emily told him with a chuckle.

'Oh, that's quite simple really,' George said as he returned to his seat. 'A Matilda's a mat or blanket for sleeping in. Waltzing is the term used for carrying it about the country with you.'

The girls were clearly impressed. 'You clever English sailor you,' Emily said sweetly.

'Yes but Gillian's got a point,' Peewee pressed. 'The waltzing bit could refer to something going on under the blanket, couldn't it?'

For a few brief seconds a shocked silence hung in the air. Then, as Emily and Gillian suddenly saw the funny side of it and burst out laughing, the sailors joined in merrily.

All too soon the final quarter-of-an-hour had passed and a barman came over and informed them that their taxi was waiting. At Kingdom's suggestion they drained their bottles in a toast to Emily and Gillian for making their first run ashore in Australia a real good one.

They were all standing, saying their goodnights and goodbyes when Gillian took Peewee's breath by planting a light kiss on his cheek.

'Thank you.' He blushed in heady surprise.

'No. 'I want to thank you. We rarely ever come to this place but I'm so glad that we did tonight or we would never have met.'

'Will you be here again during the next few days?' Peewee asked hopefully. He was already mentally planning a return visit, preferably by himself.

'No, I'm afraid not,' she replied, instantly dashing his hopes. 'Both of us are on night duty from tomorrow, but I've had the most lovely time talking to you, and we will definitely be telling your joke all around the hospital tomorrow.'

'Come along, Casanova, the taxi's on waiting time,' Toz called as the others began to make their way out into the street.

Peewee hung back just long enough to make a final, hesitating farewell before following after Toz. As they approached the exit he looked back, and saw that she was still standing, watching him leave. His heart surged when she put her fingers to her lips and blew him a dainty, silent kiss.

As the big Holden taxi bore them speedily back to the ship, Peewee was obliged to endure more good-natured ribbing from his friends who could clearly see that he was smitten. Although he smiled in reply to their well-intentioned humour, he was inwardly cursing himself for his last minute failure to summon up enough courage to ask Gillian for her address, or telephone number.

25

The Copleys

IT HAD BEEN AN easy morning for JTO Hunt. He had collated the bundle of message forms that gave the names and details of the press members coming aboard, and had typed them up into a simple master list. Apart from answering a few telephone calls there had been little else to do.

Now, sitting at the desk that had been provided for him in the compartment that had been allocated for the use of the Press Liaison Officer, he felt vaguely relieved as he worked his way through the pile of local newspapers and magazines that the PRO had instructed him to read as they awaited the arrival of their guests.

Lieutenant Spencer-Hudson was at his own desk, quietly putting together the final touches of his tour-of-the-ship speech. He had informed Hunt that once checked-off against the visitor list that he had compiled, he would deliver his welcome speech to the journalists, after which a wardroom steward would be on hand to serve everybody with tea, coffee and biscuits.

The best thing as far as the junior was concerned was that the PRO had told him that he would not be required during the tour as, to begin with, it commenced with welcoming drinks and luncheon in the officers wardroom. To any lower deck rating this was hallowed ground, and as a Junior Tactical Operator (Third Class) Peewee Hunt was not just any lower deck rating – he was the lowest. With any luck, he was thinking, he would be well away from his duties here, and he was looking forward to an early lunch himself in the dining hall.

He was making a show of reading all the material, knowing that it was just something the PRO had given him to do in order to impress the journalists with their attention to detail. In truth, he was still preoccupied with memories of the previous evening. No matter how hard he tried, he just could not stop thinking about Gillian.

Despite his lack of enthusiasm for the work in hand, as he turned over a page he could not fail to notice the boldly printed advertisement that jumped out at him from a page of *The West Australian*, the newspaper he was browsing through.

WANTED
1,000 Young Women
You are invited to
A Dance
To be given by the men of
H.M.S. ARK ROYAL
At the Pagoda

The time and date of the event was given in a short postscript, including in the detail, that admission, drinks, and light refreshments would be free of charge.

Peewee Hunt gave a low whistle and sat up, adjusting his posture as he re-read the whole item on the page.

'Something caught your attention, Hunt,' drawled the PRO, a half smile appearing on his face.

'Yes, sir, I've just seen an advertisement for the ship's dance. I don't think anyone onboard has heard about it. Not even in the main signal office. Is it true then, sir?'

Spencer-Hudson chuckled. 'I suppose that you were thinking that I had given you that heap of stuff to read for the fun of it?'

'No, sir. Of course not.'

'Well, you are to be commended for doing what you were asked. The truth is that I haven't had time to go through them myself this morning. The captain asked me to place the advertisement yesterday and I had actually been waiting to see if you would spot it, so well done.'

'I think that this is going to go down very well with the men, sir,' Hunt said politely.

The officer smiled warmly.' As I believe you men might put it, it should be the run of a lifetime. I certainly hope so as I am one of the small team of officers who have been charged with the organising of it.'

Peewee experienced a warm glow at the frankness of the officer's words. 'I'm certain that it will be an absolute brahma, sir,' he replied, using the correct lower-deck terminology, somewhat smugly.

Shortly after 1000 hours, a Royal Marine corporal stepped through the watertight doorway and indicated a group of men in civilian clothes hovering in the passageway outside. 'Press party present, sir,' the marine snapped, saluting the PRO smartly.

'Very well, Corporal. Be so good as to show our very special guests through,' the officer replied magnanimously in a voice loud enough to be heard by their visitors.

One-by-one, as they stepped through the doorway into the compartment, the PRO and the young signalman nodded and smiled greetings at them.

A boy, younger than Peewee Hunt, was the last to arrive, trailing behind a particularly hard-bitten looking man. Hunt thought that the journalist must have brought his son along with him for the ride. If so, it might be that they would be disappointed as the tour was strictly by pre-arrangement. Quickly he scanned his list but could find no sign of two people with the same surname.

The PRO was smiling quizzically at the boy. 'Is this young man on your list, Hunt?' he enquired in a mild tone.

The signalman glanced questioningly at the pair, the expression on his face clear for both to read.

257

'Don't look at me,' the older man shrugged. 'I'm here by myself.'

The boy fished into a pocket and produced what looked like a business card. Stepping across to Peewee's desk, he handed over the card for him to read. It identified the boy as Greg Copley, Editor of the Royal Australian Air force Air Training Corps magazine.

Hunt scanned his list again and with a warm flutter of relief, found the boy's name, clearly typed by himself. 'He's on the list, sir,' he informed the officer, adding, 'Greg Copley representing the Air Training Corps.'

The Press Liaison Officer chuckled. 'Well then, Hunt, I'm afraid that you're going to be required somewhat longer. As the first item on the agenda for these gentlemen…' he paused and swept a hand to indicate the huddle of men, 'is drinks in the wardroom; to be followed by more drinks in the wardroom later; I suggest that as you are of a similar age that you take this young man under your wing and show him around the ship yourself.'

It was not a suggestion, Peewee realised at once. It was an order, thinly veiled for the benefit of the young journalist.

'Does that seem agreeable to you, young man?' The PRO smiled kindly at the Australian boy.

Copley smiled back politely. 'Certainly, sir.' He turned and looked hopefully towards his personal guide-to-be who was now standing with a hand outstretched in welcome.

After introducing himself as JTO Hunt, Peewee suggested that they took advantage of the refreshments that were being served by an immaculately dressed leading steward.

Over coffee and biscuits, they chatted away cheerfully, each telling the other little bits of their backgrounds. When the rest of the journalists finally followed the PRO out of the compartment, Peewee asked the obvious question, 'Right then, Greg, where would you like to start?'

'With the aircraft,' he replied keenly. 'I understand that you've got both *Sea Vixens* and *Scimitars* onboard?'

'Well, some of them were flown ashore to Pearce airfield before we arrived, but I'm sure there's a few left to see,' Peewee answered, warming to the boy's polite attitude, as well as his enthusiasm and obvious passion for aircraft. 'Okay, let's go. Follow me. I think we'll start with the upper hangar. We've got two hangars you know, but we'll do the upper one first and then I'll take you down to the lower one.'

By the time they had reached one of the watertight doors that gave access to the upper hangar, the two of them were getting along nicely. The signalman had told the young journalist that there was no need to address him as JTO Hunt, but to call him by his nickname, unless they found themselves in the presence of any of the ship's officers.

En-route through the maze of ladders, decks and companionways, his charge showed no signs of boredom. He appeared to be fascinated and intrigued by everything his host pointed out or explained to him along the way.

Hauling the door open, Peewee stepped through first and turned to face the boy as he followed him through. 'Right, here we are then, welcome to the upper hanger,' he said, gesturing around the cavernous metal chamber.

If there really was a Father Christmas, and there was such a place as Santa's toy factory, the expression on the Australian boy's face suggested that he had just found it.

Speechless he gazed around, his eyes filled with awe and wonder as they registered the enormity of the place. Neatly parked gleaming aircraft were everywhere. *Scimitars*, *Sea Vixens* and *Wessex* helicopters, as well as the smaller *Whirlwinds* of the Ship's Flight, sparkled beneath the bright yellow glare of the hangar's lighting. A heady mixture of smells; oil, grease and spirituous fluids assailed their nostrils, lending tangible substance to an atmosphere that was already highly charged with a sense of extreme potency. It was a while before Greg finally let out a long-held breath of air and whispered, 'This is just... absolutely fantastic!'

Here and there, small teams of engineers were carrying out maintenance on individual aircraft, while other men either strolled, or strode about with purpose. One of the latter appeared to be making a bee-line towards them and the signalman, feeling rather like a fish out of water, wondered if their presence would be welcomed, or even tolerated.

'Good morning, lads. I am the duty petty officer of the day. May I ask your reason for being here?' he asked in a firm but openly friendly manner.

Peewee recognised him as former Leading Airman Robertson. He had been the original occupant of the bunk that had been allocated to Spider Webb. Quickly he explained that he had been tasked by the Press Liaison Officer to give the young Australian journalist a comprehensive tour of the ship, and that they had chosen to start here.

It turned out that the petty officer knew all about the press tour and was expecting them in the hangar later that morning. After hearing Hunt's explanation as to why they had arrived before the main body, he relaxed and after checking that the young Australian was wearing rubber, or leather soled shoes, offered to show them around personally, declaring that it would give him the opportunity for a practice run.

After a fascinating twenty minutes, during which Greg learned about Rats, Moles, and Manglers, as well as a great deal more Fleet Air Arm terminology, much of it also new to Peewee, the PO concluded their visit to the upper hangar by bringing down the forward aircraft lift. Peewee and Greg were invited to use it as transport down to the lower hangar where they were greeted by his opposite number, another young-looking petty officer.

More aircraft, including a *Fairey Gannet,* were just as neatly parked, with the exception of a *Wessex* and a *Scimitar* that were receiving more serious maintenance and repairs than those above.

The *Scimitar* was parked more or less in the centre of the hangar, and as they watched, a mechanic emerged from the open cockpit and clambered down the safety ladder that was propped against the aircraft. The petty officer excused himself and walked over to talk to him.

Greg slowly shook his head. 'I wish I could climb up into that beauty,' he sighed wistfully.

Peewee considered the boy's remark carefully before replying, 'Just hold on a minute and wait here while I go over and have a word with the PO.'

The petty officer's response to the JTO's request, was to turn to the mechanic with a, "What do you think?" expression on his face.

The aircraft mechanic shrugged, and said, 'Well I can't see why not. All the systems are shut down and the ejector mechanism is disarmed. Besides, I've got plenty of other stuff to keep me busy for the next half-hour.'

The PO turned back to Hunt. 'Go on then, call the lad over,' he smiled, adding, 'I'll leave you to supervise, but I'll still be about if you need me.'

'Thanks, PO, he's going to be really chuffed,' Peewee replied gratefully. He crooked a finger at Greg Copley who had been watching the exchange hopefully. 'Come on, Greg, I've sorted it.' He glanced at his watch as the boy re-joined him by the aircraft, 'Not too long though,' he cautioned, 'it's nearly lunch-time and there's lots more to see afterwards.'

Grinning from ear to ear the boy scampered up the ladder and climbed into the cockpit of the *Scimitar* where he remained for a good ten minutes, happily absorbing every detail of the state-of-the-art surroundings. Peewee Hunt knew that for however long he lived, he would never forget the look of pure joy on the boy's face as his warm smile glowed down at him from time-to-time.

On arrival in Fremantle the ship had re-provisioned with fresh meat, fruit and vegetables, and after a good lunch in the main dining hall shared with Robbie Robson, Toz and several other members of the tactical department, at Robson's suggestion, Peewee took his young guest down to the mess where all those present, greeted the young Australian cheerfully.

One or two of the older hands, LTO Turner included, even offered to share their cans of beer with him. To Peewee's relief, the boy politely, and sensibly, declined.

The next stop was a visit to the flag deck and the MSO where he was introduced to Knotty Ash and the other members of the duty watch.

Considering his excesses of the previous day, Ash was on good form. 'I do hope young Hunt here has been looking after you properly,' he intoned, motioning towards the in-tray piled with signals waiting to be typed and disseminated. 'Especially as we reckon that he only accepted the job in order to skive off from helping the rest of us this afternoon.

Peewee Hunt felt very silly until he noticed the sly wink that Ash directed towards Olly Green and Kingdom Hall. 'I'll just carry on then, seeing as I'm the only one that the SCO trusted,' he replied amiably.

Olly Green joined them as Peewee took Greg to the Admiral's Bridge, forward of the flag deck, then down to the Captain's Bridge below. Olly was superb, professionally but discreetly coming to the aid of his young friend by helping to answer many of the bright young journalist's many perceptive questions.

Eventually, Olly returned to the MSO while Peewee led Greg down to the flight deck where they spent an enjoyable half-hour in the company of Naval Airman Milligan who turned out to be a comically gregarious, but informative voluntary guide.

The tour ended at 1600 hours, and after escorting the youngster to the departure point, they shook hands warmly as the boy repeated his many thanks before leaving the ship via the central gangway.

Later on, Peewee, now back on duty during the last dogwatch, was surprised and concerned when the order was piped over the Tannoy system for him to report to the officer of the watch at the main gangway.

Knotty Ash and the others also shared looks of concern as such a summons usually meant trouble. 'Sounds like bad news. I reckon you'd better take your hat,' Ash told the junior soberly.

'JTO Hunt reporting, sir,' he said as he saluted the OOW who was talking to a man and woman in civilian clothes.

As the officer returned the salute, Peewee was surprised to see that he was smiling broadly. 'Well young Hunt, let me introduce you to these two very nice people who have a very kind invitation to offer you.'

Even more confused, Peewee turned to the couple who also had big smiles on their faces. 'Hi, I'm Brian Copley and this is my wife Marjorie. We are Greg's mum and dad, the boy you kindly showed around your ship today.' The man stepped forward, holding out his hand for the boy to shake.

After exchanging handshakes, Greg's parents took turns to thank him for giving their son such a good day aboard the ship. They told him that Greg had not yet come down from his place on cloud nine. However, they hoped that he would do so in time for a family roast dinner at their home the following day, to which they hoped that Peewee would accept their invitation as guest-of-honour.

It was such a pleasant surprise that it was a few moments before he was able to find the right words of acceptance, but with a little prompting from the officer of the watch he managed an almost breathless, 'Yes, I'd like to, thank you very much.'

With a promise to collect him at four o'clock the following day, and after thanking him once again, the Copleys bade a cheery farewell to Peewee and the gangway staff then made their way down to the jetty.

Much later, shortly after midnight at the start of the four hour middle watch, Knotty Ash cast a thoughtful eye over his team. 'There's far too many of us,' he concluded, indicating the empty in-tray on his desk. 'I reckon one of you can have a stand-off.'

'Well I'm happy to stay,' Olly Green yawned as Kingdom Hall poured canned milk into the mugs of coffee that Peewee Hunt had just made.

'Kingdom?' Ash enquired.

'Yeah, me too, same as Olly. I reckon that seeing as Peewee had to turn-to four hours before us this morning, you should give him the stand-off.'

263

'Fair enough,' Ash agreed, smiling at the junior. 'Besides, we want you looking half decent for your dinner date tomorrow,' he added amusedly. Using the naval slang for an offer of hospitality, he went on, 'As grippos go, we all reckon that you've dipped in nicely there. 'Now go and get your head down,' he told the delighted boy, adding, 'Mind that you're back here at 0800 sharp for the forenoon.'

After thanking the three of them, Peewee left his coffee and headed down to the bunkspace at a brisk pace. It had been a long day and he was immensely grateful to the others for giving him the opportunity to catch up on some well-deserved sleep.

Greg Copley was with his father when they arrived to pick Peewee up at four o'clock on the dot the following day. The boys greeted each other warmly and Greg was thrilled with the gift of an *Ark Royal* cap ribbon that Peewee had brought for him. They chatted away like long lost friends during the drive to the Copleys' home in Daglish, a suburb to the west of Kings Park.

A beaming Marjorie Copley and Greg's older brother, Howard, were at the door to welcome the young sailor when they arrived.

Peewee was made to feel perfectly at home, and after a wonderful dinner he was able to relax and enjoy the company of Greg and Howard while their parents were getting themselves ready to take them all out for a family evening and dance at their local community centre.

Later that night, back aboard his ship, the young man (as Greg's parents had kept referring to him) lay in his bunk and reflected on his evening out. He had thoroughly enjoyed himself throughout his time spent with the Copleys, and had lost count of their many friends to whom he had been introduced. He had also proved to be of much interest to the girls and there had been no shortage of attractive young ladies asking him to dance with them.

He smiled at the memory of Marjorie Copley arriving downstairs beautifully dressed, and doing a twirl before asking all of them, 'How do I look?' She had looked lovely, he had thought.

Quite suddenly, he began thinking of his own mother and the rest of his family, thousands of miles away on the other side of the world when, without warning, and for the first time in more than a year, he found himself sliding helplessly into the merciless grip of a long and depressive bout of homesickness. He was still crying quietly when he finally fell asleep that night.

26

A merry dance

THE RESPONSE TO THE advertisement placed in the West Australian was tremendous. Over two-thousand females of all ages turned up at the Pagoda ballroom on the night, and somehow, they were all squeezed inside to be greeted by a thousand delighted sailors. The dress code for those men lucky enough to have obtained a ticket (less than half of the ships complement) was Number One Uniform and under the colourful light that spilled down from the huge Chinese lanterns hanging overhead, brass buttons and gold wire badges glinted everywhere.

Peewee Hunt and his friends were having a great time. It seemed that everywhere they looked or turned, there was a pretty face smiling at them. Many of the girls refused to take no for an answer and even the normally cool and reserved George Allen had been unable to refuse, as one by one, each of the four signalmen were repeatedly dragged onto the crowded dance floor where the ship's own ten-piece dance band were going down a storm.

Whenever they could evade the female attention for more than a few minutes they hit the free bar where, despite the numbers in attendance, the service was excellent and their drinks were dispensed with speedy efficiency.

At about nine o'clock the band stopped playing while a hushed audience first listened, then cheered loudly after the strong voice of the Australian Master of Ceremonies announced the arrival on stage of the captain of HMS *Ark Royal*, accompanied by several local dignitaries.

Following the succession of speeches that were kept mercifully short, the band struck up again with an inspired version of *The Wild Colonial Boy* which had the immediate effect of filling the dance floor with passionately embroiled English and Australian partners.

It was shortly after this point when Toz, finally released from the grip of a very determined girl, managed to excuse himself and re-locate the others. 'By 'eck, that was getting a bit heavy,' he breathed, gratefully accepting the beer that Peewee held out to him. After taking a large swig, Toz wiped his sweating forehead on the back of his sleeve before continuing, 'You lot should see the doggo party that Squeegy's dancing with. She looks like a praying mantis.' Then, in response to the inquisitive smiles of his friends, he continued again, 'Just keep your eyes on the dance floor, they'll be coming a' waltzing round this way any minute.'

True to Toz's word, they were soon rewarded with the sight of the beefy form of Yeoman Jolly, stomach sucked in, chest puffed out, swirling round the floor with a tall, angular woman with grey, drawn-back hair tied in a severe bun, skewered through with a long pair of ivory hairpins. There was a mournful, almost funereal air of aloofness about her facial expression as she stared unblinking into the eyes of the yeoman. The hairpins that much-resembled chopsticks, stuck comically upwards and outwards like the antennae of a giant insect. As they whirled past the group of friends, her thin face and large beaky nose was so close to that of the yeoman, that Peewee found himself willing her to bite it off.

'Oh my God, just take a look over there,' Toz groaned in amusement as the mismatched couple swept on by. Toz was now directing their attention to the spectacle of naval airmen Milligan and Riley who had been taking full advantage of the free bar. They had dropped their bell-bottoms and were about to perform their party-piece, The *Dance of the Flaming Arseholes*.

'No one's going to let them do that here! Not in a place like this, surely to God,' Kingdom Hall spoke up. Nobody else seemed bothered at the prospect, especially Peewee and Toz who, by this time, were quite pleasantly drunk, while George Allen looked as if he couldn't care less.

Kingdom's concern, if that's what it was, was echoed by a good many others who by this time had acquired themselves a permanent female fixture with whom they had high hopes of ending up for the night, and the drunken plans of the Irishmen were cut short in good time with no hard feelings all round.

'Having a good time, lads?' The friends suddenly found their attention diverted by the arrival of Communications Yeoman Tom Blowers.

'We certainly are, Yeo.' George Allen replied cheerfully.

'So is Yeoman Jolly by the looks of things,' Toz chortled.

Blowers nodded and gave an understanding chuckle. 'The skinny woman he's dancing with is the widow of a mate of the chief yeoman. Some bloke he served with years ago, back in the war. Apparently he only died a couple of months ago. Lucky bugger. I think I'd rather be dead than have her to look forward to in the morning. The chief has set him up with her to keep him out of everyone else's way. Either that, or it's just to piss him off I expect.'

The friends nodded and smiled at each other with schoolboy grins on their faces at the revelation. Their eyes followed Tom Blowers as he moved off and made his way through the crowd to re-join Sam Wilcox at a large table surrounded by a number of other chief and petty officers with several women dotted amongst them.

Sitting at a table right next to the chiefs and petty officers were Robbie Robson and several other leading hands, including Topsy Turner, Tubbs McEwan and the leading radio operators, Taff Jones and Jumper Cross. They were all cheerfully enjoying the attentions of a gaggle of loudly shrieking young women bent on enjoying the party atmosphere to the maximum.

Kingdom Hall stared at the leading hands. 'It looks like all the killicks seem to have pulled,' he observed with a slight trace of sarcasm in his voice.

'Yeah. Well they're bloody welcome if that's the best they can do,' George retorted, adding, 'And talking of killicks, where's ours? I haven't seen hide-nor-hair of Knotty, or Olly either, since we got here.'

'I can answer that one,' Toz spoke up. 'I saw them both leaving the hall with two girls, right pieces of essence, while the speeches were going on. They all looked pretty friendly with each other if you ask me.'

'Well, speak of the Devil! They're back here now and heading our way,' Peewee told them. He had just spotted the two easing their way through the crowd towards them, each with an attractive young girl in tow.

It transpired that Knotty and Olly had been persuaded to go for a drive with the two girls who were introduced as Sarah and Mandy and had spent the last hour sitting in the car in what Olly described as a Lovers Leap parking area high up in Kings Park. 'The view over the river and the city from up there was absolutely fantastic,' he said, looking to Knotty for confirmation.

'Yeah, I just bet it was,' George commented dryly. He had noted the demure smiles on the faces of the two girls, and the rather cheesy one that Knotty was displaying.

The group were heading to the bar for more drinks when Peewee felt a light tap on his shoulder. Expecting to find another of their messmates, he looked round and his heart soared as he recognised the girl, Gillian, and her friend Emily, from their brief encounter almost a week ago. Gillian's eyes sparkled as she smiled at him beautifully. 'Remember us?' she asked lightly.

'Of course I remember you. Both of you.' He shot Emily a weak smile of apology and looked back at Gillian, 'I haven't stopped thinking about you ever since. I didn't think I'd ever see you again.'

'You wouldn't have done if it wasn't for this dance,' Emily told him. 'We were both stuck on night duty, but when we...'

'Emily, let me explain,' Gillian cut, in giving her friend a strange smile that might also be construed as a frown of admonishment. Turning back to Peewee, she continued, 'Since we saw the advert in the paper for tonight, the two of us have really struggled to call in some favours. Luckily, we managed to persuade a couple of our male nurses to swap shifts with us.'

'Yes, and it was damned hard work as well, 'cos the blokes in question are a pair of faggots who would rather have been here themselves,' Emily re-joined in her usual uncompromising manner.

Peewee and Gillian grew increasingly closer as the evening progressed, and neither cared as Emily and the others kept referring to them as the lovebirds. They had spent a considerable amount of time on the dance floor, particularly during the smooches in the later hours.

The dance was due to end at midnight and around ten-thirty Peewee was overjoyed when Gillian agreed to step outside with him so they could spend some time together by themselves. Holding hands, they slipped inconspicuously out into the cool night air.

It was about half-an-hour later when Emily first realised that the pair had not been seen for some time. Chaperoned by the ever attendant Kingdom Hall who had proved to be a delightful dance partner, she had been enjoying herself far too much to notice the discreet disappearance of Peewee and Gillian.

'Hey, you guys, have any of you seen the lovebirds lately?' she enquired as she and Kingdom took a break from the floor and re-joined the rest of the group near the bar.

'I thought they were with you two on the dance floor,' George Allen told her unconcernedly. 'No?' He raised an eyebrow at Kingdom's emphatic shake of his head.

'Well they won't be far away,' Toz chuckled. 'Don't worry, the bar will be closing soon, so they're bound to be back for a last drink together.'

Emily glanced at her watch. Gillian was her best friend and although Peewee came across to her as very nice, he was still an unknown newcomer into her best friend's life. 'He is alright is he, this Peewee bloke?' she asked the sailors bluntly, and was duly relieved by their nods and words of reassurance.

'Like Toz just said, they'll be here in plenty of time for last orders,' Olly Green said cheerfully.

Still Emily fretted, and after a further ten minutes had elapsed with no sign of the couple returning, she began expressing her concern again.

'I reckon they must have left the place without anyone seeing them,' Knotty's friend Sarah suggested.

'That would explain it,' George nodded, agreeing with her. After watching the way they've been with each other tonight, it would make sense for them to try and find some peace and quiet. After all, like it or not, they're probably not going to see each other again for a long, long time. If ever!' he finished matter-of-factly, giving a slight shrug of his shoulders.

Emily turned to Kingdom, a purposeful expression on her face. 'Right, come with me then. We'll go outside and find them. It's getting really close to the last dance and I know Gill won't want to miss that!' Taking hold of Kingdom's arm, she led the un-protesting sailor through the crowd towards the exit.

At the same time Peewee and Gillian were making their way back to the Pagoda, fresh from their romantic dalliance on the nearby Como beach. As they approached the entrance to the dance hall, they found their way barred by a loudly vocal and hostile crowd of about fifteen drunken men gathered outside.

'Here's another one of the Pommie bastards,' one of them cried out angrily, pointing in the direction of the approaching couple.

Gillian slowed and took hold of Peewee's hand a little more tightly 'Let's just hold back a little, this looks like trouble,' she whispered.

There were several other sailors, all with girls, who found themselves in the same position. Two of them, like Peewee and Gillian, had been heading back from the beach, while two or three other partners were returning from a small area of parkland that lay adjacent to the Pagoda building.

'What's going on?' Peewee asked the couple from the beach who had been a few minutes ahead of them on the way back.

The seaman, who sported a gold four-year good conduct stripe on his left arm, shrugged. 'Seems like a load of jealous rubbish according to this one,' he replied, nodding at the worried looking girl by his side.

'Bloody Northbridge tossers!' she snorted. 'They think they own every girl in town. Why don't they just stick to the prozzies that drink in the same dives as they do?'

Peewee studied the distance between the small group of sailors and the entrance to the Pagoda that was cut off by the gang of thugs that stood between them. It was not far, but it was going to be something of a risk he realised. He was certain that at least two of the men who appeared to be acting as ringleaders were from the pub near the railway station that he and his friends had called in on their first trip to the city. The ones who had aggressively warned them to leave the local girls alone.

This could get a bit ugly, he was thinking, but then he took some comfort at the sight of a small number of grim-looking Royal Navy Shore Patrol members swiftly alighting from a pair of Land Rovers that had just pulled up. Leading Regulator Frow stepped out of the leading vehicle while Pussy Catte, the regulator who had turned a blind eye to the antics in the cellblock during George Allen's confinement, took his time as he climbed out of the other. For the moment, both regulators cautiously held their white-belted men in check.

The sight of this sudden reinforcement might have been enough to quell the riotous behaviour of the drunken rabble had it not been for the sudden appearance of Emily and Kingdom Hall coming out of the Pagoda building together in search of their friends.

'Look! One of the slags has got a black bastard with her!' one of the ringleaders yelled. Peewee saw with horror that the man had produced a knife as he screamed, 'You filthy black nigger fucker,' and rushed forward towards Emily and the bewildered looking sailor from Birmingham. At least half of the baying crowd followed, hard on his heels.

'Shit! Stay here,' Peewee shouted the order at Gillian. Letting go of her hand he raced headlong into the melee, desperately hoping to save his friend from harm. He was just seconds too late. As he forced himself through the crowd, he was quickly overwhelmed and pushed to the ground under the weight of the bodies and hammering fists that greeted him.

Despite the fact that he was down on his knees and held firmly in the ruck, everything remained crystal clear from that moment on. Unable to prevent it, he stared in dread as seemingly in slow motion the knife was thrust into the body of his friend. As Kingdom crumpled and started to topple down over the kneeling junior, Emily came with him, holding onto him as he fell.

The vacuum created by Kingdom and Emily's fall gave Peewee the freedom of movement to lunge forward just enough to wrap his strong arms around one of the knifeman's thighs and hang on for grim death as the man tried to pull himself away.

Blows were still raining down on him from above and numerous feet kicked at him. Fortunately, this proved to be ineffectual as most of the feet were getting in the way of each other. If anything, Peewee managed to tighten his grip as he heard the warning shouts of Leading Regular Frow ordering the crowd to stop and break off.

Kingdom was groaning as his hands struggled to find the knife that was still buried in him. Somehow Emily had got hold of it and she was holding it gently but firmly in place with both of her hands. 'Leave it. Leave it where it is,' she gasped. 'You'll gush if it comes out!'

This is getting silly, Peewee was thinking. When are the shore patrol going to step in?

It did not last much longer. The bodies of the men above them suddenly began to sway violently. It was as if a bull elephant had just roamed into the proceedings, and the weight of the press seemed to lift instantly. Still hanging onto the assailant's leg, Peewee heard the sound of several meaty thwacks accompanied by a loud and familiar voice shouting, 'Piss off you bunch of cowardly bastards and leave my lads alone!'

As the view above his head cleared, Peewee was stunned to see the face of Yeoman Jolly peering down at them. 'Bunch of big girls' blouses,' he muttered as he relieved Peewee of the burden of the knifeman, thrusting him into the eager arms of two members of the shore patrol.

The rest of the crowd had fled, for as well as the maddened yeoman and the shore patrol, there were now a number of police officers arriving at the scene. A sergeant had fetched some blankets and a first aid kit from his car and Gillian assisted Emily in making Kingdom as comfortable as possible. The nurses told the sergeant that they would take care of him until the arrival of the ambulance that the officer assured them was imminent.

As soon as Hall had been whisked off to hospital the local police asserted their authority and took charge, freeing up the shore patrol to usher the few other sailors who had come out of the Pagoda back inside.

When the police sergeant informed Peewee that the alleged suspect was being held in custody he told him in no uncertain terms that the man was definitely not an "alleged" suspect. 'I saw the bastard do it. That's why I hung onto him until help came. Fucking alleged suspect, my arse!'

The police sergeant was clearly impressed, and responded by informing the boy that he would be required to accompany him to the station in order to make a statement. After taking the girls' details and informing them that they would also eventually be contacted as potential witnesses, the officer kindly ordered one of his men to drive Gillian and Emily back to their quarters at the hospital.

With Yeoman Jolly still standing, and insisting on accompanying him, Peewee was given a brief moment to say goodbye to Gillian, and to thank Emily properly for the skill and presence of mind that she had displayed.

As the police car pulled away with the petty officer and the junior sitting in the back, Peewee suddenly remembered what the yeoman had said when he had come to their rescue. 'Can I ask you a question, Yeo?' he enquired cautiously.

'Course you can,' Jolly said. 'What is it?'

'Just after you dragged that bastard off me, why did you call us a bunch of big girl's blouses?'

Squeegy compressed his thick lips and gave him a tight grin. 'I wasn't talking about you, I was talking about them.' He patted the youngster on the knee and leaned back in his seat. 'Tell you what though, if I hadn't come outside for a breath of air, things might have turned out a lot different. In a way it's turned out all right for me. At least, it's given me a bloody good excuse for escaping from that reptilian creature the chief lumbered me with. God, she hummed like a stick of gone-off celery.' He paused briefly and looked sideways at the junior. 'Believe it or not, I do have a soft spot when it comes to looking after you lot when you're ashore. And you, my son,' he said positively, 'are definitely not a big girl's blouse. You should think about joining the ship's wrestling team.' His fat face lit up with a huge, round smile as he added, 'My oppo, Wolfie, would have been chuffed to bits with the Bulgarian bedside-grip you were holding that bastard in.'

Peewee looked away and grimaced. It was the second time he had received a jokey reference to the wrestling team, and he doubted if Wolfie, otherwise known as Petty Officer Baldwin, the ship's charismatic wrestling coach who fought in the ring as the *Wolf of Baddenach,* was in any way a friend of the yeoman. Jolly simply didn't have any. Peewee was not ungrateful for the yeoman's timely intervention, but at the end of the day, he knew that his despised superior would soon revert to character. Inwardly he was chuckling. 'If only you knew,' he wanted to say, in response to the yeoman's words along the lines of, "having a soft spot for you lot". 'All of us lot have a soft spot for you. Goodwin Sands!'

27

Gillian

TWO DAYS LATER, AT 1000 hours, HMS *Ark Royal* was ready to take her leave of Western Australia. Everyone aboard, including the wounded Kingdom Hall who was making a good recovery in the ship's hospital, agreed that it had been the run of a lifetime.

Peewee Hunt watched as two pairs of signalmen, Clive Appleby with Pip Piper, and Smudge Smith with Steve Tredrea made their respective ways fore and aft to prepare to lower the Union Jack and White ensign flying at the staffs erected at either end of the ship. They were walking smartly along the side of the flight deck, occasionally waving down to the crowd of well-wishers on the jetty below.

Peewee was watching with mixed feelings. The next port of call was Hong Kong and he was unsure whether he would be there with his friends to enjoy the fabled city as he was no longer onboard the ship. At the request of the Royal Australian Police he was to remain in Perth in order to attend the trial of Kingdom Hall's attacker as a key witness.

As he stood there, craning his neck to look up at the flag deck, trying to spot who was on duty up there, he found himself reflecting over the near fatal incident with the hostile Australian thugs, but then his mind began to wander as it turned to the events of the past three and a half months. The encounters with Bloody Mary in Plymouth and the homosexual Robert in Gibraltar, were still clearly etched in his mind, as were those with the hostile Arabs in Aden, and of course, Rita and Nicole in Mombasa and Singapore. The savage beating meted out to Collins at the hands of Spider Webb would remain in his memory for a very long time, but the distress he had experienced at the tragic deaths of the flight deck engineer and the

Scimitar pilot was still very much with him. He knew that his memories of those two events alone would remain with him forever. They had been his shipmates. Family. Suddenly, the boy felt much older than his sixteen-and-a-half years and he was pleasantly distracted when he felt a soft hand slip gently into his. It was Gillian.

'How did you know that I'd be here?' he asked, surprised and delighted to see her.

'The police,' she told him simply. 'They came and took statements from Emily and me.' She went on to say that both girls were also to appear as witnesses in the Magistrates Court. 'Once they told us that you were staying behind I knew that I couldn't let you say goodbye to your ship all on your own.' She gave his hand a tight squeeze. 'Besides, the city can be a dangerous place if you don't know your way around, so somebody's got to look after you.'

From the flag deck, the brilliant white light of an Aldis lamp suddenly stabbed down at them. 'Look up there,' Peewee instructed her, 'That's Toz. He's flashing a message in Morse code!'

The couple watched until the light eventually flickered out and Peewee gave a pleasant chuckle of understanding.

'Come on then, what did he say?' Gillian wanted to know, urging Peewee with her elbow.

Peewee smiled and looked into her face, 'Oh, nothing really,' he told her, giving a slight shrug. 'Toz just signalled, "See you in Hong Kong", that's all.'

Gillian had no idea that the smile still on Peewee's face as he turned back to wave at Toz was a guilty one. "See you in Hong Kong" indeed! The message from Toz had actually read; *See you in Hong Kong you dirty lucky bastard!*

 *THE END*

WHAT PEEWEE DID NEXT . . .

Since leaving the Royal Navy I have enjoyed an interesting life. That is not to say that my twelve years in *The Andrew* was not interesting – if that had been the case I would never have been able to write this book.

I stayed aboard HMS *Ark Royal* for three and a half years, rising through the rates from JTO to TO(2) and then RO2(T) when the communications branch became amalgamated as Radio Operators with a designation letter to show the difference between a sparker and a bunting tosser. I went on to serve aboard the minesweeper HMS *Brinton* (she was about the size of the communications mess alone on the *Ark)* and then to the cruiser HMS *Tiger* for a circumnavigation cruise of South America. The Official Secrets Act prevents me from relating some service but Her Majesty's Ships *Devonshire*, *Hermes*, *Victorious*, *Naiad*, and *Blake* were among others in which I served.

In 1972 during my first year in Civvy Street, I found it difficult to adapt and worked at a number of jobs. Briefly, I was a milkman, a sales assistant for Curry's the electrical High Street chain, a foundry worker at the Singer factory in Frome (they made the *Scales of Justice* above the Old Bailey) and a door-to-door salesman selling a frighteningly expensive set of saucepans for Rena Ware, a Canadian pyramid company. This set of five stainless steel saucepans cost three-hundred and fifty quid in 1972 and I only managed to sell one set to a baker in Frome who still has them today. I blagged a job as a company car mechanic even though I knew nothing about how an engine, or a car, worked, and got away with it for several weeks before the boss of the company (Venture Carpets) sussed me out after most of the salesmen's cars had stopped working. Surprisingly, I was offered a job as a clerk in their head office that I accepted. They were nice people and obviously liked me. Except for the car mechanic one, none of these jobs lasted for more than a month but at the end of that year, I applied for, and got a job as a car salesman for a Volkswagen dealership in

Bath. I turned out to be quite good at this and eventually went on to become the senior salesman at a brand new Datsun dealership in Bristol.

Very early in my navy days I learned to play guitar and discovered that I could sing a bit, and as the years rolled by became something of an entertainer aboard all of the ships on which I served. I was keen on folk music and particularly enjoyed the humorous approach that was being taken by some professional entertainers on the thriving folk club circuit in the UK and this became a path that I followed as an amateur performer in the local clubs after leaving the service. When, in 1973, I teamed up with Alan Briars, co-organiser of the legendary Village Pump Folk Club in Trowbridge, it was not long before we turned professional and quit our jobs to hit the road as an outrageous theatrical comedy duo with the peculiar name of *Mechanical Horsetrough*.

Fondly known as *The Troffers*, Alan and I specialised in the type of humour that was referred to on the circuit as "armpit and crutch" and interspersed between songs I would tell colourful yarns about my days as a *matelot*. These colourful *sea stories* always went down well and fans would often suggest that I should write a book about my nautical past.

After ten years on the road I opened a pub, since when, wives, children, my rock band *Lucy La Stique* and other projects have kept me busily occupied.

I retired at the end of 2011 after more than thirty years in the pub trade and finally found the time to write this first story. There is more to come!

Printed in Great Britain
by Amazon